EUROPEAN POLITICS
RECONSIDERED

EUROPEAN POLITICS
RECONSIDERED

B. Guy Peters

HM

HOLMES & MEIER

New York · London

Published in the United States of America 1991 by
Holmes & Meier Publishers, Inc.
30 Irving Place
New York, NY 10003

BOOK DESIGN BY DALE COTTON

This book has been printed on acid-free paper.

Library of Congress Cataloging-in-Publication Data

Peters, B. Guy.
  European politics reconsidered / B. Guy Peters.
    p.   cm.
  Includes bibliographical references and index.
  ISBN 0-8419-1160-6 (acid-free paper).—ISBN 0-8419-1161-4 (pbk. :
  acid-free paper)
  1. Europe—Politics and government—1945–   I. Title.
JN94.A2P48   1991
940.55'8—dc20
                                                    90-40211
                                                        CIP

MANUFACTURED IN THE UNITED STATES OF AMERICA

CONTENTS

ACKNOWLEDGMENTS

A number of people deserve thanks for attempting to save me from error, although the blame for any misinterpretations and errors must remain my own. Alberta Sbragia read a draft of the entire manuscript and made many helpful comments. Members of the LOS Centre at Bergen provided useful insights into contemporary Scandinavian politics. As usual, the members of the SOG Research Committee provided a movable feast of information and interpretation of contemporary governments. Several graduate students at the University of Pittsburgh—Stanley Berard, Julio Carrion, and Michelle Egan in particular—provided timely research assistance. My family could rarely save me from factual error but did try (usually unsuccessfully) to deliver me from the bonds of the obsession to work on the book.

INTRODUCTION
What Needs
Reconsideration?

The title of this book is ambitious, but there are numerous aspects of politics in Western Europe that need to be reconsidered. Much of the conventional wisdom about European politics is now subject to a number of caveats, and some of it needs to be discarded entirely. The alterations in political life in Western Europe have been evolutionary, and have been less noticeable than the rapid and revolutionary changes in Eastern Europe or Latin America, but they still add up to significant transformations of the political systems. The kinds of issues that require some rethinking range from rather trivial facts—the names of specific ministries or interest groups—to very fundamental concepts about the organization and meaning of political life in these countries. The analysis and description of the issues presented in this book are intended to provide a foundation for the continuing need to rethink and reconfigure our conceptions of politics in Europe.

The most fundamental feature of government that has been underlying change is the role of the nation-state. Most thinking about politics in Western Europe has been based on the premise that the national state is the principal locus of policymaking and identification. That premise is no longer clearly valid, and the dominant position of the nation-state is threatened from both above and below. From above, the European Community has become a major actor, supplanting the policymaking role of the nation-state in some areas. And from below, regionalism and regional governments—whether based on language, religion, or simply geography—are claiming an enhanced role in policymaking. The changing roles of national, supranational, and subnational governments are discussed in

Chapter 2, as are specific changes in a form of European state—the Welfare State—in Chapter 8. The welfare state, or more completely the mixed-economy welfare state, has been one of the crowning achievements of government in the twentieth century. There is now some sense, however, that the programs of the welfare state no longer have the capacity to create social harmony and security that they once had. This feeling, although often rather poorly defined, has required a rethinking of contemporary political economy, and a consideration of alternatives to the existing welfare-state programs.

Most government institutions in Western Europe have remained nominally the same over the past several decades, yet have changed significantly. Prime ministers have come to behave more like presidents. Legislatures have sought to recapture some of the powers that appear to be theirs but have been lost to prime ministers and cabinets. The parliaments have sought to regain those powers through enhanced staffs, changes in procedure, and simply greater assertiveness. All political institutions have needed to find ways to control the growing powers of the public bureaucracy. These evolutionary changes in institutions will be documented in Chapter 3, and more conscious efforts at change on the part of governments will be discussed in Chapter 7. A period of economic and governmental crisis during the 1970s and early 1980s has produced numerous efforts at reform and change of governing institutions. These reforms have been more or less successful in their respective settings, but they do represent the efforts of political and administrative leaders to produce meaningful change in institutions and to make government work more effectively and efficiently.

As much as the institutions of government may have changed, the values and concerns of citizens have changed even more. Chapters 4, 5, and 6 document these changes. First, the evolution of the political attitudes and values of citizens are described. One part of the conventional wisdom about European politics is that the public has become more "postmaterialist" in its thinking about politics and public policy, and therefore less concerned with "bread and butter" economic issues. There is some evidence to support this position, and there is also important contradictory evidence that needs to be included in the record as well.

In addition to their ideas, the organizations through which Europeans express their political preferences have been changing. There is a good deal of evidence to point to a significant realignment or dealignment of political parties. The constellation of political parties that has been (relatively) stable since the end of World War II is now evolving very rapidly. Also, it appears that the system of corporatist interest representation that was so successful during the 1960s and most of the 1970s is not able to cope as well with changing political issues and values. The close intertwining of private interest groups with government that is associated with corporatism worked well during times of growing resources, but appears less suitable for managing declining or stable resources. This is true even though privatization and partnerships between government and the private sector constitute significant parts of the reform movement in the 1980s and 1990s. All of these changes then require a reconsideration of the manner in which we understand mass politics, and the options for organizing the public for political purposes.

There has been a great deal of change in politics in Western Europe. That change promises to be even greater during the 1990s as the European Community implements its plans for full economic integration by 1992, and Eastern Europe rejoins Western Europe in a "common homeland." Both of these significant events will have major impact on the politics of the individual European nation-states. It is therefore important to document the changes that have been occurring as a way of understanding the evolutionary, and perhaps revolutionary, future political course for Europe. We will begin that exercise through a discussion of the economic and social background to political change.

Chapter

1

THE CHANGED ENVIRONMENT
OF EUROPEAN POLITICS

Although the period following World War II has been one of unprecedented economic growth in Western Europe, in the late 1980s over 10 percent of the adult work force in Europe was unemployed, and many more people were working in jobs that did not utilize fully their training and skills. Also, in many European countries the future economic prospects are thought to be uncertain because of foreign competition, a declining work force, and an increasing elderly population which must be supported (through public pensions) by that declining number of working-age people. The countries that once imported foreigners to fill positions in booming industries now face unemployment as well as the tensions generated by newly introduced ethnic minorities. On the other hand, however, the prospects of full economic integration in the European Economic Community (EEC) in 1992 may make the economic future even brighter. In short, a great deal has changed, and much is uncertain, in the environment of politics in Western Europe, and those changes can be expected to have serious political ramifications.

Politics does not operate in a world of its own, but tends to reflect the world around it. The issues that arise in politics and government are the problems that afflict the economy and society; they also must appear to be solvable by governmental action. In a number of countries changes in the environment of politics in Western Europe have been dramatic, and their full impact continues to work its way through the political system. A number of economic and social conditions that had become stable components of the background of politics have now changed, so that many of the standard descriptions of European politics must be reconsidered, modified, and perhaps discarded. The impacts of these social and economic changes have not yet fully worked their way through the political system, given that institutions such as political parties, parliaments, and public bureaucracies are anchors slowing and mediating the impacts of social change, even rapid and major change. What is clear, however, is that many aspects of political life will continue to be modified to reflect the new realities that surround government.

The nature of political response to social change appears to be twofold and somewhat contradictory. On the one hand, political change will directly mirror social and economic change, and new groups and parties will attempt to occupy the "niches" it creates. Therefore, when long-term prosperity appeared to have solved the economic problems of industrialized democracies, new issues such as environmental protection and increased political participation spawned new groups and even political parties, such as the Greens in West Germany and other European countries. At times, however, the political reactions to change will be defensive, and organizations will arise to reaffirm old values and old institutions in the face of social changes that might undermine them. This can be seen in the reassertion of older religious values and the strength of religious parties despite the continuing secularization of most European societies, as well as the reassertion of ethnonationalism in the face of the homogenizing impacts of mass media (Brass 1985). It is difficult to predict the exact direction that political reactions to social and economic change will take, although the persistence of old values and institutions is usually underestimated. European societies are quite old, and contemporary politicians assume too readily that the new and the modern will be considered superior to the old and the trusted. At times they also appear to assume that just because they and their advisors can identify a trend, the voting population is ready to respond to that trend. They make these assumptions, however, at their peril.

Economic Change

The first major set of changes that influence European politics has occurred in European economies. Although there have been a number of types of change, they have been very closely interrelated. They all stem, to a greater or lesser degree, from the increasing interdependence of world economies and the inability of any government to shelter its domestic economy from international forces (Katzenstein 1985; Zysman 1983). The events that have followed the several oil crises in Western economies shattered the optimism upon which a good deal of economic policy and political hopes had been built. Those events also have forced a rethinking of politics and government policy by political leaders and citizens alike. But not only the reliance of industrial nations on imported oil has produced problems; the competition in the markets for many manufactured products then basic to the affluence of Western Europe has done so as well. No longer is there merely competition in steel, automobiles, shipbuilding, and similar industries among the European countries, and between those countries and North America and Japan. Now a new group of competitors has entered the international marketplace to challenge the industrial giants of the industrialized world with lower prices and comparable quality: the newly industrializing countries (NICs,), such as South Korea, Brazil, Taiwan, Mexico, and Singapore (Benjamin and Kudrle 1984). Even the seemingly invincible Japanese economy is now threatened to some degree by these new entrants into the world industrial economy and the acceleration of the product cycle by which production moves from innovators to lower-cost economies. As should be expected, these basic economic changes have been having political impacts. However, first we should get some idea of the types of economic change that have been occurring.

Economic Growth

One of the most obvious economic changes in Europe has been that economic growth is no longer as certain as it had been. The twenty-five-year period following World War II was one of immense and sustained economic growth for all Western European economies. Every year could be counted on to bring an increased gross national product (GNP), and with that more and more consumer goods and services. The average worker at the end of the 1960s had a level of consumption that could only have been imagined in the 1940s or even early 1950s. (See Table 1.1.) Even those economies, such as the United Kingdom, that did not do well in comparison to their neighbors did extremely well by historical standards.

The dimensions of economic growth in Europe in the postwar period are illustrated in Tables 1.2 and 1.3, which point to three important aspects of growth. The first is the rapidity of the growth that occurred until the mid-1970s. The average growth rate from 1950 to 1974 was 4.6 percent in all Western European countries, with even the lowest (the United Kingdom) having an average annual growth rate of 2.7 percent. This means that in 1974 the GNP was, on average across Europe, almost 190 percent larger than it had been in 1950. Again, even the slowest growing economy was

TABLE 1.1

Ownership of Consumer Goods in Europe[a]

(percentage)

	Home	Car	TV	Washing Machine
Austria	–	55	53	72
Belgium	59	89	97	80
Denmark	–	70	58	57
Finland	63	55	50	73
France	47	69	90	80
W. Germany	36	62	93	81
Ireland	43	63	29	63
Italy	89	–	–	–
Netherlands	45	70	72	89
Norway	–	62	52	76
Spain	69	52	92	79
Sweden	51	69	95	92
United Kingdom	54	62	97	81

SOURCE: Based on data from the Organization for Economic Cooperation and Development, *Living Conditions in OECD Countries* (Paris: OECD, 1986).

[a]Various years around 1981.

almost twice as large as it had been in 1950, while the most rapidly growing among the major economies (West Germany) was almost three times as large as it had been at that time. In historical terms, this is an immense level of growth (Denison 1967).

The second point that these tables illustrate is the regularity and certainty of economic growth during the postwar period. In the twenty-five years from 1950 to 1974, economic production on average grew every year, with only twelve instances in all seventeen countries in the twenty-five years in which there was not some economic growth. The poorest performance was experienced by the economy of Ireland, which did not grow in two of those years, while Austria, France, West Germany, Italy, Luxembourg, Norway, Portugal, and Sweden experienced growth in every single year. Thus not only was economic growth quite rapid, but it was predictable. This in turn meant that both citizens and governments could count on more to spend in each successive year. This became a real-life economic manifestation of the statement of the French philosopher Emile Coué: "Every day in every way we are getting better and better"; and it created a great deal of objective security (Bay 1965) for citizens of European democracies. This in turn allowed the healing of many of the real and psychological wounds of World War II and the movement toward a more unified and peaceful Europe through institutions such as the Common Market.

The final thing that Tables 1.2 and 1.3 illustrate very clearly is that this "economic miracle" ended rather abruptly in the 1970s. After the first oil crisis in 1973–74, things were never quite the same again. Not only were rates of economic growth lower than they had been prior to that crisis, which arose from the international environment, but economic growth was no longer predictable and certain. Current annual economic growth, on average, has been 37 percent of what it had been prior to 1974. Even in the European economy that has performed the best since the oil crisis— Norway, itself oil-rich—economic growth has not been quite as high, or as predictable, as it had been earlier. Also almost all of even the strongest economies have experienced some years of no growth or economic decline.

TABLE 1.2

Average Annual Growth Rates of Per Capita Gross Domestic Product

	1950–64	1965–74	1975–86	1982–86
Austria	5.2	4.8	2.1	1.7
Belgium	3.9	4.6	1.5	1.3
Denmark	3.9	4.6	2.0	2.7
Finland	5.1	4.8	2.8	3.1
France	5.0	5.7	2.1	1.5
W. Germany	7.0	4.0	2.0	2.2
Greece	6.5	6.4	2.7	1.4
Ireland	2.4	4.4	3.1	−0.3
Italy	5.6	4.8	2.2	2.5
Luxembourg	–	4.2	1.8	3.2
Netherlands	4.8	4.8	1.5	2.2
Portugal	–	6.1	2.7	3.0
Spain	–	7.1	1.8	2.7
Sweden	4.1	4.4	1.6	2.5
Switzerland	4.8	3.6	0.9	2.2
United Kingdom	2.9	2.5	1.8	3.8
AVERAGE	4.9	4.2	1.9	2.3

SOURCE: Organization for Economic Cooperation and Development, *Main Economic Indicators* (Paris: OECD, annual); *Economic Outlook* (Paris: OECD, monthly).

TABLE 1.3

Percentage of Years with Economic Growth

	1950–64	1964–74	1975–81	1982–86
Austria	100	100	83	100
Belgium	93	100	75	75
Denmark	93	90	75	100
Finland	93	100	100	100
France	100	100	83	100
W. Germany	100	90	75	75
Greece	100	90	92	75
Ireland	93	90	75	75
Italy	100	90	75	75
Luxembourg	93	90	83	100
Netherlands	93	100	75	100
Norway	100	100	100	100
Portugal	100	90	67	50
Spain	93	100	75	100
Sweden	100	100	83	100
Switzerland	93	100	75	100
United Kingdom	93	90	67	100

SOURCE: Based on data from the Organization for Economic Cooperation and Development, *National Accounts of OECD Member Countries* (Paris: OECD, annual).

Only Finland and Norway experienced no economic declines, although growth was very low in two successive years in each. A number of the weaker economies experienced negative economic growth in three years out of twelve. While it is wrong to blame these economic changes entirely on the energy problems that began in 1973–74, that period does constitute a useful point of demarcation. In addition, the use of those years as a point of demarcation is illustrative of the expansion of international influence in European economies—usually not for the better, at least in the short run.

Regional Structural Change

These three tables on economic change show what has happened to nations as a whole, but they do not show the concentration of those effects on regions within countries. These effects have been even more dramatic than the aggregate changes in national economies. In virtually all industrialized countries in Europe and North America, older industrial regions—the "rust belts"—have been affected very severely by economic changes. Areas such as the Ruhr in Germany, Lille and the Pas de Calais in France, Glasgow and Manchester in the United Kingdom, and even Göteborg in Sweden, which were the backbones of their nations' industrial economies, are now in the economic doldrums. They now experience high levels of unemployment, loss of industries and populations, and declines in public expectations for themselves and their families. In the late 1980s not only were the conditions in some of these regions almost desperate, they were unlikely to change rapidly, and many workers who once received handsome wages were unlikely ever to work again. The shift to high technology and to service industries, seen by many as the salvation of European economies, is unlikely to meet the needs of most of these displaced industrial workers in any meaningful way.

The differentials in levels of unemployment among areas in European countries and the massive disparities that have arisen in the face of economic change are displayed clearly in Table 1.4. Even countries that have done relatively poorly in aggregate economic terms continue to have high and growing levels of employment in some regions (for example, the southeast of England), while even those that have been doing rather well have areas of high unemployment (the Pas de Calais in France). As well as slowing the great engine of economic growth in Europe as a whole, international competition also has exacerbated regional differences within individual countries. Where areas of higher unemployment also overlap with strong ethnonationalist cleavages, such as in the Basque region of Spain, this increased regional tension could have serious consequences for the

TABLE 1.4

Variations in Unemployment by Region
(April 1986)

	High (percentage)	Low (percentage)
Belgium	Hainaut—14.2	West Flanders—7.2
France	Languedoc—13.9	Alsace—7.1
W. Germany	Bremen—13.2	Baden-Württemberg—4.0
Greece	Thessalia—8.4	Crete—4.0
Italy	Sardinia—19.3	Val d'Aosta—4.6
Netherlands	Groningen—13.2	Zeeland—6.5
United Kingdom	Northern Ireland—18.7	East Anglia—9.0

SOURCE: Based on data from European Community, *Regional Statistics* (Brussels: European Community, 1987).

political stability of some countries. And even where the consequences may be less severe, these disparities can exacerbate long-standing grievances and perceptions of inequality within a country.

The fact that these regional changes have been rather common across Western Europe has served as a justification for a greater intervention of the European Economic Community (the Common Market) into regional policy. The Community has been engaged in some forms of regional policy since their inception in the 1950s, but this activity has intensified as economic decline has become more commonplace and more severe. This policy intervention is yet another example of the impact of the international system on domestic economies, albeit this time the impact is positive. Further, it points to the declining position of the nation-state as the central actor in European policymaking, even in an area such as economic policy, which has traditionally been a central concern of national governments.

Policy and Political Change

The end of sustained economic growth in Western European economies has had a number of profound effects on the process of governing, which have been felt both at the level of mass politics and in the manner in which governments conduct their business. No country has been able to escape these changes, and no politician can afford to ignore that he or she lives in an economic world that is quite different from the one that existed just over a decade ago. The political elites cannot ignore these changes because citizens cannot ignore them. Citizens must evaluate their political leaders in part on their abilities to cope and adapt to the changes that have occurred. It appears not to matter *how* political leaders respond—they can attempt to reinvigorate capitalism or promote state ownership—so long as they do respond.

It is important to remember that not only did the end of the several decades of prosperity terminate a feeling of popular security about economic well-being, it also ended an era of security about the intellectual foundations of economic policy. Postwar economic policy was dominated by Keynesian ideas (Keegan 1984; Stewart 1971). Simply put, the Keynesian approach was that economic performance could be manipulated by manipulating aggregate levels of demand through the public budget. That is, it was argued that by reducing taxes or increasing public spending, government could put more money into the hands of ordinary citizens who would spend that money and stimulate the economy. On the other hand, raising taxes or reducing spending could take money out of the pockets of citizens and slow down an inflationary economy. These ideas apparently worked extremely successfully during the twenty-five years after the end of World War II. They were so successful that some economists could talk about "fine-tuning" the economy, while assuming that its basic ability to produce stable economic growth was not then in question.

The period of "stagflation" beginning in the mid-1970s challenged and then destroyed the Keynesian consensus about economic policy. Before that period inflation and unemployment were assumed to be traded off along the Phillips curve (Phillips 1958), so that high levels of both undesirable conditions should not occur at the same time. By the end of the 1970s they did, and the prevailing wisdom could offer no means of understanding or, more important, counteracting this predicament. The field was then open for new economic approaches. Most candidates for replacing the Keynesian theoretical consensus came from the political and economic right—ideas such as monetarism and supply-side economics—although interestingly, even the political right appeared to accept the fundamental obligation of government to regulate the economy. To be changed were only the degree of intrusiveness and the role of market forces in that regulation. Despite the changes that have occurred in the practice of economic policy, currently there is no intellectual foundation such as that which was provided by John Maynard Keynes.

Thus the end, of affluence during the 1970s put governments into a double bind. First, they appeared responsible for poor economic performance; having taken the credit for good performance in the past, it was difficult for them to escape blame for the current problems. Further, at least in the early days of the crisis, governments assumed that their old remedies would work and promised "cures" for the economy. Over time, however, governments learned that the instruments they usually had employed in attempts to correct the poor economic performance appeared ineffective at best and counterproductive at worst. Governments not only had a bad situation on their hands, but they appeared to have little to offer to ameliorate or solve the difficulties their citizens were experiencing.

MASS POLITICS. At the level of mass politics, reintroduction of scarcity into European political thinking (it never really went away but it certainly appeared to) first has affected the manner in which individual citizens behave in politics and react to politicians. One popular characterization of politics in advanced industrial societies in the 1960s and 1970s was as "postmaterialist" (Inglehart 1977; Lafferty and Knutsen 1985; Marsh 1975). That is, it was argued that economic bread-and-butter issues could no longer mobilize voters into two rival left and right blocs that would engage in political conflicts over the distribution of the society's resources.

Somewhat earlier a similar form of change in the behavior of the mass public was referred to as "the end of ideology" (Bell 1960; LaPalombara 1966), but in Europe that characterization of political change had significantly different connotations.

The underlying conception of postbourgeois politics was that the older economic issues that had served as the basis of politics and political parties for generations appeared to have been solved, with sufficient economic resources available to provide "treble affluence" (Rose and Peters 1978). During the 1960s and into the 1970s, there had been sufficient total economic growth to allow both expanding levels of government spending on whatever was considered important and high levels of private consumption on automobiles, television sets, vacations, and so on. There seemed to be no effective budget restraint in either the private or the public sector, and it appeared that economic growth could easily pay for any new spending.

With the basic production and distribution problems "solved," politics could become concerned with such issues as the protection of the environment, rights for minorities and women, and political participation. The assumption was that new political cleavages were emerging that would divide the population very differently than did the older economic issues, and in fairness the empirical evidence appeared to substantiate such an assumption. Economic issues declined in importance in public opinion surveys in the 1960s and 1970s (see Table 1.5), while the postbourgeois issues of equality and participation increased in importance. It did indeed appear as if politics was being altered in a very fundamental sense and that new political alignments were emerging.

The idea of the end of ideology, on the other hand, implies to some extent the end of politics as we have become accustomed to it. Not only would the issues that divided people politically be changed, but partisan politics as a means of making decisions would be of declining importance. Instead of partisan conflict and the political process, public decisions would emerge from a more rational, bureaucratic, and technocratic consideration of the evidence and alternatives. It was assumed, according to this school of thought, that old political ideologies could not compete with modern science, including the economic science apparently so cleverly steering the economy, and therefore would all but disappear from public consideration. Parties espousing ideologies might continue their vestigial functions of recruiting elites to fill positions in government and perhaps of socializing the mass public with their slogans, but the real impact of party and ideology would be declining.

The reassertion of the inevitable truth of scarcity has brought the whole idea of postbourgeois politics into severe question. Not only did the reality

TABLE 1.5

Indicators of Postmaterialist Attitudes:
Percentage Agreement with Goals

	Materialist Goals			Postmaterialist Goals					
	G1	*G2*	*G3*	*G4*	*G5*	*G6*	*G7*	*G8*	*G9*
Belgium	52	19	10	18	17	11	17	15	7
Denmark	24	23	31	20	17	8	11	7	7
France	43	18	21	13	28	9	14	9	11
W. Germany	44	24	18	12	11	9	11	4	3
Ireland	44	29	16	20	8	15	6	5	3
Italy	41	31	17	9	14	11	9	3	5
Luxembourg	29	33	28	22	11	19	7	7	9
Netherlands	26	14	18	24	26	14	13	10	10
United Kingdom	50	29	11	15	12	15	11	6	5
United States	25	16	20	16	12	16	10	18	8

SOURCE: Adapted from R. Inglehart, *The Silent Revolution: Changing Values and Political Styles Among Western Politics* (Princeton, NJ: Princeton Univ. Press, 1977), 49.

G1	=	Fight Rising Prices	G6	=	More Say in Government
G2	=	Economic Growth	G7	=	Protect Free Speech
G3	=	Maintain Order	G8	=	More Beautiful Cities
G4	=	More Say on Job	G9	=	Ideas Count
G5	=	Less Impersonal Society			

of economic life change, but the manner in which it was perceived changed as well—back toward a more conventional, bourgeois concern with economic distribution and the basic issue of getting enough from the economy to be able to live something approaching a comfortable life. The conflicts were being fought by new people and in a somewhat different manner, but important to European politics were many of the same issues that had dominated it for years during the twentieth century. Postbourgeois ideas have not died out totally, and "Green" political parties continue to flourish, perhaps indicating a growing economic and social division brought about by industrial decline and the creation of knowledge-based service industries.

It is especially interesting that the consensus on the mixed-economy, welfare-state structures in the public sector has been shattered in a number of European countries; in its place a neoliberal doctrine extolling the role of the market has been institutionalized, although without the intellectual foundations that had supported Keynesian policies (but see Eatwell and

O'Sullivan 1989). The Thatcher government in Great Britain is the most obvious example of this change, although less dramatic but nonetheless real changes of that sort have occurred in West Germany, France (after 1984), and to some degree even Sweden, Norway, and the Netherlands. These changes represent a very clear and strong reassertion of an ideology, though not as well developed philosophically as Marxism. Further, it is an ideology largely about economic management and the reduced role of government in social life. This ideology is used by politicians in office both as a guide for action and as a mechanism for justifying policy choices and results that might otherwise be problematic politically. Thus, despite British voters' historic aversion to unemployment (Strümpel 1969), the Thatcher government has been able to maintain its popularity and its voting strength in the face of extremely high levels of joblessness. The availability of an ideology has certainly helped Mrs. Thatcher's government to explain its actions and has provided a basis for promising a better future if the very obvious short-term hardships are endured.

While the assertion of the neoliberal ideology by Margaret Thatcher and others certainly gives the lie to the end-of-ideology idea, even earlier events had brought it into severe question. In particular, the events of 1968—most notably in Paris but to some degree all across the industrialized world— pointed to another form of ideological movement, which was to a great degree a product of postmaterialist ideas. It asserted the importance of the individual, participation, and freedom in the face of what were characterized as bureaucratic and monolithic governments and societies. The year 1968 in many ways represents postmaterialism on the march. The ideology being espoused was not very well developed, probably even less developed and less integrated than that of the neoliberals a decade later, but it was powerful nonetheless. It and its adherents were able to shake the very foundations of government in a number of well-institutionalized and seemingly stable political systems.

When the negative economic changes began to take place in the 1970s, concerns with peace, freedom, and justice quickly appeared quaint and outdated, even to many of the young, who were now flocking to attend business school rather than to occupy university administration buildings. The real changes in economic circumstances have produced equally real changes in the political concerns of the young. Yet the postmaterialist concerns of the 1960s and 1970s have not vanished entirely. To some extent they live on in the cohort of citizens and voters who came of age politically then. Although this cohort is aging and generally becoming more conservative, it is fundamentally different on some political dimensions from those that preceded and those that have followed it (Inglehart 1981).

Further, as that cohort reaches the age when it may be expected to take major leadership positions in economic and political life, we may expect to see the impact of its past political experiences. Postmaterialist ideas also survive in the new peace movements, environmental groups, and rights advocates that dot the political landscape of the 1980s and 1990s. The most obvious manifestation has been the "Green" political movement, with parties representing many of the ideas associated with postmaterialism winning seats in at least five national parliaments.

Postmaterialist values are also embodied in a set of governmental institutions that still exist and have some real policymaking powers. Agencies concerned with environmental protection, civil rights, and women's rights, and laws containing enhanced rights of public participation are continuing legacies of the 1960s and 1970s. As with so much of government, few things ever really disappear, but rather they become enmeshed in a web of other organizations and laws. These organizations may lose their initial vigor (Downs 1967) or even change their ostensible purposes, but they will persist and perhaps to some small degree continue the fight that was begun years before. Further, governments may use new or invigorated agencies to pacify the Greens and other similar movements.

While the political struggles of the 1960s and 1970s are now institutionalized, contemporary political struggles are attempting to create their own institutions and laws for coping with the problems of the economy. One manifestation of this effort has been an increasing concern with industrial and regional policy designed to ameliorate some of the concentrated impacts of economic change on the older industrialized regions. At one end of the policy spectrum, this has meant appeals for protective tariffs to reduce the impact of foreign competition on domestic and, by international standards, inefficient producers. At the other end have been labor market policies directed at retraining and relocating individuals affected by international competition. In between those extremes have been a number of policies directed at improving the competitive positions of industries or ameliorating some of the worst effects of economic change on individuals. These policies are becoming increasingly associated with the work of the European Economic Community and the 1992 goal of full economic integration. All of these policies, however, represent a reaffirmation of the importance of basic economic issues in European politics, largely brought about by the perceived scarcity resulting from changes in the international marketplace.

Besides regional policy changes, the policy agenda of government has had to change regarding revenue and expenditure plans. "Austerity" has become a popular word to describe how governments now budget. The creativeness with which governments have responded to their revenue and spending "crises" is remarkable and should dispel the common mythology that governments cannot respond effectively to novel problems. Almost all industrialized countries have adopted new budgeting programs (Peters 1989a; Tarschys 1985); some of these programs have radically altered the manner in which government has been making decisions for years, and all have attempted to reduce or at least control levels of public expenditure. Further, the deficits that many industrial countries have accumulated during the economic slowdown will narrow the options available to future governments. Current deficits imply future debt interest payments, and in European countries larger and larger shares of public expenditure are now required simply to pay interest on the national debt.

Again, it is necessary to point out the extent to which the agenda of government has been altered. Budgetary change in the 1960s and 1970s generally meant the adoption of mechanisms such as Planning Programming Budgeting Systems (PPBS), which would improve the "rationality" with which expenditure decisions were made. It was assumed at the time that governments could make optimal decisions about expenditures to maximize the utility of each marginal unit of currency spent. That technocratic optimism now appears naive, and budgetary changes in the late 1970s and 1980s frequently were mechanisms to force governments to spend less, often by such simplistic devices as across-the-board cuts (Tarschys 1981, 1985). As appealing as rationalistic mechanisms may be intellectually, events may overtake them when it is perceived that the public sector is in deep financial trouble and that the economy will not grow rapidly enough to take care of the problem painlessly.

Finally, the impact that these economic changes may have on the welfare state in Europe needs to be considered. The European welfare state is in many ways a social insurance state, and depends therefore on workers making contributions throughout their working lifetime to develop eligibility for benefits and to fund the benefits for those currently receiving them. When a significant sector of the labor force is put out of work for a long period of time, those people not only do not develop eligibility themselves, but they place a strain on current and future benefit structures. When a large number of (formerly well-paid) workers becomes almost permanently unemployed, social insurance loses much of its meaning. Concurrently, the welfare state as a major legitimating agent for contemporary democracies also loses some of its potency.

In summary, the economic miracle that characterized postwar Europe is for the most part over. In its place is a period of slower and less certain growth, as well as almost certain death for some industries and unemployment for groups of industrial workers. The service and high-technology industries of the 1980s offer some relief from these problems, but they tend to be relatively slow growing when compared to manufacturing and to provide a large number of low-paying jobs. While the service industries may include a number of well-paid stockbrokers and computer scientists, they include many more waitresses and retail clerks. Thus for both national economies and the household economies of individuals, the future is uncertain and far from promising.

Demographic Change

While the economic changes that have affected European politics have been influenced by international events to a significant degree the demographic changes are primarily—although not entirely—domestic. Though a number of changes in the population structures of these countries are relevant, the most important single demographic fact is the aging of the populations in almost every European country, except a few surrounding the Mediterranean (OECD 1988). This increasing population age comes both from fertility rates that have been below replacement rates and the increasing life expectancy of those now in or approaching their retirement years. In short, fewer babies are being born each year but, once born, people can expect to live longer. The reasons for the lower fertility rates are multiple. They include women delaying or avoiding having children in order to pursue their own careers, a feeling of responsibility to limit the world's population in order to conserve scarce resources, and some feelings of foreboding about the future of the world because of technological (especially nuclear) hazards. For whatever reasons, however, there are fewer young Europeans.

Some idea of the magnitude of the change in the European population can be gained from Tables 1.6 and 1.7. These tables show the percentage of the population in certain age groups in a number of Western European countries as well as the birthrates and life expectancies in these countries over time. All the evidence points to a "demographic time bomb" almost exactly opposite that predicted for Third World countries. Rather than having too many young people who will shortly be demanding an education and jobs, the demographic crisis in industrialized countries is more often too many old people who will be demanding public retirement and medical benefits. Either way, the simple fact of the changing age distribution of a population can impose real problems for a government.

One crucial problem that the aging population imposes on government

TABLE 1.6

Population by Age
(1986)

	Under 15	15–64	65 +
Austria	18.6	67.1	14.3
Belgium	18.6	67.3	14.1
Denmark	20.7	66.3	13.0
Finland	19.5	68.1	12.4
France	21.5	65.7	12.8
W. Germany	15.6	69.7	14.7
Greece	21.9	65.5	13.2
Iceland	26.4	63.5	10.1
Ireland	29.6	59.8	10.6
Italy	17.6	69.2	13.2
Luxembourg	16.8	69.8	13.4
Netherlands	19.9	68.1	12.0
Norway	20.0	64.3	15.7
Portugal	23.7	64.6	11.7
Spain	24.4	64.3	11.3
Sweden	17.4	64.7	17.9
Switzerland	17.9	68.4	13.7
United Kingdom	19.5	65.7	14.8
AVERAGE	20.5	66.2	13.3

SOURCE: Based on data from the United Nations, *Demographic Yearbook, 1986* (New York: UN, 1988).

has already been alluded to: the number of elderly persons eligible for, and indeed entitled to, social security payments and public medical programs. As the number of elderly has increased, the number of workers paying to support them has been decreasing, or at best remaining constant (see Table 1.7). This change would present less of a problem if social insurance programs were, as many people conceptualize them, actuarially sound programs that save and invest the contributions of individuals while they are working and then pay them back (perhaps with interest?) when those individuals retire or become disabled. This is not, however, the case; most social insurance programs have become direct intergenerational transfers from those who are working to those who have retired. Thus when the relative number of workers to elderly decreases, each worker has to pay (through taxes and social insurance "contributions") for the support of more and more elderly. This, in turn, conflicts with the ideological and practical desires, at least of many contemporary governments in Western Europe, to hold the line on taxation.

Thus a simple change in the age structure of the population has produced the potential for yet another major challenge to the welfare state and its system of social insurance that, along with economic growth, has been a cornerstone of postwar European political stability. On the one hand, governments can ill afford to renege on the promises they have been making for decades to their workers that an adequate public pension would await them once they retired. On the other hand, short-term political pressures

TABLE 1.7

Birth Rates, Death Rates, and Annual Percentage Population Change[a]

	Birth Rate	Death Rate	Annual Percentage Change
Austria	11.5	11.8	0.0
Belgium	11.5	11.2	0.1
Denmark	10.6	11.4	− 0.1
Finland	13.2	9.2	0.3
France	14.1	10.1	0.3
W. Germany	9.6	11.5	− 0.2
Greece	11.7	9.3	0.4
Iceland	15.8	7.0	0.6
Ireland	18.2	9.0	1.3
Italy	10.1	9.5	0.1
Luxembourg	11.1	10.0	0.1
Netherlands	12.3	8.4	0.3
Norway	12.1	10.6	0.2
Portugal	13.0	9.6	0.6
Spain	14.6	7.4	0.6
Sweden	11.8	11.3	− 0.1
Switzerland	11.5	9.1	− 0.1
United Kingdom	12.9	11.7	0.0

SOURCE: Based on data from the United Nations, *Demographic Yearbook, 1986* (New York: UN, 1988).

[a] Number of births and deaths per 1,000 population per year; population change figure ignores effect of migration.

make tax increases unpalatable, even when those increases are packaged in the form of insurance contributions or other earmarked taxes that presumably have greater appeal and legitimacy for citizens (Lewis 1982). These demographic changes have produced a real dilemma for government; choosing either horn can produce very real political consequences, not to mention the human consequences that reducing social security payments might produce for the elderly. Most governments have chosen short-term palliatives for their problems, leaving untouched the underlying disparities between commitments and resources.

The other side of the demographic problem arises when governments attempt to meet their defense commitments with a declining population of young males. Most Western European countries are members of the North Atlantic Treaty Organization (NATO), which, along with the welfare state and economic growth, has been a stable anchor for postwar European politics (Ravenal 1985; Rush 1979). One obligation arising from being a NATO member is assigning a specified number of troops to NATO command for the defense of Europe. There is now a declining pool of young men who would normally fill those ranks, and governments are faced with some interesting policy options. Even countries that are not members of NATO command, most importantly France and Sweden, have significant military establishments and will face the same problems in filling their military ranks as do the NATO member states.

The policy responses of the NATO states to this problem are potentially quite important. One option is to employ higher technology weapons, a choice that some believe may bring much closer the use of tactical nuclear weapons in any European war. Simply put, if there are not enough conventional forces available and the European front is to be defended, the only option available may be nuclear. Not only is this fearsome by its very nature, but governments may be in the additional bind of being involved in negotiations that would reduce the availability of nuclear weapons in Europe, so that even more conventional forces would be needed. Fortunately, changes in East-West relations have made these difficult choices almost moot. The other option, which is being put into practice, is to replace manpower with womanpower. Military forces are now using an increased number of women in positions much closer to actual combat than would have been acceptable even a few years ago. Thus again seemingly simple demographic changes may be having significant social effects, in this instance hastening changes in gender roles, especially in societies where those roles have been clearly delineated for a number of years.

Finally, the declining number of young people entering the labor force each year presents more interesting options and problems for governments in the area of job training and labor-market policy. With fewer new workers, and indeed fewer workers in total, each must be as productive as possible. That is certainly an economic goal at any time, but the changes in demography makes it all the more compelling. Each worker will have to be trained to the highest degree possible and perhaps frequently retrained as the economy becomes more technologically sophisticated. Some European governments, most notably Sweden (Lindbeck 1974; Rydén and Bergstrom 1982), have already initiated active labor-market policies that attempt to keep the labor force in the most productive positions possible and to facilitate movement among jobs. Such policies, as well as changes in educational policy so that education can be a lifelong enterprise rather than something that terminates in early adulthood, will almost certainly have to spread throughout the industrialized world if the relative, or even absolute, standard of living in these countries is to continue.

In addition to the changes in the age structure, the demography of Western Europe has been changing significantly with the growing number of foreign workers, frequently referred to by the euphemistic German word *Gastarbeiter*, or guest workers. In some cases host countries have allowed these workers in because of the declining numbers of their own workers. In many European countries the actual number of guest workers is lower than it has been in the past, especially during the rapid economic growth of the 1960s and 1970s. What is different, however, is that the "guests" have become permanent rather than transient additions to the labor force, and to the host societies. Besides the men who initially came to work have been added women and children, and the guests are now stable parts of the society. Thus many European societies that had been quite homogenous racially, such as Scandinavia, suddenly have acquired significant racial and ethnic minorities.

As with any country that has an ethnic minority, the immediate question that arises is what sort of policy responses (if any) are necessary to deal with the new population. This is especially true when the ethnic minority has developed (in historical terms) rather quickly and may have only economic ties to the country. Even in countries that have significant divisions along ethnic lines, such as Belgium, ethnic community members have more than a little allegiance to the nation (Delruelle-Vosswinkel and Frognier, 1980); they think of themselves as Belgian as well as Flemish or Walloon. This may not be the case for the *Gastarbeiter* who came primarily to make a better living than would have been possible in their home country, but who grew accustomed to that income and the life-style of their adopted country and stayed on.

In addition to the problems that any multiethnic society might encounter, European countries have faced some special difficulties in coping with their *Gastarbeiter* populations. Even though the economies of many European countries have become partly dependent on these workers, who now make up a significant portion of their population and do primarily the dirty, poorly paid jobs that few natives want anymore, the governments may not know what to do with them. What are their political rights? (After a period of residence *Gastarbeiter* can vote at least in local elections in many countries.) What are their civil rights? Should attempts be made to assimilate them into the dominant culture through education for their children, language training for the adults, and so on? What are their entitlements for social services and even for retirement? Finally, with the economic uncertainty already mentioned, the poorly paid jobs performed by the guest workers may look better and better to many unemployed nationals. Few if any European countries have come to final or satisfying answers to most of these public policy questions.

Although not *Gastarbeiter,* the influx of Germans from East Germany and of other ethnic Germans from Eastern Europe and the Soviet Union has presented some special problems for West Germany. These Germans are all citizens once they arrive, according to the constitution and laws of West Germany, and they speak the language and most are culturally similar to West Germans. Further, they help meet the nation's future needs for skilled labor. Still, this is an addition of thousands of people each week to a population already living in a limited land space (population density in West Germany is ten times that of the United States and more than double that of France). And the needs for social services, housing, and employment counseling will place additional burdens on the German taxpayer. While welcomed as fellow Germans, this migration may be a mixed blessing in the long run.

In summary, gradually and almost imperceptibly the populations of most European countries have been changing. These small changes, however, are accumulating into major ones, and are forcing some major rethinking of basic public policies and to some degree basic political principles. European countries that a few decades ago appeared young and growing are now becoming increasingly elderly. Many programs founded with an implicit if not explicit assumption of a stable or even increasing number of workers to fund social insurance are now faced with genuine financial difficulties. Likewise, defense programs founded on the assumption of a stable if not growing pool of young male recruits are also in jeopardy. Clearly, European governments will have to adjust their manner of doing business if they are successfully to take into account these very fundamental changes in their environment.

Technology

Technological change has been both the boon and bane of contemporary industrialized societies. While producing benefits in the form of a higher standard of living, longer life expectancy, and an expansion of cognitive limits that would have been the subject of science fiction only a few years ago, technology has had serious unintended consequences and unanticipated effects. These have brought into question the desirability of always pushing back the frontiers of possibility and indeed the very idea of "progress" itself in many European countries. At the most extreme, nuclear technology, even in its peaceful forms, also offers the prospect of annihilation, and new biomedical technologies present possibilities that few people appear prepared to cope with ethically. Even very familiar forms of technology, such as coal-burning electrical power stations, present real problems of controlling effluents and of restoring the damage that has already been done to forests, lakes, and even people. And such seemingly benign technologies as television have had significant effects on social and political life.

The real and potential negative impacts of technology were brought home to most Europeans during the 1980s. First, there was the decision to base American cruise missiles with atomic warheads in several European countries, thereby increasing the perceived threat of nuclear war in Europe. The concern about the dangers of nuclear technology escalated with the disaster at the Soviet nuclear power station in Chernobyl; radioactive waste fell across almost all of Europe, sometimes in dangerous concentrations. In Britain those fears were compounded by the continuing investigation of the Sellafield nuclear accident. Less dramatically but nonetheless real, acid rain coming largely from coal-burning power stations day by day is killing forests in Germany and poisoning lakes in Scandinavia and in other parts of Europe. And acid rain and the several poisonings of the Rhine River by chemical spills are but a few of the more obvious examples of environmental degradation in these industrialized societies.

It is now difficult or impossible for governments to proceed with plans for technological advance without the population being involved and questioning those decisions. While many working in government might question this statement, popular mobilization concerning technology (for example, protests against nuclear power) may have some real political side benefits. The most important of these is increasing the political involvement of people, especially the young, many of whom have been politically apathetic and uninformed. The environmental movement, especially in its more vocal manifestations such as the "Greens" in West Germany and

Scandinavia, and the antinuclear movement have been in many ways movements of the young. They represent a reemergence of the youth of these countries as significant political forces, in the manner of the 1960s. While generally not as politically powerful as the antiwar and even environmental movements of the 1960s, the contemporary antinuclear and pro-environment movements are channeling energies into the political system and making politics more salient for a segment of the population that often has been disaffected and apolitical. Even those who disagree with the intentions of these mobilizations, but who do want to preserve effective political deomocracy, cannot help but see some benefits from them. In the terms of Harvard economist Robert Reich (1988), the process of "civic discovery" may be an important side benefit of mobilization around technological issues.

In addition to highlighting a set of problems and issues for the political system, the ever-expanding nature of contemporary technology must also have a significant effect on the distribution of power within government and the manner in which governments make decisions. The policy agendas of European governments are now crowded with numerous technological issues: regulation of nuclear power and of biotechnology, telecommunications policy, the internationalization of financial markets because of rapid telecommunications, and many others. Few parliamentarians or even the responsible ministers have sufficient technical background to make informed decisions about these complex issues on their own. The increasing technical content of policy issues, combined with the sheer volume of work required in contemporary government, means that the permanent bureaucracy and special policy advisors must assume an ever greater significance in decision making in industrialized democracies.

The increasing technocratic and bureaucratic nature of policymaking will clash with other changes that are occurring in these European democracies. In the first place, their populations are now increasingly well-educated and feel they are increasingly competent to participate in policy debates. However, even very well-educated people may be at a severe disadvantage in dealing with experts about significant scientific issues. Further, those issues that may be the most difficult and controversial scientifically and technically may be the very ones about which there is the greatest political mobilization, such as nuclear safety or genetic engineering. This is especially true, as noted earlier, of the young, who happen to have become politically mobilized primarily about those very same issues. Thus the increasing technical content of policy may further alienate the mass public from politics and make people feel that they are incapable of really influencing what goes on in government, no matter how educated and skilled they may be (Huntington 1974).

As well as altering the manner in which decisions are made in government, technology may also be altering the manner in which political elites appeal to the mass public. Although not as pronounced as in the United States, European political campaigns are becoming media events, and the appeal to the voter is ever more through the broadcast media, rather than more personally and directly. The development of electronic campaigning affect the political process in several important ways. One is to accentuate the extent to which elections are perceived as the selection of a single individual as prime minister or president, rather than simply being an election of members of Parliament. This is a change from usual practice in parliamentary governments in which the prime minister has been considered "first among equals" rather than a national figure on his or her own. This combines with the tendency toward technocracy mentioned earlier seriously to devalue parliaments as effective decision-making institutions in democracies, pushing power even more toward political executives and their bureaucracies.

Besides being associated with a shifting balance of power among institutions, communications media may influence the types of people who are successful in politics. To be successful, it is increasingly important to be effective on broadcast media, especially television. Although campaign laws in European countries limit or forbid purchasing of advertising time on radio and television, even the limited free time permitted is extremely influential as citizens receive a larger portion of their political information from those media. And because political events may be covered as news, leading candidates' actual exposure may be much greater than their allotted free time. This shift in the source of information and in the centrality of information sources in campaigning has also resulted in candidates' media personalities becoming as important or more important than policy issues. Hence, to be a good campaigner requires good presentation of self on television, rather than the skills that might make one a successful prime minister or parliamentarian. While the characteristics important for being elected may always have differed from those necessary for effectiveness once in office, this gap appears to have widened as broadcast media become more important in campaigns.

This widespread use of television as a source of news may influence even more than the selection of candidates. The importance of an issue may be decided by its ability to be compressed into a thirty-second or one-minute news segment with interesting pictures. Arguably, relatively few really important government issues can be presented adequately in such a brief manner. Yet this is how citizens will view the public policy world that surrounds them. Thus there may be a tendency toward oversimplification of very complex issues. Politics frequently forces the choice of simple solutions for complex questions, but this may be exaggerated as more and more people rely on broadcast media as opposed to printed media as their primary source of information about government and public policy.

A Melting Cold War

Finally, although it is currently highly speculative, the changes in Eastern Europe and the Soviet Union may have profound consequences for Western Europe. Although the postwar period has been one of immense economic and social development in Western Europe, it also has been a period of profound uncertainty. World War II was followed very quickly by the outbreak of the Cold War between two armed camps, and some of the early skirmishes of that "war" were fought in Europe—the Berlin blockade and airlift is a very obvious example. The tensions between East and West led to the formation of NATO, and for much of the postwar period Western Europe, especially West Germany, has been armed and prepared for a possible attack from the East. That all appears to have changed in 1989, and the East is becoming very much a copy of the West.

With large political and economic changes in the Soviet Union, and even more fundamental changes in Eastern European countries such as East Germany, Poland, and Hungary, Western European countries face a number of new opportunities and challenges. Europe is again becoming one economic and political area rather than two. The transformation of Eastern European politics may open huge new markets to Western businesses, although most people in Eastern Europe do not yet have sufficient buying power to participate as consumers in any economic change. The reduction in tensions between East and West may also free Western nations of some of their burdens of military spending, just at a time when demographics (fewer young males in the population) and economics (tax resistance) have made commitments to NATO more difficult for the European countries to maintain.

The challenges to political leaders arising from changes in Eastern Europe are also important. First, removing the Cold War threat destroys one of the foundations of appeal for a number of political parties, especially on the political right. Interestingly, however, it may also remove some of the appeal of parties of the left, such as the Greens, a good deal of which is based on peace and accommodation to the Eastern bloc. Second, any significant reduction in tensions between East and West very quickly raises the question of what to do about the two Germanies and to what extent, and how quickly, reunification is possible. In 1990 the two Germanies represent the heights of capitalism and the heights (however crumbling) of Marxism, but both are still Germany, and it is unclear if other European countries (East or West) want a reunified Germany with almost 80 million inhabitants. The first major step toward reunification occurred on July 1, 1990, and the future remains clouded. Finally, the reduction of tension between East and West has diminished the need for an American presence in Europe and therefore also loosens the Atlantic connection that has been a mainstay of postwar international politics for both the United States and Europe.

It is still the early days of any lessening of tensions between the Eastern and Western blocs in Europe. While much has already happened that would have been inconceivable even in the early 1980s, a great deal of tension and suspicion remains. There is also a real chance that the economic and political reforms will fail or be curtailed by conservative forces in the Soviet Union or other Eastern countries. However, if the changes do proceed and are successful, they will force a fundamental reexamination of our understanding of European politics and of international politics considered more broadly.

Summary

This chapter has pointed to a number of important changes in the environment of politics and government in Western Europe. Although few of the changes discussed have occurred overnight, they have accumulated to produce a rather different setting for politics from that which would have been found ten or even five years earlier. No longer is economic growth rapid and sure, and no longer are there large numbers of young people waiting to enter the labor force. Further, the powers within government itself have been redistributed as technological advances have altered the issues about which governments must make policy as well as the manner in which politicians must appeal to voters. Finally, the political changes occurring in Eastern Europe may generate a fundamental rethinking of Western European foreign policies. No longer will foreign policies be based upon the existence of two armed camps in Europe. Foreign aid to countries in Eastern Europe has become as significant an issue of foreign policy as defense against possible aggression had been. This ending of the Cold War may also promote an even stronger identification with Europe, and the common European home, and speed the process of supranational integration. By no means are all the foreign policy problems of Europe solved, but they appear much less threatening than they did before the events of 1989.

These environmental changes have produced a wide variety of political responses, which we will be exploring in the chapters that follow. Some of the responses, although perhaps not directly related to the environmental changes just described, produce a declining utility of the nation-state as a mechanism for understanding what happens in Western Europe. That entity, which has served as a major institutional anchor for thinking about government for several centuries, is threatened from both above and below. In addition to institutional changes, there have been immense changes in mass politics. Formerly stable alignments of voters and political parties have been forced to change in order to reflect both changes in the socioeconomic cleavages that have divided parties and voters and, to a somewhat lesser extent, changes in the manner in which politics is presented to them through the media and election campaigns. It can even be said that traditional party systems have become dealigned as voters tend to follow individuals rather than parties, or perhaps are more concerned with the activity of interest groups rather than of political parties.

Finally, public policy has been changing and will continue to change in Western Europe. Some change is inevitable, but major policy complexes such as the "mixed-economy, welfare state" and the North Atlantic alliance are now being placed under considerable strain. Clearly some policy components will have to be altered if the fundamental nature of these complex structures that have served so well for almost four decades is to survive. In addition, some politicians and a portion of the mass public now no longer want all of these institutions to survive. Thus governments in Western Europe are presented with fundamental challenges to their creativity and to their durability as they attempt to adjust to the changing world in which they now must live and govern.

We have been discussing the numerous changes in the political environment of Europe. We should not, however, permit ourselves to assume that governments are defenseless against these changes. Governments have a substantial capacity to act effectively to cope with, or even avert, institutional and policy problems. Because of the greater prestige and power accorded the public bureaucracy, that anticipatory capability appears better developed in Western Europe than in the United States. Therefore, although we begin our analysis of politics in Western Europe with a description of changes in the socioeconomic environment and in mass politics, we should not underestimate the power of government institutions to respond. Although by now very old organizations, frequently with ancient and quaint traditions, these institutions have demonstrated remarkable resilience and a remarkable capacity to make policies, and to make those policies work.

Chapter

2

THE DECLINE OF THE NATION-STATE

One of our most comfortable generalizations about European politics is that it is the politics of nation-states. In Britain, France, Spain, the Netherlands, Sweden, and a few others, these nation-states have histories that extend back for centuries. Even in the more recent additions to this family of nations—West Germany, Italy, and Norway, plus several smaller examples—the concept of the nation-state appears well entrenched and well understood by the populations. After all, it is these entities for whose sake millions have gone to war and died, to whom millions pay taxes, and from whom millions now receive benefit checks. Further, many of the political pressures within existing nation-states arise from groups that want to form a new nation-state. It is not the concept of the nation-state that ethnic separatists reject, only the one to which they may belong at the time. When we look at a map of contemporary Europe, we see a collection of nation-states, and that image appears to be burned into the consciousness of most people.

Unfortunately for our comfort and ease of analysis, however, this image of nation-states as the primary actors in Western Europe is becoming increasingly outdated, and we must begin to think about European politics, economics, and society somewhat differently. In fact, the viability of the nation-state as the dominant political actor in Europe appears to be eroding, both from above and from below. From above, the European Community (EC, or more commonly the Common Market) is an increasingly influential economic actor, and thus economic importance is being gradually translated into political importance as well. The significance of the European level of policymaking is accentuated as Europe moves toward full economic integration in 1992. The full implications of this target date are currently only dimly understood and its full impact may be comprehended only years later. What does appear clear, however, is that Europe as a whole, or at least those countries that are members of the European Community, will in policy terms behave increasingly like a single country, especially regarding economic policy, but perhaps in other policy areas as well. As policies become more European, citizens of the individual countries may have to begin to act that way as well.

The dominance of the nation-state is also under attack from below. Ethnonationalist and regional movements in many European countries are claiming their rights of policymaking, especially over educational and cultural issues. These policies are especially important because centralized national policies may reduce, and often actively have sought to reduce, the opportunities for perpetuating minority cultures and languages. Although contemporary maps of Western Europe may show a relatively small number of nations, a century or slightly longer ago maps would have shown many more splotches of color; and maps for a century before that would have been extremely colorful. What is now Italy, for example, as late as the 1850s was divided among eight separate political units, some of which were controlled by foreign powers. While a century may appear to be a sufficient time in which to produce nationhood, it may not be when the things that may divide nations—language, religion, and a sense of belonging to a distinctive group—persist alongside an apparently unified political system. Even several centuries of unity have not been capable of reducing the appeal of ethnic distinctiveness in Spain and the United Kingdom. What may be more surprising than the strong reassertion of ethnicity in European nations during the 1970s and 1980s is that it did not occur sooner (Allardt 1979; Krejci and Velimsky 1981). Further, the appeal of ethnic distinctiveness, as well as basic appeals for political freedom, has generated the formation of a number of new nation-states in Western Europe since World War II (see Table 2.1). Many of these are very small nations, but they have all the trappings and legal powers of larger nation-states.

The ethnic and regional groups asserting their separate social and cultural identity are joined by economically based groups demanding control over, or at least some greater participation in, aspects of government policy that affect their livelihoods. As we will discuss later, the great age of corporatism in Western Europe appears to have come and gone. However, a number of manifestations of corporate policymaking remain. These organizational and procedural institutions for the influence of traditional eco-

TABLE 2.1

European States

States in 1875	Additions between 1875–1919	Additions between 1919–1945	Additions since 1945
Andorra	Albania	Czechoslovakia	Greek Cyprus
Austria	Bulgaria	Estonia	Turkish Cyprus
Belgium	Montenegro	Finland	East Germany
Denmark	Norway	Ireland	Faroes
France	Romania	Latvia	Greenland
Germany	Serbia	Lithuania	Iceland
Greece		Poland	Malta
Hungary		Yugoslavia	
Italy			
Liechtenstein			
Luxembourg			
Monaco			
Netherlands			
Portugal			
Russia			
San Marino			
Spain			
Sweden			
Switzerland			
United Kingdom			

nomic interest groups have been supplemented by other more subtle institutional and legal changes granting some access and power to consumers, environmentalists, and other less traditional economic interests. For example, consumer groups are often now given the same representation as business and labor on advisory committees. Other nontraditional interest groups, such as women and homosexuals, have also come to play manifest political roles when previously they were largely quiescent. It is increasingly difficult to say that the nation-state in Europe can make an economic or social policy in an autonomous and authoritative way. The linkages of individual nations to the global economic system (Katzenstein 1985), and the internal power of economic interests, makes such policymaking difficult if not impossible. That difficulty is exacerbated by the awakening interests of noneconomic groups and their recognition of political mechanisms for achieving their ends.

In short, the policymaking action in Western Europe appears to be shifting away from national capitals and toward Brussels (the headquarters of the EEC), regional capitals, and even interest-group headquarters. Public policy formation in Europe is now rooted in a more complex and variegated set of institutions than would have been the case only a few years ago. National governments appear to have lost a good deal of their ability to act autonomously and to make decisions that will be binding for their citizens. This, in turn, may be affecting the manner in which those citizens regard government and the nature of policy itself. This chapter will discuss two of the three previously mentioned pressures pushing decision making away from the nation-state, but the question of the role of interest groups in policymaking will be reserved for discussion in chapter 6.

European Politics: The Emergence of a New State?

History would not make anyone very optimistic about the future of political integration in Western Europe. At least since the Thirty Years War (1618–1648), Europe has seen a succession of wars involving some or all of its nation-states.[1] When active hostilities were not occurring they were being prepared for, or more subtle forms of competition for dominance were being undertaken. Ongoing enmities lasting decades or even centuries have existed between some pairs of nations—France and Germany, Britain and France, Italy and Austria. War was a major activity of the European nation-state, and anyone who expected this history of conflict to be replaced by cooperation and by an elimination of nationalism might have appeared naive even a few decades ago.

World War II was a watershed for the history of nationalism in Europe. Although World War I actually cost the lives of more European combatants, World War II brought the horrors of modern warfare and the depths of human depravity home to the ordinary citizen. At least 10 million Western Europeans who were not in uniform died in World War II—from bombings, systematic extermination, or starvation; over 30 million civilians died in the war on all fronts (Gilbert 1989). Further, although it did not fall on Europe, the use of the atomic bomb pointed to the immense destructive potential that would be available if future European conflicts broke out. Many ordinary citizens, and many statesmen, believed that the pattern of frequent warfare established through the centuries could no longer be allowed to continue if European civilization were to survive.

The feeling of the European in the street was matched or surpassed by the ideas of some remarkable postwar European political and economic statesmen. These leaders included Winston Churchill who, although he was virtually a symbol of British nationalism during World War II, advocated an end to destructive nationalism at the end of the war and in 1946 called for "a kind of United States of Europe" (de la Mahotiere 1970, 20–22). The three most noted leaders of the movement toward European economic (and perhaps eventually political) union were Paul-Henri Spaak (Belgium), Jean Monnet (France), and Robert Schuman (France). These leaders, along with many more, believed that the only viable future for Europe was as a single entity. Such a belief was, however, difficult to implement even in the face of the war's destruction.

The leaders of the European movement understood the difficulties inherent in attempting to overcome centuries of nationalism and believed that a *functionalist* approach to unification might be the only means of achieving their ends. The functionalist approach argues that making a frontal assault on nationalism would almost certainly fail; the psychological attachments to existing nations were strong, and governmental institutions were almost entirely oriented toward the single nation. What was needed, the functionalists argued, was a gradual approach, based on first integrating (making common among all nations) a single function—usually economic—and then letting that integration "spill-over" into additional forms of integration (Haas 1964; Mitrany 1946). The strategy was to capitalize on the "problems all nations have in common" (Lindberg and Scheingold 1970). The functionalists believed that if some significant portions of the economy were to be integrated, then there would be a need eventually to integrate all portions of the economy. Then, when full economic integration was achieved, there would be a need and the possibility to integrate the political systems that guide those economies. From this functionalist perspective, politics as usually practiced is conceived of as a barrier to integration that should be avoided in favor of patient work to unify the economy. Economic unification was assumed eventually to produce demands for political unification.

The functional approach to integration in Western Europe won out over a *federalist* approach that argued for immediate political unification along federal or confederal principles before the nations could recover from the war and reestablish their old ways of dealing with each other (Spinelli 1957). To be successful, the federalist approach would depend on the existence or development of a popular identification with the new political unit that was being envisaged. In the terminology of students of nationalism, the federal political unit would have to become a *terminal community*, or the highest level of organization to which the individual citizen gives allegiance (Deutsch 1952). Such a sense of identification did not appear to exist for Europe in the early 1950s; or if it did, it was not nearly so strong as continuing identification with the individual nation-states. This absence of a terminal community appeared to make a functionalist solution the better approach to unification.

The first major functional integration in Western Europe was in the area of coal and steel—the so-called Schuman plan. After rebuilding its destroyed plants, Europe was capable of producing more coal and steel than it needed, and if it did so competition and/or restrictive trade practices might revive much of the old nationalist sentiments. If an agreement among the coal- and steel-producing countries could be reached, steel could be produced more cheaply and Europe would be better able to compete in the world market (rather than produce only subsidized steel for domestic consumption). Following an initial agreement between France and Germany, the European Coal and Steel Community was established in 1951, with those two countries plus the Benelux countries and Italy. This organization served as a successful model[2] for the Treaty of Rome and the founding of the European Economic Community (EEC), otherwise known as the European Common Market, which was founded in 1957 along with Euratom, a unified atomic energy association.

The Treaty of Rome was signed in 1957 by France, West Germany, Italy, Belgium, the Netherlands, and Luxembourg. Despite the early interest of Churchill and other leaders, Britain decided to remain outside the community. It had not become involved with the Coal and Steel Community because the postwar Labour government wanted to rebuild its own nationalized industries, and it remained outside the EEC in part because it wanted to ensure its ability to maintain its special economic relationships with its commonwealth. The six nations that signed the treaty pledged to search for a new economic future. They promised first gradually to remove all internal barriers to trade among themselves, especially tariffs (import taxes), and then to erect a common tariff on goods imported from non-EEC countries. They further promised over time to develop a common policy toward industry and especially toward agriculture (Body 1982). They also promised to harmonize other national policies that infringed on the central goal of economic integration and fair competition. These barriers to integration included such policies as taxation, labor laws, health and safety laws, and professional licensure. In short, they promised gradually to integrate their economies and with them possibly their political systems as well.

Since the original signing of the Treaty of Rome, six more countries have joined the EEC. After having been twice rejected (Kitzinger 1973), Britain joined in 1973, along with Ireland and Denmark. In all three nations national referenda had approved the idea of membership. In the 1980s Greece, Spain, and Portugal joined the EEC. This expansion still leaves six substantial European countries outside the Common Market: Sweden, Switzerland, Finland, Austria, Norway, and Turkey.[3] All but Turkey are members of the European Free Trade Association, an economic organization with much more limited goals than the EEC. Sweden and Switzerland have opted to stay out of the EEC largely because of their historical neutrality; the requirements for referenda to validate many significant policy decisions form an additional barrier to Swiss membership. Finland has remained out because of, among other things, its special ties with the Soviet Union. Austria has many of the same concerns as Sweden and Switzerland, especially because of strict neutrality provisions in the treaty granting it its independence in 1955. Norway considered membership at the same time that Denmark joined, but a national referendum produced a majority no vote (Orvik 1975; Valen 1973), based to some degree on the desire to maintain the cultural values of a small and largely rural country. With the exploitation of its oil reserves in the North Sea, the Norwegian economy appears strong enough, at least in the short run, to survive outside the EEC. Finally, Turkey has applied for membership but the vast economic differences between it and the rest of the EEC—per-capita income in Turkey was $1,142 in 1986 compared to an EC average of $9,742, and the poorest country currently in the EC (Portugal) has a per-capita GNP more than twice that of Turkey—plus Turkey's political instability make admission unlikely soon. Several smaller European countries, such as Malta, may be permitted to join before Turkey.

The movement toward complete economic integration of the EC by 1992 has placed more pressure on the nonmember countries to consider membership. Austria actively considered applying for membership during 1988, but internal conflicts within the governing coalition did not allow any significant movement in that direction; the idea was revived in 1989 and 1990. Sweden has applied successfully for an upgrading of its observer status in Brussels, perhaps with the view to an eventual application for membership. Finland still must be cognizant of its special relationship with the Soviet Union, but the warming of the Cold War makes that much less of a difficulty if it wants to pursue membership. More than in any other country, however, possible membership in the EC is a divisive political issue in Norway. The failure of the referendum in 1972 left deep political scars, especially within the Labor party that had advocated membership, and any movement toward reopening the question appears unlikely in the complex and divisive political environment after the 1989 elections. If full integration of the EC has the profound effects that many politicians and scholars expect, however, all nonmembers will have to seriously reconsider their positions.

The Institutions of European Government

To manage the EC, the Treaty of Rome established four major political institutions: a two-part executive, a European Parliament, and a Court of Justice. The member countries pledged to support these institutions with "contributions," but now the EC is financed by its "own funds" derived from the common tariff on imported commodities and a levy of 1.4 percent of the value-added tax in each country.[4] These political institutions began their existence as small and weak players in a nationalist ballgame. However, as the anticipated course of functional integration has in fact taken place, the institutions have gained in power and confidence. The further integration mandated through the Treaty of Rome has facilitated this increasing role for these European organizations; the movement toward integration in 1992 is in some ways only an elaboration of the treaty. While the functionalist approach served as an intellectual background for European integration, the framers of the treaty also mandated additional steps to ensure that progress toward integration would be made.

A complex set of institutions has been designed to govern the European Community. The executive branch of the governing institutions is divided into two parts: the Council of Ministers and the Commission. The Council of Ministers, as the name implies, is composed of ministers from the member countries. The membership will vary depending on the issues being decided: ministers of agriculture may appear for agricultural issues, and prime ministers may appear for especially important issues. There is a committee of permanent representatives and a staff to manage the day-to-day business of the council. The council is the most nationalist of the institutions. It serves as the final check on community policy and as the place where the individual nations can ensure that their prerogatives are not being trampled upon by aggressive, pro-European members of the other governing institutions; no significant policy proposal can become Community law without being approved by the council. Votes on the Council of Ministers are by simple majorities of the twelve members, by majorities weighted by the size of the country,[5] or by unanimity. Unanimity is required for particularly important issues, such as admission of new members to the EC.[6] With the move toward full integration in 1992, more issues will be subject to decision by a simple majority vote.

The Commission is the other executive branch institution. At the top of ths institution is a Commission of some seventeen members, two each from

France, Germany, Italy, Spain, and the United Kingdom, and one each from the other countries. The Commission is headed by a president who serves for two years; the president selected by agreement among the member states with each member nation having the presidency in rotation. The members of the Commission are proposed by their own countries but must be agreed to by the other members. Unlike the Council of Ministers, however, once in Brussels for their four-year terms, members of the Commission are supposed to look after Europe first and particular national interests second if at all. The evidence is that the members of the Commission do take their role as Europeans very seriously and do become strong advocates for increased integration. This has been especially true of several British commissioners, who have been accused by Mrs. Thatcher's supporters of "going native" and becoming too European.

The Commission is also responsible for the bureaucracy of the European Communities. The EEC now employs over 20,000 people, most permanent employees of the Communities and some on loan from national civil services. As would the civil service of a national government (see chapter 3), these European civil servants are responsible for the implementation of the law of their government—the treaty and rulings of the Council of Ministers and the Commission—and in the process must make a number of decisions interpreting those basic laws. Thus, just as in national governments, civil servants make secondary legislation in the process of implementation. In the end, however, rule-making through regulation is often insufficient, and the Commission has to propose new European legislation to the council. The Commission also formulates this new legislation, giving members substantial influence over its final character.

It can be argued that it is through the detailed work of the Commission that a great deal of the progress toward European integration has taken place. The push for full integration in 1992, for example, was largely the initiative of the Commission contained in 286 proposals to the Council of Ministers. Although the leaders of this institution receive their office through nomination by their national governments, once in Brussels they are expected to act supranationally, and usually they do. Unlike the Council of Ministers, members of the Commission are *not* supposed to represent their nations but rather Europe and good administration. The European civil servants—whether permanent or on loan—tend to become absorbed in the content of the policies they are administering and in attempting to make those work as intended. This usually means that they will press toward harmonization of national laws and toward European standards.

The third institution of the European Communities, the European Parliament, is located in Strasbourg, France, rather than in Brussels. This Parliament is elected on a national basis but is organized along partisan and ideological lines rather than on nationality. Members are now elected to the European Parliament directly,[7] with representation being roughly proportional to population. When the Parliament is organized, however, members are seated by partisan affiliation rather than country. In 1989 the Parliament had nine partisan groups and a few unaffiliated members. The partisan groups included some very familiar labels such as socialist and communist, but also some more unusual new ones like the "Rainbow Group" (Greens from Germany, Belgium, and France along with some nationalists from Belgium and Italy). By the 1980s, the partisan groups in the European Parliament were beginning to act like political parties that operated across national borders (Pridham and Pridham 1979, 1981). The parties now have a common platform for all their members running in the different countries in the European elections and receive campaign funds from the EEC. Some of the future of European integration may lie in the integration of organizations such as these, rather than in more dramatic and visible acts of governments.

The primary functions of the European Parliament are to pass the budget for the Communities and to consider laws that are binding on member nations that fall within the scope of powers established by the Treaty of Rome and subsequent agreements. These decisions are only advisory, however, as the council remains the final power on EEC law. As in national parliamentary regimes, however, there is a growing notion of executive accountability to the European Parliament. The Commission can, in principle, be forced to resign en masse, and individual members can be called before the committees and required to attend question time in the Parliament. However, as the Council of Ministers remains the ultimate power between the two executive bodies, full parliamentary accountability has yet to be achieved, although Parliament continues to enhance its powers.

The final political institution of the European Communities is the European Court of Justice (Hartley 1988). This body, which sits in Luxembourg, is responsible for determining whether decisions made by the Commission are in accordance with the Treaty of Rome and whether the member nations are living up to their obligations under that treaty. While in the United States the Constitution serves as the basis for Supreme Court actions, the Treaty of Rome, the European Convention on Human Rights, and several other supranational documents (now including the Single Europe Act) are the basis for most Court of Justice actions. Like the U.S. Constitution, these documents have at least a limited supremacy over national laws. The Commission, the governments of member nations, and now individual citizens can bring cases to the European Court, whose decisions are binding on the member nations.

The decisions of the European Court, now reach very far down into the daily business of governing the member states, as two decisions affecting Britain illustrate. In one, the Court ruled that the use of whipping as a form of punishment for crimes on the Isle of Man (part of the United Kingdom but with some residual powers to make local laws) violated the European Convention on Human Rights. In 1988 the Court ruled that the practice of H. M. Customs and Excise in Britain not to charge tax on construction materials violated Britain's commitment to a common system of value-added taxation and therefore gave British firms a competitive advantage not permitted under the Treaty of Rome (*Financial Times,* June 20, 1988). In both instances the British government eventually acceded to the decision of the European Court. Thus not only through bureaucratic but also through judicial decision making the economic and, to some extent political, unification of Europe is being extended steadily.

Major Policies and Programs

The Treaty of Rome provides a basis for the economic integration of Western Europe. The primary thrust of the treaty is to eliminate barriers to trade among the member countries and then to erect a common tariff barrier to external trade. The EEC is, however, more than merely a customs union; it is intended to eliminate *all* barriers to trade among its members, including barriers to the free movement of capital and labor as well as tariffs. In addition, its power now extends very broadly through the economies, and it has a widespread influence on economic and social life in the member countries. Thus, another Community activity is creating greater economic equality in the EC through regional policy. Here we will discuss very briefly three of the Communities' major programs: the Common Agricultural Policy, the Regional Fund, and the Social Fund.

THE COMMON AGRICULTURAL POLICY. The one EEC policy that most Europeans can identify most readily is the Common Agricultural Policy (CAP). Just as the potential for massive overcapacity in the steel industry led to the Schuman plan, there is massive overcapacity in agriculture, especially in the dairy industry and in wine. The problem politically is that a large number of Europeans are employed in agriculture, in some instances very unproductively. Agricultural employment varies significantly among the member countries (see Table 2.2), as does the level of productivity for each

TABLE 2.2

Agriculture in the European Economic Community

	Agricultural Employment as Percentage of Total	Agriculture as Proportion of Gross National Product
Belgium	3	3
Denmark	8	6
France	8	4
W. Germany	6	2
Greece	29	16
Ireland	16	11
Italy	12	7
Luxembourg	4	3
Netherlands	5	4
Portugal	24	11
Spain	18	9
United Kingdom	3	2

SOURCE: Based on data from the International Labour Office, *Year Book of Labour Statistics* (Geneva: ILO, annual); and the Organization for Economic Cooperation and Development, *National Accounts of Member Countries* (Paris: OECD, annual).

agricultural worker and the contribution of agriculture to national income. As is common for agricultural policies in many countries, the CAP attempts to support the prices for agricultural products so that farmers can make a living. At the same time the program encourages rationalization of agriculture for greater productivity and eventually perhaps lower prices for consumers. The major way in which agricultural prices are supported is through buying up surplus commodities, creating a "butter mountain" and a "wine lake."

The Common Agricultural Policy costs member nations a great deal of money—in the late 1980s, some $24 billion annually.[8] The costs and benefits of CAP are distributed far from equally; countries with large numbers of small and relatively inefficient farmers benefit most and countries with smaller numbers of more efficient farmers provide the subsidy. So it is estimated that Italy received $231 million as an agricultural subsidy in 1984 and France some $170 million. On the other hand, Britain paid some $45 million more in agricultural contributions alone than it received in that same year, and West Germany some $40 million. The expansion of the EC to include three more heavily agricultural countries—Spain, Portugal, and

Greece—has added significantly to the costs of the CAP, as well as exacerbated the perception of unequal benefits flowing to the less efficient agricultural countries.[9]

In addition to the perceived inequality among countries created by the CAP, the program's actions may produce some additional disparities. By subsidizing the price of commodities, prices for food are higher than they might otherwise be. The British Treasury estimated that food prices in Britain increased 190 percent during the first ten years of its membership in the EEC. Although most of this increase was due to increases in world commodity prices, many perceived the EEC to be responsible. The subsidies provided to agriculture mean that industrial workers to some extent must pay twice for the program—once when they pay their taxes and again when they buy their food. This feeling of injustice is felt most strongly in the countries that are efficient and largely self-sufficient agriculturally, but industrial workers in all the countries may share this attitude.

THE REGIONAL FUND. The EC also subsidizes industrial development through the European Regional Development Fund. This fund, initiated in 1973, provides grants and loans to assist less prosperous member nations to develop. Its work is supplemented by loans from the European Investment Bank and is coordinated with rural development funds administered through the Common Agricultural Policy. The total value of regional economic aid available in Europe approaches the amount made available to the Third World through the World Bank (Buchan 1989). Financing from the Regional Fund is available both for areas that have not been industrialized, such as southern Italy and virtually all of Ireland, and areas that have been industrial but are now declining, such as Scotland in the United Kingdom and the Ruhr in Germany. Although not nearly as expensive as the CAP, regional policy expenditures in 1984 were some $2.5 billion and have been increasing rapidly.

Regional Fund grants and loans appear somewhat more equally distributed among the member countries than do funds in agriculture, as almost all countries have some significant areas that can benefit from industrial subsidies. Further, the countries themselves can designate the areas in need of funds. The expansion of the Common Market to include Spain, Portugal, and Greece has added many more regions in need of development assistance to the Community and thereby also added to the costs of this policy. In addition, some economists predict that the movement to full integration will result in an increased need for regional assistance to areas negatively impacted by greater competitiveness among the member countries.

Politically, the Regional Fund has been important for shifting some of the focus on policymaking from national capitals to Brussels. Rather than lobbying their own governments, local and regional governments increasingly send delegations to lobby Brussels for money from the fund. Further, subnational governments increasingly approach Brussels directly, rather than working through their national governments. Apparently much of the policymaking activity (or perhaps more exactly grant-getting) has become European rather than national, and Brussels will be increasingly a central object for all levels of government.

THE SOCIAL FUND. Given that most member states of the European Communities have well-developed social programs, it might be expected that the EEC would have very little need to engage in a large-scale social policy effort. That is indeed true. Yet while Social Fund expenditures are smaller than the CAP or the regional policy program, they still are a significant amount of money. In 1984 the EC spent approximately $2.15 billion for its social policy initiatives. The Social Fund was a component of the original European Communities plan, in part because it was believed that there would be a great deal of employment displacement in the early days of economic integration and in part because the fund was perceived as a means of assistance for adjustment to increased competition enabling individual citizens to feel greater identification with Europe. The Regional Fund now offers more, but the movement to full economic integration may revive that role for the Social Fund.

In addition to coping with the direct effects of the EC, and despite the existence of the national programs, the EC can still do a good deal with social policy. The Social Fund is especially active in attempts to equalize access to social services among the member nations and to spread standards of "best practice" among those countries. This is, in part, because only if there is relative equality among social services will there ever be the free movement of labor envisaged by founders of the Communities. The Social Fund is also active in some social and industrial policy areas, such as industrial democracy, equal pay for women, and child care for working women, that have not always been central components of many member states' social and labor policies. While the EC may not be the major actor in social policy that it is in agricultural policy, it can still have a significant impact on social conditions.

SUMMARY. The European Community is now a major policy actor in Western Europe. It is perhaps the dominant actor in agricultural policy and is playing an increasingly significant role in a number of policy areas. It has clearly extended its character beyond a simple customs union to become involved in a wide range of economic and noneconomic areas. The policymaking capacity of the EC makes more difficult this role for national governments. They must attempt to do what they want to do, while at the same time keeping their policies coordinated with Europe-wide policies. There are numerous spillover effects from one policy area to another, and many predictions of the functional theorists appear to be becoming reality. Once begun, it may be difficult to restrain the growth of supranational policymaking power and activity. This is even more true as many decision makers in European institutions are not passively reacting to the effects of integration but are rather actively seeking new opportunities to expand the influence of the European Community. The move toward full integration in 1992 is the most obvious example of this expansion. To some degree 1992 is a symbol for an ongoing series of changes that have the level of nationalism in Europe, but in other ways 1992 represents a real movement by design toward a more European future.

The Creation of a European Identity

The functionalist logic of the founders of the EC appears to have been correct in policymaking terms, but it is less clear if it has had the social, political, and psychological effects intended. If a united Europe is to replace centuries of nationalism in Western Europe, then the individual European in the street will have to transfer his or her identification from the nation-state to the new supranational entity. Although the evidence is still rather sparse, it appears that this shift in identification has been occurring to some degree (Hewstone 1986). When asked, many citizens are giving answers that are less nationalistic and more pro-European (see Table 2.3). Further, those citizens' answers show less hostility toward other European nations, even those with which their country may have had years of hostility and active warfare. This decreased hostility and more positive friendship is especially pronounced among French and Germans. Apparently something has been happening in the European political psyche to produce a new terminal community, with Europe being the ultimate source of identification rather than the nation-state.

Of course, progress toward this new European identity is by no means smooth and uniform. It varies a good deal across time and across countries, and there are some ardent Europeans as well as some ardent nationalists in all these countries. The evidence available from regular surveys of EEC member countries shows that Luxemburgers tend to be the most ardent

Europeans, while the British, Dutch, and Irish tend to have the least identification as citizens of Europe rather than their own nations. Interestingly, French and German respondents, despite their histories of nationalism and nationalistic wars, also show very high degrees of identification with Europe, and low hostility toward one another (Inglehart and Rabier 1978). Also, in the latest surveys respondents from the most recently admitted countries—Spain, Portugal, and Greece—show a high degree of identification with Europe.

The data reflect what has been called the British problem with the European Communities. Britain is a major European country, but psychologically it is by far the most remote of them. Why is this? Britain's psychological isolation appears to result from several factors. First is the tortured history by which Britain gained entry to the EC and its difficult relationship with the French government of that time. Second is the activity of British political leaders who have been confrontational toward the EC and pressed national demands over things such as the Common Agricultural Policy. These nationalist feelings may have been heightened by the Falklands War in 1982. The British also have rather general negative feelings toward the CAP and some other European programs that have infringed on their traditional political ideas, such as the sovereignty of

TABLE 2.3

National Perspectives on the European Community
Is Membership in the European Community . . .

	A Good Thing? (percentage)	A Bad Thing?[a] (percentage)
Italy	71	3
Netherlands	64	3
Belgium	57	3
France	64	4
Luxembourg	65	7
Germany	56	8
Ireland	50	20
Britain	47	21
Denmark	36	25

SOURCE: Reprinted, by permission of the publisher, from R. Inglehart, *The Silent Revolution: Changing Values and Political Styles Among Western Publics* (Princeton, NJ: Princeton Univ. Press, 1977), 353.

[a] Remainder undecided or no answer.

Parliament. In 1988 Mrs. Thatcher was using the same language—"a Europe of nations"—to oppose further integration that Charles de Gaulle had used when opposing British membership. What is not yet known is if the passage of time will produce a more European Britain.

Despite the high identification with Europe in some nations, the degree of identification with Europe by citizens of member nations—not just the British—does not appear to have increased substantially during the past decade, and in some cases it has actually declined. Several factors may account for this. In the first place, the novelty of European integration may have worn off, and citizens may believe that many of the same social and economic problems that exist will be present whether Europe is unified or not. In addition, as the functional logic of integration has been played out, some adjustments required of individual nations due to European policies and standards have become evident and have provoked citizen backlash. Finally, as the generation who survived World War II is thinned by death, the memory of the immense destruction that can be wrought by nationalism is dimming and the real virtues of supranationalism are less evident. For whatever reason, the functionalist success of the EEC does not appear to have been matched fully with psychological success, and national sentiments remain somewhat alive.

In addition to the psychological identification people may or may not have with Europe, other changes are occurring that may make their political life more European. A major factor is that political parties and interest groups are becoming more internationalized and are having to direct a greater portion of their attention to dealing with European matters than to strictly national issues. We noted earlier that seating in the European Parliament is by party, not by country; and this arrangement requires parties to have a supranational means of deciding on party programs. Representatives of the major parties from around Europe meet regularly, and there are some nascent versions of international political parties.

Even more clearly, interest groups are having to focus their attention on European capitals rather than their own national capitals. Agriculture is the principal example, now that the Common Agricultural Policy is so important for most farmers' livelihood. As more complete integration approaches with 1992, other interests will also have to focus on Brussels. Given that product standards for almost all commodities will become European, both industrial and consumer groups will have to go to Brussels if they want changes. A focus on Europe may be especially important in the field of environmental policy, since many of the most visible environmental problems—acid rain, pollution in the Rhine, nuclear wastes—have very clear cross-national implications and may not be fully soluble except on a broader European level.

Summary

European integration has come a very long way since the end of World War II. A viable economic community has been created and, if the promise of 1992 is fulfilled, an economically powerful entity will function almost as a single national economy. Many of the economic rivalries and political conflicts that have characterized European history have been submerged in this flurry of economic activity. There are, however, major challenges remaining for Europe. Some of these are policy problems. Economic integration may require additional unification of monetary policy, but the creation of a European Monetary System is opposed by several nations that want to maintain control of this economic lever. Also, there is a question about what to do with defense policy and the relationship of the EC to NATO; this is especially important if historical neutrals want to join the EC. The more basic question of creating a common European identity and a psychological attachment to the Community is a more difficult process. It may be successful only after several generations have come to live with the concept of being European rather than British, Dutch, or French.

Regionalism in Europe

The nation-states of Western Europe appear clearly defined on a map, but if we look closely at the history of their formation and their internal politics, we find that often they are not unified wholes. Many European countries are better understood as composites of a number of regions rather than integrated nations. Subnational allegiances remain strong in many countries, and in several, regional interests are demanding separate nation-states. Two large European countries—Germany and Italy—were formed only slightly more than a century ago, and at least in the case of Italy unification may be less than complete (Haycraft 1985; LaPalombara 1987). A number of other countries—the United Kingdom, Spain, France, Belgium, the Netherlands, Switzerland—have significant regional sentiments based on language, religion, history, or a combination of all of these (Sharpe 1987). Some fifty different languages are spoken in Europe, and in the European Economic Community it is estimated that at least 50 million out of the 320 million people speak a language other than the dominant language of their country (O'Riagain 1988). Further, even the Scandinavian countries that appear more uniform to outsiders are divided socially over industrialization and urbanization,[10] factions that serve as a basis for political mobilization. Some idea of the degree of division and diversity that exists among regions within Western European countries is given in Table 2.4.

It is worth noting that although it is not strictly a regional phenomenon, Europe has created its own new ethnic divisions by bringing in foreign workers to do jobs that many Europeans no longer wanted to do, or by increasing immigration from former colonies (Heisler and Heisler 1986; Layton-Henry 1988). Almost all European countries now have significant populations of foreign nationals, many of whom intend to remain in Europe and to raise their children there. Some, as in Germany, were encouraged to come in as *Gastarbeiter* to work when there was a labor shortage, but they have found ways to remain even when unemployment has increased. Others, as in Britain and France, came from former colonies and have certain (often ambiguous) citizenship rights in their "mother country" (Davis and Peters 1986).

These foreign nationals do create something of a new regionalism. They tend to be concentrated in the large cities, and even then in certain parts of the country. Some cities in the north of England now have virtual majorities of non-English residents, and Marseilles and other cities in the south of France have large populations of North African immigrants. In France, the longtime residents of these areas gave strong support to Jean-Marie Le Pen and his extreme right political party *(Front National)*, which advocated expulsion of immigrants in the 1988 elections. In addition to provoking political mobilization, the new immigrants tend to be large consumers of social services and to create other service demands, such as teaching English as a second language in inner-city schools in Britain. Thus a new set of ethnic and language problems has been added to the already diverse mixture in Europe, even in such countries as Sweden and Norway, which had been homogeneous societies.

Regional issues need not, however, be entirely cultural (language, religion, or whatever) in their basis. In some countries the economic disparities among regions of the country are sufficiently pronounced to produce political mobilization. These regional disparities also produce a real need for differential economic policies for various parts of a country. Even in Scotland, for example, which is itself treated as a separate region in the United Kingdom, there are huge economic disparities among the urban and industrial "Central Belt" running between Glasgow and Edinburgh, the vast and largely unpopulated areas in the highlands and islands, and the energy-producing region around Aberdeen. Part of this one "region" must

TABLE 2.4
Regional Variations

	Religion		
	Protestant	Catholic	Other/None
Swiss Cantons			
Bern	76.8	17.5	5.7
Aargau	45.1	46.5	8.4
Valais	4.7	92.8	2.5
W. German Länder			
Schleswig-Holstein	86.5	6.0	7.5
Baden-Württemberg	45.8	47.4	6.8
Bavaria	25.7	69.9	4.4
Northern Ireland Counties[a]			
Antrim	75.5	24.5	–
Armagh	52.5	47.5	–
Londonderry City	33.3	66.7	–

	National Identification		
	Nation	Language Group	Canton
Switzerland			
German Speaking	53	16	31
Romance Speaking[b]	40	40	20
	Nation	Region	
Spanish Regions			
Asturias	93	5	
Aragon	61	31	
Galicia	38	53	
	Belgian	Other	
Belgian Legal Regions			
Flems	32.5	67.5	
Brussels	56.5	43.5	
Wallons	50.3	49.7	

SOURCE: Based on data from Rose (1971); Kerr (1974); Blanco et al. (1977); Delruelle-Vosswinkel and Frognier (1980); and official statistics.

[a] Percentages exclude other or no religions.
[b] Romance = French, Italian, and Romansch speakers.

47

be treated as a declining industrial area, while another part must be treated as a traditional agricultural area; the third portion should be considered as a local boom economy with an insecure economic base. Thus the economic and social textures of most countries are far from uniform, and those differences have some real political implications.

Finally, regionalism may develop simply as a reaction to the centralizing tendencies of the welfare state in most European countries. Government in postwar Western Europe has become, in many eyes, increasingly bureaucratic and remote, and there is a perceived need to recapture some control over that government (Rokkan and Urwin 1982). Many citizens view the movement toward supranational government through the European Community as making government even more remote and more bureaucratic, and it may be no accident that supranationalism and regionalism have appeared to vary together. Further, as the activities of the state have expanded, efficiency requirements have prompted numerous reorganizations of local governments (Gunlicks 1981). Many politicians perceived local government only as a service delivery unit for central government, and this dismissive attitude provoked some backlash among Europeans (Sharpe 1987). People do live in space as well as time, and often citizens identify with a physical territory regardless of any ethnic ties. If central government tramples on the perceived rights and privileges of those areas, then some reaction may be expected.

Implications of Regionalism

The regionalist sentiments that exist in European countries can have a number of ramifications that are relevant for the conduct of government. One of the most relevant is voting for regional political parties. Parties of this sort exist in almost all European countries, and in some they are significant political forces. As shown in Table 2.5, in several European countries parties with a cultural basis (which are almost always regional in focus) draw a substantial vote, and in some countries they have been a part of governing coalitions. When votes for rural parties, which also have strong regional overtones, are added, the regional vote in European elections can be very substantial. Further, if we concentrate on the vote-gathering capacity of these parties within their own regions, their impact is even more pronounced. For example, while the Scottish National Party gets just over 1 percent and Plaid Cymru just under 1 percent of the total vote in the United Kingdom, they get 14 percent and 8 percent of the vote within Scotland and Wales respectively. The Scottish National Party is still capable

TABLE 2.5

Ethnic and Regional (predominantly rural) Parties

Belgium	*Spain* (among others)
Volksunie	Basque Left
Wallon Assembly	Basque National Party
Denmark	Galician People's Party
Schleswig Party	Democratic Left of Catalonia
Venstre	*Sweden*
Finland	Center Party
Swedish People's Party	*Switzerland*
Rural Party	Swiss People's Party
Italy	*United Kingdom*
South Tyrol People's Party	Scottish National Party
Val d'Aosta Party	Plaid Cymru (Welsh Nationalist)
Norway	
Center Party	

SOURCE: Based on data from T. T. Mackie and R. Rose, *International Almanac of Electoral History* (New York: Facts on File, 1982); and J.-E. Lane and S. Ersson, *Politics and Society in Western Europe* (London: Sage, 1987).

of mustering substantial support, even in the urban areas of Scotland, and of winning seats in Parliament and even in the European Parliament.

Very few of these regional parties would ever expect to form a government, although a few have been a part of governing coalitions. These parties do, however, have an opportunity to carry their ideas into the national parliaments and directly represent the political wishes of their supporters. To the representation provided by these parties must be added the effects of regional differences that may exist within national parties. Factions from different parts of the country within a party represent varying conceptions of what their party means and of what government policy should be. For example, the Communist party in France, Italy, Finland, and several other countries has both urban and rural membership. In urban areas it is largely the party of the industrial proletariat, while in rural areas it tends to function as a party of protest by agricultural workers and to some extent by rural and anti-industrial interests more broadly.

As well as having political parties representing their concerns, regional interests also form pressure groups to advance their views in national politics. At times these may be branches of nationwide interest groups, such as the Scottish TUC in Britain, or they may be separate regional organizations. As with the regional political parties, cultural issues and especially education constitute a major portion of the agenda for interest groups of this type. And again as with political parties, farmers and rural interest groups in many ways function as regional organizations to protect their way of life against the encroachments of modernity and industrialization. Further, certain institutions associated with different regions in a country, such as churches of different denominations, may also function as regional interest groups centered around issues of cultural and religious freedom.

Making Regionalism Work

Governments have always had to devise some mechanism for governing their territory. For a small country divided by few geographical barriers—Belgium, for example—this is quite easy, and a relatively centralized form of government could, in principle, be effective. For larger and more diverse countries this could not be effective, and means of governing in the provinces had to be developed. One means has been, of course, just to let the provinces govern themselves in many matters that do not seriously affect the central government or that do not require national uniformity. Yet the leaders of most European countries have thought that there were few things that did not concern the center and have sought to enforce their rule directly. They have done so by locating powerful central government officials in the field—for example, prefects in France and Italy (Machin 1977)—or by mandating standards of service for functions performed by subnational governments—for example, the United Kingdom or West Germany. During the 1970s and 1980s the centralization of power in European governments was under serious attack, a number of new subnational governments were formed and some existing ones strengthened.

The political pressures placed on central governments by regional groups in European countries produced a substantial degree of decentralization of power and authority in the 1970s and 1980s. Some countries—for example, the Federal Republic of Germany, Austria, and Switzerland—already were designed around federal or confederal principles, which naturally include a great deal of decentralization. Others, such as Sweden and Norway, which are nominally unitary, actually allow a great deal of local autonomy. Belgium also was nominally unitary, but strong demands to give separate treatment to the two linguistic communities have produced a solution that is in essence federal.

The most striking changes have occurred in countries that have been constructed on centralized, Napoleonic models of governing but have felt the need to form a regional tier of government and give those new subnational governments real policymaking powers. The major examples of this type of change are France, Italy, and Spain (Keating 1988).[11] While the particulars of government form and powers are different in each of these countries, the general pattern is that a tier of government was created in the 1970s and 1980s. Those new governments have powers that would have been totally unthinkable earlier. Regional governments also have viable participatory systems with meaningful elections and have citizens who identify with them even if there is no underlying regionalist sentiment. Once this popular participation is implemented, and regional (or local) governments can make some claims of legitimacy, a central government has difficulty in reasserting its control over policies. In fact, only in the United Kingdom has there been a significant reassertion of the power of central government (Jones 1988; Rhodes 1988). There, to gain control over public expenditure and to some extent over specific policies, the Thatcher government has centralized most policy areas. Some local governments (usually controlled by the Labour party) have fought back, however, and demanded greater autonomy. In short, regional government now appears to work where it had not worked or even existed previously.

Some idea of the powers of regional governments can be gained by looking at the levels of taxation and expenditure that occur at this level. As is to be expected, regional governments spend more money than they collect in taxes (see Table 2.6). National sources of revenue tend to be more buoyant than the revenue sources allotted to local and regional governments. Further, by retaining control over taxes, and therefore being able to withdraw funds, the national government can still retain ultimate control over regional governments' activities. What is noticeable, however, is the increase in the proportion of taxation taken by regional and local governments in many countries during the 1970s and 1980s. These governments are now becoming significant actors and can make an increasing number of decisions on their own.

The degree of autonomy of regional and local governments is even more pronounced for expenditures than in taxation. Because of transfers among levels of government, a substantial pool of money is created for subnational governments to spend in excess of what they received from taxes. In many instances, the central government mandates subnational governments to spend for certain purposes, but the latter tend to have substantial autonomy over how expenditures are made within these functions. Again, the autonomy to spend how one wishes may be especially important in policy areas such as education and culture, which are directly associated with the

TABLE 2.6

1985 Taxing and Spending by Subnational Governments
(percentage of total public revenue or expenditure)

	Revenue	Expenditure
Austria	23.8	32.2
Belgium	7.7	12.0
Denmark	28.3	52.6
Finland	26.0	42.5
France	8.7	15.9
W. Germany	30.8	34.2
Greece	1.3	14.5
Ireland	2.2	29.3
Italy	2.3	31.8
Luxembourg	11.6	12.3
Netherlands	2.4	33.2
Norway	17.9	30.2
Portugal	3.5	5.5
Spain	11.5	21.7
Sweden	30.2	41.8
Switzerland	39.2	46.8
United Kingdom	10.2	25.7
AVERAGE	15.2	28.4

SOURCE: Based on data from the Organization for Economic Cooperation and Development, *The Tax/Benefit Position of Selected Income Groups in OECD Member Countries* (Paris: OECD, annual), and OECD, *National Accounts of OECD Member Countries* (Paris: OECD, annual).

preservation of minority cultures and values. In addition to traditional local government functions such as streets and sanitation, economic development has become a major function of subnational governments. This is especially true in France, where regional governments are given substantial powers in economic planning and in microeconomic policy (Hayward 1983, 200–202; 1986). Regional governments in Italy and Spain also have some substantial economic development functions, and the Scottish and Welsh Development Agencies are major actors in Britain. Just as the EEC targets a good deal of its financial aid to regions rather than to national governments, national governments have found that many economic policy questions may best be addressed in a territory smaller than the entire nation.

Although regional policy instruments are in place to make regionalism work, there are still questions about the viability of this level of government as an important focus for governance. As with the European Economic Community, a major question is the level of psychological attachment ordinary citizens have to their regions. This is easy enough to see where the regions correspond to well-established historical and ethnolinguistic boundaries. It is less clear when the regions are modern creations. For example, Scots may readily identify themselves as Scots. However, many find difficult to grasp the notion of a region such as Strathclyde, which is composed of what had been Ayrshire, Lanark, Argyll, and other more familiar place-names. Likewise, in Germany, although some of the *Länder*, such as Bavaria and the city-states, have historical roots, others, such as North-Rhine-Westphalia, may have very little identity for citizens. Some evidence indicates that regional identification is developing (Putnam 1988), but most areas have a long way to go to create a sense of citizenship and belonging among their residents. The effective and efficient provision of public services by regional governments may be one means by which they can create that sense of legitimacy they require to be viable political entities.

Summary

One of the most fundamental changes occurring in European politics is the relative decline of the powers of the nation-state. Once the central mode of political organization in Europe, the nation-state now finds its centrality challenged. Its powers are being drained off supranationally toward the European Economic Community and subnationally toward regional and even local governments. The nation-state still has quite a lot of latitude in governing its territory, but its powers are now more circumscribed and require greater consultation and compromise. Of the two changes, the increased power of the EEC appears the more significant change. Once it began to gather momentum, the EEC demonstrated the viability of the functionalist logic that has guided it for a good part of its development. It is in the economic interest of current members to cooperate fully with the Community and with each other. Further, it appears to be in the economic interest of nonmembers to gain admittance, even if that presents serious political difficulties. Major psychological hurdles still will have to be jumped, but there is movement toward European integration. In several generations, European politics may be just that—European.

We should not expect the nation-state in Western Europe to vanish in the near future, but it is clear that politics is becoming somewhat different.

Many central questions of economic policy will be decided in Brussels, and many social and cultural policy issues may be decided in the regions. The nation-state is a form of organization particularly suitable for the conduct of war. If so, and if to some extent the formation of European political institutions is about the end of war, at least among member nations, then the nation-state may eventually become a less useful mode of political organization. The large-scale economic issues may be better handled at a higher level, and it is clear that many domestic policy issues can benefit from decentralization. While the face of European politics may change greatly, that change may also be a very long time in coming.

Notes

1. Wars certainly took place prior to this time, but during the Thirty Years War at least one protagonist emerged (Sweden under the Wasas) that looked like a modern nation-state (Samuelsson 1968).

2. An abortive attempt in 1952 to form a European Defense Community to integrate all the armed forces of Europe slowed progress toward integration. This effort ran afoul of traditional nationalist sentiments, especially in the French Parliament, which rejected the treaty. In particular, the French wanted to retain full control over their army to deal with colonial concerns in Vietnam and Algeria (see Deutsch et al. 1967).

3. We will not be considering the roles of very small countries, such as San Marino, Malta, Andorra, Liechtenstein, or territories, such as the Faeroes and Greenland, that are moving toward statehood.

4. These contributions are still collected by the nations and therefore can be withheld for political and financial leverage over the EC. The United Kingdom, under Mrs. Thatcher, has been especially prone to use its contributions as a form of blackmail to attempt to coerce the EEC to do what it wants.

5. In a weighted vote, France, Germany, Italy, and the United Kingdom receive ten votes; Spain has eight; Belgium, Greece, the Netherlands, and Portugal receive five; Denmark and Ireland, three; and Luxembourg, two.

6. This veto power was how Charles de Gaulle was able to keep Britain out of the EC for so long after it had decided to apply for membership (Kitzinger 1973).

7. The movement to have direct popular elections had to overcome a good deal of opposition from national governments. It was implemented only with the 1979 Parliament (Lodge 1986).

8. Budgeting within the EEC is done with the European Unit of Account, with its value linked to a shopping basket of the currencies of member countries. The value of this unit varies against the dollar, so all the spending figures in dollars given here can only be approximate.

9. Although they are heavily agricultural, admitting these countries to the Common Market does bring in some agricultural products, such as citrus fruits, that are not produced in abundance in the rest of the Community.

10. Interestingly, much of the theoretical literature on central-periphery relations in Western Europe grew out of work on these countries rather than countries divided more clearly along ethnolinguistic lines. See particularly the work of Stein Rokkan (1966, 1967, 1970).

11. It was in these very countries that the Napoleonic system of local government was established to break attachments to regions. The naming of the *départements* in France for geographical features, for example, was an attempt to break the bonds of citizens in such regions as Burgundy and Brittany to regional government.

Chapter

3

THE INSTITUTIONS OF GOVERNING

We have now described the centrifugal pressures driving power and authority away from national institutions in Western Europe. While these pressures are certainly powerful, we cannot afford to forget that national governments continue to make most public policy decisions. Even when unitary national governments choose to decentralize and to give regional and local governments more power, they reserve the right to reclaim that power at a later date. Likewise, even though European integration proceeded rather quickly in the late 1980s, most decisions still had to be approved by the representatives of nation-states sitting in the Council of Ministers, and nationalism is certainly alive in that institution—especially in the hearts of the British representatives. Even as the Commission of the European Community was pushing toward greater unification in the summer of 1988, Mrs. Thatcher was very clearly expressing her perception of the national interest in keeping Britain as independent as possible (Riddell 1988), and she has continued to search for alternatives to full economic unification. In virtually a restatement of the language Charles de Gaulle had used when denying British entry to the Common Market, she has stressed the importance of the concept of a "Europe of separate countries working together," rather than a Europe as a single political entity itself.

Further, some important policy areas have not even begun to be integrated and are unlikely to be so in the foreseeable future. Defense remains national, except through North Atlantic Treaty Organization (NATO) linkages. Both the French, with their independent *force de frappe,* and the British, with the history of the Falklands war still fresh in their minds, appear very reluctant to relinquish any meaningful control over their defense forces. These countries, along with West Germany, provide the bulk of Western European defense forces. Going along with these independent forces are independent diplomatic representation of differing national interests. In addition, justice and police remain national, although the European Convention on Human Rights is beginning to have some impact on the administration of justice. Finally, although under some pressure to form a European Monetary System, the monetary policies of the member nations may remain largely autonomous. Nation-states are threatened but are still significant policymaking actors, especially with respect to what Richard Rose (1976) called the "defining functions" of government.

Parliamentary Democracy

From an American perspective, the styles of policymaking in Western European countries are rather unusual. In particular, to someone accustomed to the separation of powers among the branches of government, the parliamentary regimes found in Europe offer a different approach to managing the affairs of state. Rather than require a (possibly) conflicting set of institutions to reach an agreement after due deliberation, and thereby slow the work of government, a parliamentary regime enables the party or coalition of parties with a majority in the lower house of the Parliament to make policy relatively easily. This is especially true given that European political parties have greater cohesion and discipline than American ones. This means that a majority in Parliament is likely to be an effective voting majority when issues arise. Checks on possible abuse of this policymaking power tend to come after the fact, in the next election, rather than through another government institution.

There are other important differences between Europe and American approaches to government. One is that the public bureaucracy is a more central policymaking actor in most European countries than is the case in the United States. European countries have a history of powerful and capable civil service systems that could provide that commodity called "government" when the elected political leadership was too fragmented or indecisive to rule itself (Diamant 1968). Further, unlike the United States, there is no tradition of giving executive responsibility in government to a large number of political appointees who are not Parliament members

(Neustadt 1966). The partisan political leadership in most European governments is a thin veneer on top of the career bureaucracy. Those bureaucrats themselves may have political views and certainly will have policy views, but they are members of a respected career service rather than politicians. The economic and governing problems we have already discussed have brought the policymaking role of the civil service in European countries into some question, but it remains more powerful than its counterpart in the United States.

Another major difference between North American and European government is the role that law and the judiciary play in governance. This is not to say that somehow European governments are not concerned with the rule of law. What it does mean, however, is that the judiciary in most countries (West Germany is a major exception) is not so independent and activist as that in the United States. Hence, when Parliament makes a policy, that is the law, and in most countries it is not subject to constitutional challenges that laws in the United States might face. As with the separation of powers discussed earlier, when considering the role of the judiciary, the ability of a Parliament to decide and make a decision stick must be weighed against other values, such as civil liberties and accountability. Further, the well-developed systems of administrative law that exist in continental European countries provide an avenue for countering government power that is no less effective than the methods available in the United States or other common-law countries (Nedjati and Trice 1978). That remedy, however, applies to the procedures used to apply the law much more than to its substance.

Another major difference between European and North American countries is the volume of activity in which the state is engaged. In most Western European countries, many functions that are performed in the private sector in the United States or even Canada are public. The most obvious of these are economic activities—telephones, steel, electricity, and so on—carried out through nationalized industries in Europe, and the much better developed set of welfare-state programs. All this activity adds up to a much larger public sector in Western Europe, whether measured by revenues or expenditures (see Table 3.1). It further means the management of government and its massive level of public expenditure is a more difficult, and more important, task for elected governments. While European governments have been privatizing a number of these economic functions as neoliberal ideologies sweep that continent as well as North America, government there remains a more significant economic actor than in the United States.

The Political Executive: Prime Ministers and Cabinets

The executive branch in European governments typically is composed of a prime minister and a cabinet. Although the exact details of the institutional relationships do vary, in essence this executive is a committee of the Parliament and serves at its pleasure. The term government is also used to describe the executive, and includes the cabinet as well as any other members of the Parliament given executive responsibility but who do not sit in the cabinet. The executive receives office through election by the Parliament and, again with varying details, can be dismissed by Parliament by a vote of no confidence or by the rejection of an important piece of legislation. Thus rather than having any separation of powers, in a parliamentary

TABLE 3.1

Public Revenue and Expenditure, 1987
(as percentage of Gross Domestic Product)

	Revenue	Expenditure
Sweden	50.5	58.3
Denmark	49.2	53.4
Norway	47.8	41.2
Belgium	46.9	61.4
France	45.6	52.0
Netherlands	45.0	54.6
Luxembourg	42.8	46.6
Austria	42.5	48.4
Ireland	39.1	58.0
United Kingdom	38.1	46.5
W. Germany	37.8	41.6
Finland	37.3	39.3
Greece	35.1	55.4
Italy	34.7	59.2
Canada	33.1	50.3
Switzerland	32.1	26.0
Portugal	31.1	53.8
United States	29.2	40.1
Spain	28.8	46.3

SOURCE: Drawn from: Organization for Economic Cooperation and Development, *Economic Outlook* (Paris: OECD, June 1989).

regime the powers of government are fused. Being able to exercise one set of powers (the executive) depends on being able to command the other (the legislature). The executive is not at the mercy of Parliament and can shape the latter's work, but it does still have to maintain a working majority. This parliamentary arrangement also makes the dynamics of politics and governing different from those that are usually found in a presidential regime.

In the first place, in a parliamentary regime the executive does not necessarily have the mandate that an independently elected president can claim to have. A prime minister may be the leader of the party that wins an election and may be particularly visible during the election campaign, but in the end he or she is voted for directly only by the voters in one constituency out of several hundred. Voters in the other constituencies may vote for a candidate from a party because they want a particular person to be prime minister, or for any number of other reasons. The prime minister is therefore more obligated to the party and the other party members in Parliament than would be a president. Thus prime ministers are as much or more leaders of political parties and legislative bodies as they are politicians appealing directly to the public.

It has been argued that the premiership in most European countries is becoming more presidentialized (see Hennessy 1986). This assumed change is in part a function of the changed nature of the electoral campaigns by which parliaments, and hence prime ministers, are currently selected. Partly because of expanded coverage by the electronic media, the leading candidates for prime minister are increasingly visible to all voters, and the style of campaigning is increasingly dependent on the personality of party leaders. Rather than expressing broad ideological views about policy as they were once expected to, European political parties appear more and more to be focused on the personality and leadership potential of the probable prime ministers. Those leaders are often not devoid of policy ideas, as indicated by Mrs. Thatcher in Britain, Olof Palme in Sweden, or François Mitterrand in France, but much of their electoral appeal has become personal rather than ideological or party-oriented.

The style of governing once in office also appears to have become more presidential, with an accretion of powers around prime ministers. Some West German scholars (for example, Bracher 1974) have gone so far as to refer to their system of government as "Chancellor Democracy," because of the central role of the chancellor (prime minister). Prime ministers have, for example, tended to expand their personal staffs and to make more policy decisions through their own office rather than in full cabinet. Some prime ministers have had significant staffing for a longer period of time, for example, the *Bundeskanzlersamt* in West Germany, and others have created or expanded staffs. Prime ministers have also been attempting to place more of their own loyalists in important positions in government rather than continuing to rely on the career civil service. Again, in many continental European countries this practice has been relatively normal, and civil servants themselves can choose to make their partisan affiliations known. The practice of checking political preferences of civil servants has become extensive, however, producing some concern about excessive politicization of the civil service (Derlien 1988). Cabinets also have become less balanced among factions in countries where coalition politics permit, with only true believers being given executive positions. Prime ministers now appear to want to extend their personal powers down into government to a much greater extent than has been true in the past, and have developed the tools to do so.

The necessity of having a majority in Parliament to become prime minister usually also implies the need to create a coalition. Only rarely and in a few countries in postwar Europe has any single party received sufficient votes and seats in Parliament to be able to form a majority government on its own. Even parties with very long periods in office, such as the Social Democrats in Sweden or the Christian Democrats in Italy, often have had to govern in coalitions. A coalition with a dominant partner may be very different from the multiparty coalitions in Belgium or Denmark, but it is still a coalition. Some countries, such as those in Scandinavia, have been able to function with minority governments, but in most a majority coalition must be formed. The need for a majority government means that the period after an election may be as important politically as the period leading up to it, and issues that could not be solved by appeal to the voters will have to be accommodated in the creation of a coalition government. In the language of the structural-functional approach to comparative politics (Almond and Powell 1966), *interest aggregation* may have to occur after the election among political parties rather than before the election within parties.

The academic debate about the basis on which coalitions are formed has been long and intense. We will not attempt to summarize all the schools of thought here (but see DeSwann 1973). What is most important for our purposes is the debate over whether the size of the final coalition, or its ideological composition, is more important in determining which parties belong and which do not. The "size principle" (Riker 1962) argues that politicians would attempt to form a coalition that is as small as possible while still constituting a majority. Given the multiple political cleavages that divide parties in Europe (see Chapter 5), including more parties and/or party members increases the number of concessions on policy ("side payments" in coalition theory) that the coalition will have to make in order to be formed and to remain together. On the other hand, it can be argued that size is not nearly so important as the degree of ideological or policy consistency among the members of the coalition; with a higher degree of ideological consistency, fewer side payments may have to be made regardless of the coalition size. In practice, both of these factors appear to have some importance (Franklin and Mackie 1984), but the political wrangling to form coalitions is still particular to each setting and each set of circumstances and continues to defy simple explanations. For example, coalitions in Switzerland tend to be larger than needed, because traditionally they are expected to have something approaching proportional representation of the many ethnic and ideological groups in the society (Steiner and Dorff 1980).

When thinking about coalition governments, it is important to remember that there are at least three distinct varieties, which in turn have rather different dynamics. One variety, characterized by coalitions in West Germany, has a large party as the dominant partner, with one or more small parties (the Free Democrats in Germany) as subordinate albeit crucial members. This pattern also appears in Sweden when the Social Democrats form the government (with the aid of the Left Party Communists) and to some extent in Ireland (with Labour at times alternating as coalition partner with Fianna Fail and Fine Gael). A second variety of coalition is the amalgam of many small parties. The party from which the prime minister comes may take the lead in such a coalition, which is a grouping of *relative* equals. While the first form of coalition does depend on several parties, it behaves more like a single-party government; the multiparty coalitions are characterized by more internal bargaining and greater instability. The third form of coalition is the "grand coalition" that includes all the major parties and therefore is much larger than the size principle would predict. Grand coalitions tend to be formed during times of crisis, or when there is a transformation between parties after a long period of domination by a single party, such as in Germany in 1966 and in Austria in 1987.

The need to form coalitions and the need to generate majorities in Parliament both tend to produce a third crucial political difference between parliamentary and presidential governments: the degree of party discipline. It is not uncommon for political parties in presidential regimes, most notably the United States, to have multiple factions and to allow individual members to behave in idiosyncratic manners. That freedom of action can rarely be permitted in parliamentary regimes, where continuing in office will depend on the ability of a party to command a majority on every significant vote. Further, if a coalition is to be successful, the members must be able to count on one another's support. A failure of party discipline could only weaken the trust among parties necessary to make the coalition function and further undermine the chances of a less disciplined party's being selected as a coalition partner in the future.

PRESIDENTS AND PRIME MINISTERS. In the typical European state the roles of head of state and head of the government are separate, unlike the president of the United States, who occupies both roles. For European countries the head of state is either a constitutional monarch (as in Spain, Britain, Belgium, the Netherlands, Denmark, Sweden, Norway, Luxembourg, plus a few smaller countries) or a president elected either directly by the people or by the Parliament. In the cases of both monarchs and elected presidents, however, the post is largely ceremonial. The duties involve receiving diplomatic credentials and visiting heads of state, formal openings of Parliament, and other necessary duties that have little impact on public policy. The head-of-state powers come to the fore if the monarch or president must choose whether or not to dissolve the Parliament or to exercise some discretion about whom to ask to form a new government after an election. Even then, in most instances these are not real choices; constitutional or consensual principles govern decisions. However, after a close election or in a confusing situation in Parliament, the head of state can sometimes make a real choice, although to make too obvious a personal political choice might threaten the continuation of some hereditary monarchies.

In European countries the prime minister is the effective executive power. As the leader of the largest party in the lower house or the obvious leader of a probable majority coalition, he or she is usually asked to form a government after an election. In forming a new government the prime minister has the power to dispense office and thereby to create a coalition among parties or among factions within a single party that can consistently command parliamentary majorities. This coalition is also the prime minister's power base. Once this cabinet is formed, the prime minister expects to be its leader and increasingly is expected to be more than the old British description of the prime minister as *primus inter pares* ("first among equals"). The media, the development of prime ministerial staffs, the ability to reshuffle the cabinet, and a perceived need to act "presidential" have all pushed prime ministers out in front of their cabinets as the most central actors in European politics. This leadership role has been highlighted by economic summits and even meetings of EEC heads of governments, which in addition to being media events show political leaders meeting together to attempt to solve their common problems.

Although almost all European governments have exhibited a tendency toward presidentialism, the roles prime ministers have adopted do differ. This is often a function of the personalities of the leaders who have occupied the office during the period of expansion of media coverage and increased focus on the executive. Some like Margaret Thatcher have been able to project a strong image, while others like Helmut Kohl (in contrast to Helmut Schmidt) are not good media personalities. In some political systems, as in Italy, the average prime minister is in office a rather short time and is not able to project a personal, presidential role. Further, even in stable coalition governments a prime minister may have to be somewhat less presidential to preserve the participation of other parties and other leaders.

Despite the powers given to a prime minister, he or she may not be able to hold together a coalition, or may even lose support from members of a single governing party. Therefore, parliamentary systems require provisions for dissolving a sitting government and selecting a new prime minister. In many cases the government is legally and/or morally bound to resign when it loses a major vote in the lower house of Parliament (or the single house in unicameral legislatures). In most instances this would involve dissolving the Parliament and calling a new election, although the practice in the Scandinavian countries has been to form a new government (even if a minority) from the current Parliament and proceed until the next scheduled election.[1] It has become common practice, however, for governments not to resign unless they lose a specific vote of "no confidence"; if the government loses a policy vote, it may then ask for a confidence vote. If it is successful on that vote, it will retain office.

West Germany is the principal exception to these statements about the procedures for replacing a prime minister. The constitution of the Federal Republic requires that there must be a "constructive vote of no confidence" to force a chancellor to resign. The lower house (Bundestag) must elect a new chancellor before the old one is forced to leave office. For example, in 1982 the Free Democrats grew tired of Chancellor Schmidt's policies and decided to break their coalition with the Social Democrats that was keeping him in office. The Free Democrats then voted with the Christian Democrats to elect Helmut Kohl to replace Schmidt. This constitutional provision was designed to prevent the instability of the Weimar regime (1919 to 1933) that contributed to the rise of Hitler and the Nazi party. Bringing down a government under the 1949 constitution is more difficult, and there would always be a government in office, not the long interregnums and periods of coalition building that had characterized the Weimar Republic.

The differences in rules about causing a change in government, in party systems, and in the decision-making loads being placed on governments have produced very different levels of government turnover among the European democracies. As shown in Table 3.2, Greece has had the most unstable executive since 1945, with some forty-six changes in government and thirty-two changes in the prime minister. Finland, Italy, and France are close seconds, along with Switzerland if the annual planned changes in the executive there are counted as instability. On the other end of the scale,

TABLE 3.2

Changes in Government, 1950–88

	Any Change in Top Three Posts[a]	Change of Prime Minister	Elections
Austria	18	6	13
Belgium	25	18	14
Denmark	26	14	16
Finland	40	29	12
France	42	32	13
W. Germany	16	6	10
Greece[b]	46	32	13
Iceland	17	15	13
Ireland	18	13	12
Italy	42	26	11
Luxembourg	12	6	12
Netherlands	21	14	11
Norway	21	13	11
Portugal[c]	15	7	6
Spain[d]	9	3	4
Sweden	18	7	13
Switzerland[e]	42	42	10
United Kingdom	33	11	12

SOURCE: Based on data from Cook and Paxton (1986); Mackie (annual); and *Facts on File.*

[a] Prime minister, minister of finance, or minister of foreign affairs.
[b] Ignores period of 1967 to 1974.
[c] Period after 1975.
[d] Period beginning in 1976.
[e] The vice-president, in many ways the prime minister, is elected for a one-year term from the Federal Council. The Federal Council itself stays the same, and this is hardly as unstable as it looks.

Sweden, Austria, and West Germany have been extremely stable, with very few changes in government since 1945, most of which occurred at the time of regularly scheduled elections. Spain has also been rather stable since it began democratic politics.

We must be careful, however, not to make too much of apparent government instability in Western Europe. When asked how many governments Italy had had in the postwar era, one commentator replied "One," meaning that although there were numerous changes in the partners and in the ministers, the Christian Democrats had dominated the Italian government (see the discussion in Cassese 1980) since 1946. It may be that, particularly with coalition governments, changes in government are merely minor shifts around a core set of policy principles—and a core set of actors—rather than fundamental changes in the direction of government. Although the surge of neoliberal ideologies in many countries has challenged the postwar consensus on policy, it remains a powerful force for stability.

A DUAL EXECUTIVE. France, which has both a powerful, popularly elected president and an influential prime minister, is the major exception to the roles just discussed for presidents and prime ministers. The constitution for Fifth Republic France was designed to rectify the problems (as perceived by Charles de Gaulle) of the Third and Fourth Republics, especially government instability. It was thought that if there was a president of the Republic who could govern almost without the parliament,[2] then there would be less instability, or at least any instability that did occur would not be as damaging. The possibility of government instability was further reduced by a constitutional provision that any member of Parliament who accepted a ministerial post had to resign his or her Parliament seat, so that if the government fell he or she might be out of a political job.[3] These constitutional provisions were another way of attacking the same problem of instability that the German constitution addressed with the idea of the constructive vote of no confidence.

The Gaullists who designed the constitution of the Fifth Republic were, if not hostile toward traditional parliamentary democracy, certainly cool toward it and especially toward its perceived excesses. The Fifth Republic was designed to be able to make decisions, through the president and his or her power to issues decrees, even if the Parliament continued to be plagued by the instability that had afflicted it in previous regimes. The system of an independently powerful president and prime minister functioned relatively smoothly as long as both were from the same political party. Even then, however, at times there was friction over specific policies. The possibility of that friction became very pronounced when, in 1986, the voters returned a right-wing (Gaullist and Republican) majority to the National Assembly after having elected a Socialist president, François Mitterrand, some five years earlier. Mitterrand still had two years left in office. The stage was set for a possible constitutional crisis, or for government by presidential decree.

This possible confrontation did not happen, however, and "cohabitation" (Duverger 1987) appeared to function very smoothly. A number of articles of the French constitution specify how a prime minister is to be selected and the scope of independent authority of both the president and the prime minister. Mitterrand followed these, apparently to the letter of the law, and proposed the Gaullist Jacques Chirac as prime minister. After Chirac's election by the National Assembly, the two executives made laws within their own spheres and appeared to coordinate their activities successfully, using the elaborate machinery already in place (Fournier 1987). The peculiar bicephalous arrangement of the French constitution functioned even when placed under this severe partisan strain. The events of 1988, with widespread public service strikes after a Socialist (Michel Rocard) replaced Jacques Chirac as prime minister, made it appear that cohabitation had worked better than having executives from the same party in the two offices.

WHO IS IN THE CABINET? The size and composition of cabinets vary substantially among Western European countries. Cabinet members are, most often, members of Parliament who have been given the executive task of running one of the government departments. Some cabinet members may, however, not have direct executive responsibility for an organization but rather are included to provide general advice for the prime minister, or to provide a balance among various party factions. For example, the British cabinet includes the "Chancellor of the Duchy of Lancaster," a post that itself is largely a sinecure, although it may be held along with another real executive post.

In most instances the size of the cabinet is up to the prime minister. He or she can decide which executive posts to include and which to exclude, and usually can reorganize the executive branch of government almost at will. In 1988 cabinets ranged from seven (set by law in Switzerland) to thirty (Italy) members. Cabinets with the most members tended to have either a number of posts for nationalized industries or for specific industrial sectors, or to have ethnic divisions in departments that are reflected in multiple cabinet seats for essentially the same function. So, for example, the large Greek and Italian cabinets both contain a minister for the merchant marine, and in the Belgian cabinet there are separate French and Flemish ministers for education and institutional reform. Another reason for a particularly large cabinet is to provide enough spaces for all the political parties, or factions thereof, that must be rewarded adequately for coalition participation.

The demographic characteristics of most cabinet ministers are hardly surprising: Most are well-educated, middle-aged men from the dominant social groupings (class and ethnic) in the country. There are, however, an increasing number of women in high executive posts. In addition to two women serving as prime ministers (Margaret Thatcher in Britain and Gro Brundtland in Norway), some cabinets (especially in Scandinavia) have up to 35 percent female representation. Most cabinet ministers have been involved in politics for a long time and have served long apprenticeships before attaining a cabinet position. In these apprenticeships, they generally have moved around among different ministries and performed different governmental tasks, often for very short periods. This experience is at once a strength and weakness for them when they become members of the cabinet, as we will discuss later.

THE OPPOSITION. Another facet of parliamentary government that is quite different from what would be expected in a presidential regime is the institutionalization of the opposition. In a parliamentary regime the government of the day may be out of office the next day. Those out of office may have only a few weeks to campaign in an election, to prepare for governing, and actually to take control. Therefore, it makes a great deal of sense for the opposition parties to be organized for governing and to be prepared to take office. Most parliamentary regimes have a formalized opposition, organized very much like the government, with a "shadow cabinet" to monitor the actions of incumbent ministers. This practice of shadowing also makes organizing parliamentary activity easier, as the shadow minister is expected to be prepared to debate the incumbent minister's proposals. The opposition may be institutionalized to the degree of being provided some staff and the shadow ministers being given extra pay and allowances to do their jobs properly. Even with an institutional opposition, however, the rapid changes of government possible in a parliamentary system further enhance the power of the public bureaucracy as the repository of an "organizational memory" for government and as the source of continuity in periods of change.

In addition to the practical matters of being prepared for government and organizing parliamentary debate, the principle of opposition may have some deeper, philosophical meaning in parliamentary government. Especially in the United Kingdom, it is assumed that better legislation will emerge from an adversarial system of government. If the opposition is not well organized, vigilant, and properly staffed, then parliament runs the risk of passing poor legislation. The opposition must be "Her Majesty's *Loyal* Opposition," but it must still be the opposition. Even if the opposition agrees with legislation in principle, it has the duty to present alternative means for achieving the same ends or to present alternatives to the government's program. The opposition is also expected to be responsible in the future for the policy alternatives it presents, and parliamentary debate is to some degree the opening round of the next election campaign.

PARTY GOVERNMENT. Democratic politics presumably is about translating the wishes of voters expressed on election day into public policies. In the simple model of democracy, voters are choosing a bundle of policies as much as they are choosing a set of political leaders. The problem is that in the institutional design of governments many intervening factors make it difficult for this simple model of democracy to function in the real world. Unfortunately, as the responsibilities of modern governments have grown both more numerous and more complex, the disparity between the idealized model of partisan government and the more confused reality has increased.

The first thing that must occur for the model of political democracy to be effective is for the political parties campaigning for office to give the voters clear choices among goals and means to reach them.[4] We will discuss what has been happening with European party systems in Chapter 5. Here we will only point out that political parties may be willing or able to do this less adequately than in the past. The issues that governments must confront are more complex and frequently defy simple explanations in mass campaigns. The tendency of the mass media to report short, pithy comments by candidates rather than detailed discussions of complex issues exacerbates that difficulty.[5] In addition, campaigns have become increasingly about the personality (and perhaps the capabilities) of prime ministerial candidates rather than about issues, and political parties—at least the traditionally ideological parties of the Left—have become less ideological. This gives the voters less of an anchor for their judgments of the policy proposals being offered. Finally, the rise of more single-issue parties (such as the "Greens") participating in politics has meant that a number of issues may be discussed more outside the campaigns of the principal parties that have a real chance for election. These smaller parties have injected ideology back into politics, but also may divert attention away from the more likely party options for government. In short, mass politics may not be much concerned with the selection of public policies but more with the expression of sentiment about parties and leaders.

Once the mass stage of politics is completed, those who are chosen for office have to get about the business of governing. One question is whether they have the skills necessary to perform the tasks before them. First, although this is tending to change, those who are given ministerial office rarely have any significant amount of education or experience in the policy area for which their ministry is responsible. The cabinet typically will be formed to balance a number of political considerations and to provide jobs for proven party leaders, whether or not they have any particular policy expertise (Headey 1974). One study of ministers in the democracies of Western Europe and North America concluded that only about 20 percent had any expertise in the policy area for which they were responsible (Blondel 1985, 196). In fact, the practice of working one's way up in the political executive by performing a number of different tasks, while certainly giving someone in government "the big picture," does not often equip him or her to manage any particular program.

Although there may be some common patterns and problems, governments do differ in the extent to which their ministers are capable of dealing with substantive policy issues. There are some variations across time, with some ministers adopting "technocratic" styles of governing. However, the major variance appears to be across countries (Blondel 1988). For example, Austrian ministers (as might be expected from the stability of governments there) tend to stay in office for long periods and to come from the civil service or from outside government rather than from Parliament. Very often they are selected for their expertise rather than solely for political reasons. Belgian ministers, on the other hand, are politicians who are in office for short periods and arrive there with little advance knowledge of the programs they will administer. Everything else being equal, we should expect the more managerial Austrian ministers to be able to provide better governance than the more political Belgian ministers.

In addition to their frequent lack of policy expertise, those selected for cabinet positions often lack managerial expertise as well. A political career rarely permits people to gain significant experience managing a large organization, and in government they will be called upon to manage some of the very largest organizations in their societies. There are exceptions, of course. Some conservative parties have ministers who have managed large businesses, and some labor or social democratic parties have ministers who have been leaders of large labor unions. Also, in continental European countries where political and civil service careers are not incompatible, civil servants may be ministers; over half the ministers during the Fifth Republic in France have been civil servants (Antoni and Antoni 1976; Birnbaum 1985). The typical minister, however, will have had a political career and, unless he or she has been a minister previously, probably will not have had experience in managing a large organization. Even if he or she has managed in the private sector, a potential minister will not have encountered the peculiar difficulties of managing in government—civil service laws, budgeting restrictions, requirements for public disclosure, and so on. Of course, the civil service is there to keep the organization running on a day-to-day basis, but if the minister is to have the impact necessary for party determination of policy, he or she probably needs some management skills.

In addition to a potential deficit of skills, ministers in parliamentary governments also frequently lack the time to perform adequately all the tasks for which they are responsible. The job of a minister in a parliamentary system is a difficult one. He or she remains a member of Parliament and therefore must attend many parliamentary sessions. Regular attendance is especially important for a cabinet member who may be expected to speak on the policy issues affected by his or her department. He or she also has constituency duties and must return periodically to tend to the concerns of the voters. Although usually not as well developed as in the U.S. Congress, parliaments do have committees and the minister may be a member of one or another of those. And as a member of the cabinet, the minister will have at a minimum weekly meetings and will also have to meet with numerous committees (Mackie and Hogwood 1985) to conduct the cabinet's business. Once in his or her department, the minister will have to receive numerous deputations and individuals who are making requests of the department. Finally, when all that is done, the minister may have time to think about ministry policy and management. It is little wonder that a former cabinet minister in Britain described his existence as "a dog's life in a ministry" (Marples 1969).

Of course, there are variations in the extent to which ministers in individual countries are faced with all these duties and in the extent to which they have assistance in carrying them out. These variations are in addition to those in recruitment discussed earlier. Perhaps the best equipped to handle the tasks are ministers in the Fifth French Republic. Not only do they have to resign their parliamentary seats if they accept a ministerial post, thereby relieving them of a great deal of work, but they also have sizable personal staffs to assist them in managing their departments (Remond, Coutrot, and Boussard 1982). Ministers in France (and in Belgium and Italy, among others) have personal *cabinets* to advise them and to assist in pushing their own program through the department. Italian ministers face formidable managerial tasks within their departments, but the government can co-opt members from outside Parliament (Cassese 1980) who can deal with policy and management issues full time. In other countries (West Germany and Sweden most clearly) the ministers do not have a large department to manage. In West Germany, most ministries are small planning organizations, with public policies being implemented by state *(Land)* governments. In Sweden, the ministries are also small, with most implementation being done by semi-independent boards *(styrelsen* and *ämbetsverk)*. Finnish administration is a compromise between the decentralized Swedish style and direct ministerial management (Lundqvist and Ståhlberg 1983). In instances when there is devolution of administration to state governments or quasi-autonomous bodies, the minister may be responsible for the ultimate execution of policies, but does not have to manage a large bureaucracy directly.

At the other extreme, ministers in the British and Irish governments probably face the most difficult tasks. They have direct responsibility for management working within a (now weakening) tradition of ministerial responsibility for everything that occurs in the department. They have little or no personal staff, but must depend on the permanent civil service. Further, their parliamentary duties must be carried out with little or no staff; a member of Parliament in Britain receives only a tiny annual staff allowance. The task is especially difficult for Irish ministers because of the well-developed tradition of constituency service by members of the *Dáil* (Parliament) as a means of circumventing the civil service. An Irish parliamentarian is expected to spend a great deal of time and energy on the individual problems of constituents if he or she wants to be reelected (Chubb 1963).

Finally, after a "policy" has been formulated in a ministry and passed by the Parliament, it must be implemented. The ministries can make all the policies they wish, but if nothing happens with them farther down the organizational hierarchy, then they are not really government policies. In the process of implementation, the minister must be able to influence members of the organizations that actually put the policies into effect. In most countries lower echelons of the same organization that the minister heads conduct much of the implementation activity. Even then, however, resistance is possible if the policy adopted is contrary to the organization's established procedures and norms (Peters 1981). Large public organizations make millions of decisions each year, for example, about eligibility for social benefits or whom to arrest, and most of those are made by the very lowest echelons. Ministers in most political systems lack the tools and the personnel effectively to counter any resistance of the career civil service to new programs as they make those millions of decisions.

Controlling implementation may be even more difficult when it is performed by organizations beyond the minister's direct control. We noted earlier that the managerial workload for Swedish and West German ministers is less than for ministers in most other countries, but they pay for this luxury with less direct control over implementation. Fortunately, both countries have legalistic political cultures that enable the law itself to exercise a major controlling and coordinating function (Steinkemper 1974), but that may be insufficient in some cases, especially when a *Land* government is controlled by a different political party from the central government. Further, even in countries where most implementation is more centralized, subnational governments still perform a substantial portion of the administrative work. Local authorities in most countries have responsibility for implementing a broad array of national programs, with social services, police, and education as common examples (Rhodes 1988). Reliance on subnational governments constitutes a major source of slippage between official pronouncements and actual practice, especially when local authorities are controlled by different political parties from the central government and utilize implementation as a form of guerrilla warfare against the central government.

In summary, governments are elected to do the things that they promised during the campaign. When they actually get to office, however, they encounter a number of barriers to their actually doing those things. In most instances the barriers are not the result of civil servants or local governments trying to sabotage the governing party. They tend to result more from inertia, from habit, and also from the inability of those in government to organize for effective policy control. The nature of most parliamentary systems places such huge demands on ministers that only the exceptional ones have the mental and physical capacity to perform all that they are expected to do. Democratic government is a difficult commodity to produce, and it may be growing more difficult day by day as quantitative and qualitative demands on government escalate. The difficulty and complexity of governing have placed the public bureaucracy in a position to acquire (whether it wants it or not) power over public policies.

Parliaments

The legislative work of Western European governments is carried on by parliaments. In most countries, even those that have achieved the status of full-fledged democracies only recently, there is a history of an assembly of notables. The British Parliament, for example, grew out of an assembly of the nobility and then later knights of the shires, usually called together when the king needed more revenue. In Spain the *Cortes* traditionally was an assembly of the several estates (nobles, clergy, burgers, and so on) in society that met when called by the king. Only more recently have parliaments as popularly elected legislative bodies responsible for writing laws and for controlling the executive become central features of government. They are now the central democratic institution of government, although the executive does much of the actual work of governing.

The Structure of Parliaments

Parliaments are organized differently in each Western European country. These differences are usually not that great, and structures and procedures in one would be largely recognizable in another. There are, however, several structural features that do merit a brief discussion because of their impact on the quantity and quality of legislation that the Parliament is able to produce.

SIZE. The first feature to be considered is the size of the Parliament, especially relative to the size of the country's population. This factor is important for the role of parliaments as representative institutions. As shown in Table 3.3, parliaments in Western Europe range in size from 59 to 650. The average member of Parliament in Luxembourg represents only some 6,000 people, while the average member in France, West Germany, and Spain represents more than 100,000 people. All the figures on representation are, however, substantially lower than in the United States, where the average member of the House of Representatives has over 500,000 constituents, while the average senator represents approximately 2.4 million citizens. Another factor that must be remembered about European parliaments is that they are not as constrained by rules about equality of representation as are American legislatures, and therefore seats can be apportioned to meet needs of government other than strict numerical equality. For example, in the United Kingdom, Scotland, and Wales are overrepresented in the House of Commons to take into account their particular ethnic and historical differences from England. While the average member of Parliament from England represents approximately 93,000 people, those from Scotland represent around 72,000 and those from Wales around 76,000. Equally sharp differences, largely overrepresenting rural areas, occur in other European parliaments.

While their smaller size apparently makes European parliaments more directly representative of their publics than the U.S. Congress, the fact that most of the parliamentarians are elected by proportional representation

TABLE 3.3

Sizes of Parliaments

	Seats in Parliament	Citizens per Seat	Method of Election
Austria	183	41,000	PR
Belgium	209	47,400	PR
Denmark	175	29,100	PR
Finland	200	24,500	PR
France	489	111,900	PR
W. Germany	498	122,300	Mixed[a]
Greece	300	33,000	PR
Iceland	60	3,200	PR
Ireland	166	21,700	PR
Italy	630	90,900	PR
Luxembourg	59	6,200	PR
Netherlands	150	96,700	PR
Norway	155	26,400	PR
Portugal	250	40,800	PR
Spain	349	110,300	SM
Sweden	350	24,000	PR[b]
Switzerland	200	32,000	PR
United Kingdom	650	86,300	SM

PR = proportional representation.
SM = single member.
[a] One-half by proportional representation; one-half by simple majority.
[b] 310 in constituencies; 40 in compensatory pool for national representativeness.

from large constituencies tempers this to some degree. The parliamentarians therefore may be more connected and more responsive to the national political party that placed them on the electoral list than to the local voters. Further, even when the members of Parliament are elected in single-member constituencies, as in Britain, they may not be local residents and may have only the most tenuous contacts with their constituency. So, more than the U.S. Congress, European parliaments are national rather than collections of "ambassadors" from localities. There may be some localism, especially from regional and ethnic parties, and to some degree all politics is local. Even in centralized states, such as France, local notables have had substantial political advantages. Yet the prevailing forces in European politics are national.

While representativeness is an important quality for a legislature in a democratic country, there may be some trade-off between it and other attributes of a working legislature. As greater representativeness will also mean a larger Parliament, it must be traded off with the efficiency with which the Parliament can function. A large Parliament such as that of the United Kingdom may not really be able to function as a deliberative body. It may do a good job of organizing an adversarial contest between the front-bench leadership of the two large parties, but rarely can it take into account the views of most of the membership. Thus, somewhat paradoxically, although citizens may be somewhat closer to their member of Parliament than in a smaller legislature, that may make little difference if the member is little more than a pawn of the leadership of his or her party.

BICAMERALISM. Except for the Scandinavian countries of Sweden, Denmark, Finland, Iceland, and Norway, European parliaments are bicameral. In the Scandinavian model of democracy, referenda often serve the function of checking the Parliament that might be served by a second chamber (Elder, Thomas, and Arter 1983). Although elected as a unicameral body, the Norwegian parliament *(Storting)* does divide into two houses for certain types of issues, and the organizational pattern in Iceland is similar. In all cases in Western Europe, the lower house of Parliament is popularly elected, and it is that house to which the prime minister and cabinet are responsible. While the second houses may have equal power in making legislation in most countries, the business of selecting a government and holding it accountable will occur in the lower house only.

The second chambers in European parliaments are selected on a number of principles and fulfill several different purposes. The House of Lords in the United Kingdom is a vestige of the nondemocratic past, with its membership composed of hereditary peers, clergy, and peers appointed for life. Lords does consider legislation and is a institution in which the government can accept modifications to its legislation, or even a defeat, without its control of office being threatened. The powers of the House of Lords are now reduced to a suspensive veto, with no power over money bills. In contrast, the Irish Senate is a corporate body, containing representatives of various interests in the society—business, labor, agriculture, the universities, and administration—rather than popularly elected representatives. We will point out in Chapter 6 that corporatism is a continuing feature of politics in most European countries, but few go so far as to have corporate representation in a parliamentary body.[6] In several other countries, the second chamber is composed of directly elected representatives, usually representing a larger geographical area than the larger lower houses.

The second chamber in West Germany, the *Bundesrat,* is the most important of the second chambers in Western Europe. It is designed to meet the needs of the federal constitution, with representation being of the constituent states *(Länder)* rather than of individuals. The *Länder* do have, however, different numbers of seats, based on population.[7] The *Bundesrat* is a full partner in lawmaking for at least 60 percent of legislation—those laws that affect the states and their spheres of responsibility. The *Bundesrat* is conceived of as an expert body as well as a place to represent the interests of the *Länder.* The *Länder* send permanent representatives to the *Bundesrat,* but may substitute experts in the policy area being discussed and change the representatives to meet the legislative needs of the time. In practice, civil servants spend more time in the *Bundesrat* than do the nominal political representatives. This is seen as a way of ensuring that the legislation that is passed is not only acceptable to subnational interests but also well conceived on technical grounds.

Several other second chambers of European parliaments also represent territorial interests. The Council of States, the second chamber of the Swiss parliament, is a powerful legislative body with representatives elected popularly from the cantons and half cantons. Also, the Dutch second chamber is elected by provincial assemblies and has retained a significant role in policymaking. The second chamber of the Austrian legislature, called the *Bundesrat* as in West Germany, is elected by *Land* legislatures but on a partisan basis. This tends to make the Austrian *Bundesrat* more of a partisan rather than a federal body. In countries governed with federal or confederal principles, second chambers tend to be important mechanisms for defending the prerogatives of the constituent units in the federal union, and retain full legislative powers.

COMMITTEES. The feature of a legislature that most students of the U.S. Congress would want to know about would be the presence and strength of parliamentary committees. The committee system is the source of much of the strength of Congress, and also the source of much of the power of the individual congressmen. In most European countries, however, legislative committees are not the significant instruments for policymaking that they are in the United States.

The Congress of the United States relies on committees to do a good deal of the detailed deliberation and writing of legislation and to perfect laws before they are passed. In European countries that function is fulfilled primarily by the government (who are, of course, themselves members of Parliament), with the assistance of their civil servants. If committees were to be given too free a hand in modifying legislation, this would be seen in several countries as violating the principles of ministerial responsibility and cabinet government. The constitution for Fifth Republic France goes so far as to limit the National Assembly to six committees with very limited powers, in order to prevent committees from seizing too much power from the Parliament as a whole (and perhaps more important, from the executive). Those committees are forbidden, as are legislative committees in many other European countries, from holding on to legislation and must report it back to the full Parliament after a specified time period. In a parliamentary political system, the government must prepare legislation and is then judged in Parliament, and subsequently at the next election, on the basis of that legislation. For this type to work, it must be clear whose legislation it is that is being considered, and the government must be able to have *its* bill passed.

Yet there are committees in European parliaments, and in some cases they do have some real power. In West Germany, for example, the committees of the *Bundestag* receive legislation prior to the principal political debate and are active in considering, and at times modifying, that legislation (Johnson 1979). In part because of the volume of private legislation and opposition bills, the Italian parliament has also developed a powerful and effective committee system. The Swedish and Finnish parliaments also have well-developed committee systems that shadow the ministries and are central features in the legislative process. The Netherlands also has a well-developed committee system, but it is less central to legislative activity. Denmark has committees corresponding to the ministries but uses them primarily for oversight; legislation is handled in ad hoc committees for each bill. This is somewhat similar to practice in the United Kingdom, with the select committees monitoring the activities of government (Drewry 1985) and with membership on parliamentary standing committees adjusted somewhat for each bill.

What Do Parliaments Do?

In modern governments, parliaments are sometimes considered endangered species. Despite the important role they have traditionally played in democratic governance, some see them as being rather old-fashioned and inefficient. Many of the same constraints that afflict cabinet ministers also afflict parliaments. The members often do not have the background to understand complex policy issues and, unlike the U.S. Congress, do not have the staffs and strong committees to help them. Further, they often do not have the time to master the details of most of the legislation that they must pass. The procedures parliaments employ to do their work appear inefficient, antiquated, and hopelessly out of touch with the demands of a modern decision-making body. Despite all those problems, parliaments do survive, and some are even making a comeback against the power of the executive. In addition to their symbolic function as representatives of the people in a democracy, parliaments continue to do at least three important things in government: make laws, adopt budgets, and oversee the executive branch.

LAWMAKING. The most obvious function of parliaments is to pass legislation. This they do, and in some volume. Parliaments continue to be the basic source of legitimate rules for European societies. Further, their debates on legislation constitute a major public record about the policies that governments are making for those societies. The openness of parliaments, as contrasted to the secrecy of the executive branch in many European countries, serves as a source of public education on the policy problems that those countries confront. Perhaps most important, citizens still think that legislatures are important. One study (*Eurobarometer*, 1983) showed that, on average, one-third of European respondents thought that Parliament was very important, while less than one-fifth thought that it was not very important or not important at all. Scholars appear to have dismissed parliaments much more quickly than ordinary citizens.

Still, one can question whether the legislature itself is doing the legislating. More than a decade ago, one scholar described legislatures in Europe as being engaged in the process of ". . . mere registration of decisions taken elsewhere" (Grosser 1975). This assertion is based on the assumption that parliaments are really the rubber stamps for prime ministers and cabinets and lack the resources to initiate and pass effective legislation on their own. For example, one study reported that over 85 percent of all legislation in France was initiated by the government, while in Britain the figure was almost as high (Drewry 1981; Frears, 1981). In the Scandinavian countries a government bill has a 99 percent chance of being passed, while a private member's bill has a very low probability of being passed (Elder, Thomas, and Arter, 1983, 124); similar odds face private members' bills in most other countries (see Table 3.4). Italy and Germany are principal exceptions to this generalization. In Italy the number of *leggine* ("little laws") passed as private members' bills and bills initiated by opposition parties rival the amount of government legislation. In addition to bills coming directly from the ministries, political parties (especially the governing parties) through their own research offices may be generating, and then advocating, legislation. While parliaments may have the power to generate and pass legislation, most of the initiative has passed to the executive.

TABLE 3.4

Sources and Success of Legislation

	Government Bills as Percentage of Total	Percentage of Bills Passed[a]	
		Government	Private
Austria	65	96	50
Belgium	23	137[b]	7
Denmark	59	84	6
Finland	48	102[b]	1
France	22	82	3
W. Germany	74	101[b]	58
Greece	87	77	0
Ireland	9	90	10
Italy	29	51	9
Luxembourg	94	100	24
Netherlands	98	85	16
Norway	90	99	12
Portugal	70	14	48
Spain	58	81	13
Sweden	app. 99	–	app. 1
United Kingdom	92	92	10
AVERAGE	58	86	17

SOURCE: Based on data from the Inter-Parliamentary Union, *Parliaments of the World* (New York: Facts on File, 1986).

[a] Percentage of bills introduced in each category that are passed into law.
[b] Greater than 100 percent because of bills coming from upper house.

   Although the record is spotty and difficult to read, it appears that legislatures are attempting to fight back against executive domination in policymaking. Legislatures have begun to develop more of their own staffs so that they can conduct their own policy research and analysis (see Table 3.5). They still have a very long way to go, and no European Parliament has anything like the staff support provided individual congressmen and committees in the U.S. Congress. In addition, more mavericks are showing up in parliaments with their own ideas and with the capacity to see those ideas actually enacted. These mavericks may be individuals or they may be political parties—"Greens" and sometimes the extreme Right—with agendas very different from those of the governing parties. While these counterattacks may never produce a real return to parliamentary domination of public policy, they do represent some move toward greater balance in power between the executive and the legislature.

Another point worthy of note is that although parliaments do make most things with the title "law" (in whatever language) attached to them, a great deal of additional rule-making is occurring in European countries. The products of this rule-making have the force of law, but are developed without the direct action of parliaments. Most laws now passed by parliaments are actually framework laws that require additional rule-making before they can be implemented with any real effect. For example, parliaments may pass industrial safety legislation outlawing exposures to dangerous chemicals above safe levels; someone else must determine what safe levels are and perhaps which chemicals are dangerous. That "someone

TABLE 3.5

Staff Support for Parliaments

	Personal Staff[a]	Committee Staff	Legislative Reference and Research
Austria	from party	no	very limited
Belgium	no	yes	yes
Denmark	from party	yes	yes
Finland	yes, also from party	limited	very limited
France	yes	yes	yes
W. Germany	yes	yes	yes
Greece	limited	limited	no
Ireland	limited	limited	very limited
Italy	from party	yes	yes
Luxembourg	yes	very limited	no
Netherlands	limited; also from party	yes	very limited
Norway	from party	yes	limited
Portugal	no	very limited	very limited
Spain	from party	yes	very limited
Sweden	limited	yes	yes
Switzerland	limited	yes	limited
United Kingdom	limited	very limited	limited

SOURCE: Inter-Parliamentary Union, *Parliaments of the World* (New York: Facts on File, 1986).

[a] Paid for by government.

else" is almost always the public bureaucracy. Secondary legislation produces a much greater volume of law than the primary legislation issued by parliaments. It cannot be written without a legislative peg to hang it on, but as a broad interpretation of laws is common, there is a great deal of latitude for action. Parliaments can always go back and pass new laws if the bureaucracy's interpretations are not what was intended, but without careful supervision of the bureaucratic rule writers, legislative purposes can be deflected during the implementation process. To meet the need for supervision, parliaments have organized themselves—usually through the creation of a special standing committee—to review all secondary legislation being issued. The same sort of mechanism is being used to monitor the effect of European legislation and secondary legislation on national policies.

BUDGETING. We mentioned earlier that parliaments historically gained a good deal of their power by control of money and the government's purse strings. Those purse strings continue to be a major source of parliamentary power. The executive receives the right to spend money, and with it implement programs, through an act of Parliament. In addition, the fact that in most societies the auditing of government accounts is done by officers responsible to the legislature serves as a significant check on the powers of an executive that wants to spend according to its own priorities rather than those of Parliament.

When compared to the executive branch, parliaments may be at as much, or more, of a disadvantage in budgeting as they are in legislating in general (see Table 3.6). Most parliaments lack the analytic staff that executives have in their treasuries or ministries of finance to advise on budgeting and on the economics of public expenditure and taxation. Further, the legislative process tends to divide the consideration of revenue and expenditure, even though these categories should be considered together to have any control over the public deficit. Appropriations tend to be considered at one time in one or more spending bills, while taxes are considered at another time in another bill. Where committees are important legislative actors, there are almost always separate ones for taxation and appropriations. Finally, as money bills are almost inherently issues of confidence, the legislature is often forbidden from altering them unless it is seeking a dissolution of the government, and individual members are often prohibited from introducing bills with budgetary implications. With strong party discipline a dissolution may be difficult to achieve, and moreover for most policy issues legislatures may be rubber stamps for budgets.

Although European legislatures in general are not well prepared to cope with the control of the public budget, some are better prepared than are others. For example, as shown in Table 3.6, some parliaments have separate budget committees, can amend budgetary propositions, and have staff to assist in analyzing the budget. Others have none of these attributes and therefore will have much less chance of influencing the budget sent to them by the executive. They may have the formal power to refuse the budget (in France even that would not matter in the face of a determined executive) but little capacity to carefully scrutinize the budget.

Again like the case of general legislation, legislatures are making efforts to become more equal partners in budgeting. They have begun to ramify their staffs and have begun to include some budget analysts on them. Parliaments have used the fiscal problems that have plagued most European governments since the mid-1970s as a lever to develop new procedures

TABLE 3.6

Strength of Parliaments in the Budgetary Process

	Right to Amend	Separate Budget Committee	Referral to Functional Committee	Staffing	Summary
Austria	yes	yes	no	low	medium
Belgium	yes	yes	yes	medium	high
Denmark	yes	yes	no	medium	medium
Finland	yes	yes	yes	medium	high
France	no	yes	no	low	low
W. Germany	yes	yes	yes	high	high
Greece	no	yes	yes	low	low
Ireland	no	yes[a]	no	medium	medium
Italy	no	yes	yes	medium	medium
Luxembourg	yes	yes	no	medium	medium
Netherlands	limited	no	yes	low	low
Norway	yes	yes	yes	medium	high
Portugal	yes	yes	yes	low	medium
Spain	yes	yes	no	high	high
Sweden	yes	yes	yes	high	high
Switzerland	no	yes	no	high	medium
United Kingdom	no	no[b]	no[b]	low	low

SOURCE: Based on data from the Inter-Parliamentary Union, *Legislatures of the World* (New York: Facts on File, 1986).

[a] Several.

[b] Referred to various select committees rather than to standing committees.

giving them a greater voice in budgeting (Schick 1988; Tarschys 1985). Finally, legislatures have taken the postaudit power more seriously and have used it as a handle to attack executive power. This may be a blunt power, because usually it can be invoked only after the money is spent, but it is a power nonetheless. Further, to the extent that legislatures have begun to follow the American practice of including efficiency auditing along with financial auditing, they have been able to expand their influence over public expenditure. In short, legislatures have begun to take "the power of purse," the original source of their power, more seriously again.

OVERSIGHT. The final power of the legislature is oversight over the political executive (the cabinet) and the permanent civil service. The whole idea of parliamentary government and ministerial responsibility is that the ultimate powers reside in the legislature and that the executive has power only so long as the legislature retains confidence in it. Parliaments have developed a number of mechanisms to investigate and control the executive. Some of the more important of these come through their power over the budget mentioned earlier. There are, however, means through which the legislature can exercise power even on matters of day-to-day administration.

One mechanism for legislative oversight is the committee system. We have already said that few parliaments have as well-articulated and powerful committee structures as those of the U.S. Congress. What some have been developing, however, are special oversight committees responsible for monitoring the activities of the executive and reporting any perceived malfeasance or nonfeasance to the whole parliament, and thereby to the public. The new Select Committees in the British House of Commons (Drewry 1985) are examples of this type of committee, while in Sweden and Finland the Committee on the Constitution has been performing the same task for a much longer time. The powers of these oversight committees to punish malfeasance are very limited or nonexistent; the committees depend on Parliament and public opinion for any real effect on the executive. The power to generate publicity, however, can be in itself an important weapon for keeping the behavior of the executive within bounds.

A second parliamentary tool for controlling the executive is interpellation, or question time. In all parliamentary systems, some time is set aside for members of Parliament to question ministers about their actions and those of their ministries. These questions can range from the most trivial details of administration to matters of high policy. While there are varying grounds for ministers to refuse to answer—such as national security or privileged communications—ministers will usually reply and sometimes must respond with very embarrassing information. Again, this method of control relies for the most part on publicity and other parliamentary actions to have any real effect. In addition, the norms of ministerial responsibility are weakening, so political executives may no longer be responsible for the actions of their civil servants. The simple fear of public exposure of wrongdoing, however, can be an important tool in controlling an executive.

A final tool at the disposal of many legislatures is the ombudsman, or parliamentary commissioner (Rowat 1985). The ombudsman is typically an officer of Parliament with powers to investigate complaints against the executive branch. The powers granted to these officials vary widely. In some countries, such as the Scandinavian countries, the ombudsman can investigate what he or she wishes, while in others, such as the United Kingdom, the ombudsman cannot investigate unless requested to do so by a member of Parliament. In some settings the ombudsman can initiate legislation as a matter of right, while in others he or she depends on the Parliament members to introduce remedial legislation. The scope of their powers also varies. In some countries they can intervene only in civilian administration, while in others there are special officials for the military and for prisoners (West Germany), and for consumers (Sweden). Further, the level of staffing allowed the ombudsman varies, and with inadequate staff little real investigation can be done. While a good deal of the power of these officials depends on publicity and exposing malfeasance to Parliament, in the countries where the institution is most ingrained—largely the Scandinavian countries—it can have some direct impact on the executive.

SUMMARY. Parliaments may not be the all-powerful institutions that formal statements of parliamentary sovereignty make them appear. Neither, however, are they the weak and purposeless puppets that their critics portray. The real picture of their role is more balanced. Parliaments have indeed lost some of their powers and prerogatives to the executive, just as within the executive branch itself full cabinets have lost some power and prestige to prime ministers. Parliaments are not, however, powerless and have been attempting to reassert their powers in a number of ways. They must face the formidable task of attempting to combine their deliberative functions and complex procedures with the demands for quick decisions on complex issues that now characterize contemporary governments.

The Public Bureaucracy

Up to now we have been using the public bureaucracy as a foil for the powers of the political executive and to some extent for those of the legislature. We shall now discuss this important policymaking institution itself in some detail. Bureaucracies have become more important in policymaking in almost all countries, but their powers are perhaps especially pronounced in Western Europe. This is true for several reasons. One is that traditionally the state has been perceived more positively in Western Europe than in most other portions of the world, and consequently the state's servants, the bureaucracy, also have been given a higher status (Armstrong 1973). Thus in Germany, Austria, and some other continental countries, senior civil servants have the stature of judges or legal officials in other countries. Associated with this high status is a selection process emphasizing merit and legal qualifications rather than political patronage. In much of Western Europe the public bureaucracy is an elite institution, not a set of political hacks given public jobs as a reward for faithful partisan service.

A second reason for the powers of the public bureaucracy has been the relative inability of other institutions, at times, to provide governance (Diamant 1968; Peters 1989a). We have already pointed out that few political officials in ministerial positions have any special knowledge of the issues over which they must preside. This leaves the field clear for the permanent civil service to exercise influence. Further, few parliaments are organized to supply independent expertise in the consideration of policy issues, and in many countries those parliaments, and the governments coming from them, have been very unstable. The bureaucracy has become the only institution capable of supplying continuity and stable government. Even in countries that do not have a strong *étatist* tradition, such as the United Kingdom, the expertise and continuity of career civil servants have been important to effective and efficient government.

The Nature of the Public Service

There is a tendency to speak of *the bureaucracy* as an integrated whole, while in reality it is a complex and multifaceted institution. It is as diverse as the activities of the contemporary state and is growing increasingly professionalized and expert as the demands placed on government are now also more complex. Although spoken of collectively, rarely does the bureaucracy act together on any policy issues, unless it is on the issue of their own pay and perquisites.[8] One central activity of civil servants is to protect the interest of their own organization and thereby their own clients. Defending their own programs frequently brings one group of civil servants into conflict with others over such issues as the budget and the best approaches to providing public services.

This brings us to an important consideration about the civil service in modern states. This is that the majority of public employees are service providers rather than paper pushers (see Table 3.7). For every person sitting behind a desk making policy decisions or checking forms, the government employs perhaps a dozen doctors, social workers, teachers, police officers, and the like who actually provide direct services to citizens. In many countries these service providers are direct employees of the central government—not of local or regional governments—while in others they may be employed by quasi-governmental organizations, as in the National Health Service in Britain. Many governments have been attempting to disguise their true size by "hiving off" a number of their activities to seemingly independent bodies (Hood and Schuppert 1988; Peters and Heisler 1983). To the government social service providers just described must be added employees in nationalized industries such as electricity, gas, railroads, and telecommunications who are also involved in providing different types of services directly to the public. If all these social and economic service workers are excluded, and the military is excluded, European governments do not really employ very many people, despite the image of their being very large and ever-expanding.

Although the bulk of public employment is composed of workers who provide services directly to the public, the most important positions are usually thought to be the "decision-making" positions in the senior civil service—the mandarins (Aberbach, Putnam, and Rockman 1981; Dogan 1975). In every civil service system there is a cadre of several thousand people at the top of their respective organizations who advise the ministers,

TABLE 3.7

Public Employment as Percentage of Labor Force
(early 1980s)

	Total	Other than Military	Other than Military and Service Providers
United Kingdom	28.3	27.1	5.4
France	29.8	29.2	8.6
W. Germany	24.9	23.5	6.4
Italy	22.3	20.7	5.6
Sweden	37.4	35.6	8.2
United States	16.6	14.7	4.9

SOURCE: Based on data from R. Rose et al., *Public Employment in Western Democracies* (Cambridge: Cambridge Univ. Press, 1985).

link the political and the career components of the executive, and are managerially responsible for most public organizations. Although there are some important differences among these officials in the several European countries (Page 1985; Peters 1989a), there are also some important similarities as well. In general, the senior civil servants in European countries:

1. Have received an elite education. Further, that education will be distinctive in each country: law in Germany, the Scandinavian countries, and others with the same legalistic traditions; the École Nationale d'Administration (ENA) in France, and so on.

2. Will spend almost an entire career within government, preparing to occupy a post at the top of the organization in some ministry or other large public organization. They are also prepared to be associated directly with ministers and other political officials as advisors and so on.

3. Will develop policy expertise even if they did not receive it by education. The education of most civil servants is general, but on the job they will specialize and spend most of their career in a single policy area.

4. Will regard the job as political in the broadest sense and in some cases may be partisan political. Most civil servants will understand their role in making public policy and will be happy with that role and responsibility. They will differ, but tend to accept political decision making as appropriate within a political democracy, even if at times they may devalue the planning and other analytic information the bureaucracy provides.

All these factors combine to make the career civil service in Western Europe a formidable institution in the policy process.

The Role of the Bureaucracy in Making Policy

We can examine the role of the public bureaucracy in making policy in much the same way as we looked at the capacity of ministers and political executives to make policy. Each of the several stages we outlined with respect to ministers can be also be considered for the civil service and will sum to an important role for the bureaucracy. That role, however, may not be so important as analysts of the shortcomings of contemporary political democracy might expect. The civil service has more of a policymaking role than traditional models of political democracy would predict, but it is not the dominant feature of the more critical portrayals either.

First, to be said to govern, an institution must have ideas about policy. Generating ideas is not usually considered the role of the public bureaucracy, but it often is. Policy ideas come forth from the bureaucracy in two ways. One is that the status quo itself is a powerful idea for what to do in a policy area, and the bureaucracy often is the implementer and defender of that status quo. This is especially true for bureaucracies operating in countries with legalistic administrative cultures and with a status quo embodied in law. In most cases, the civil service should be expected to defend the programs that are already in place. The public bureaucracy should also be expected to be the source of some new policy ideas. Civil servants increasingly are trained in a profession, or some other specialty, and have the knowledge and professional networks that would produce new ideas about how to shape policies. In addition, their long experience in a policy area is likely to produce some ideas about how existing programs could be improved. Given that at least senior civil servants work in a policy advisory capacity, they may be able to push those ideas onto government policy agendas for action. Even at the lower levels of a public organization, the ability to write the secondary legislation required to implement a program provides the bureaucracy a substantial influence over new policies.

If the generation of policy ideas might be thought to be the weakness of the public bureaucracy, the management of organizations and the implementation of policy once decided might be thought to be their strong points. This is certainly true when contrasted to most politicians, but it may not be absolutely valid. The management of any large institution is difficult, but it may be even more difficult in the public sector where there are more regulations on hiring and firing of personnel, spending money, open hearings, and public disclosure of information than are found in the private sector (Allison 1986). In addition, as noted earlier, political executives have come to understand that civil servants gain a great deal of power in their day-to-day management of policy and have begun to place (whenever possible) more of their own partisan loyalists in those managerial positions (Derlien 1988; Meyers 1985). Thus to the extent that career civil servants do have their own interests to protect in the perpetuation or improvement of existing programs, they will have to engage in some process of conflict or collaboration (Peters 1987) with the political appointees who are now being imposed upon them.

When the bureaucracy attempts to control the implementation of public programs, it may face some of the same problems encountered by political managers. The principal problem is that the members of most organizations do not march to the same drummer. The field service of an organization, in constant contact with clients and conditions throughout the country, may identify more with client needs than with the "policies" coming from the central office. They may consider what goes on in the home office as out of touch with reality and disregard it in the interest of doing what they "know" is best. Professionals with different education and training within the same organization may bring different values with them, and therefore also may make different policy decisions (Gormley 1982; Slayton and Trebilcock 1978). In short, large public organizations may be no more controllable by the permanent civil service than they are by political elites. What the permanent civil service will bring to the problem is a greater understanding of the policy issues, more experience, and more time to devote to the issues.

Legal Institutions

We commented at the beginning of this chapter that the courts play a much less significant role in policymaking in most European countries than they do in the United States. While this is true, we should not totally disregard their role (see Hogwood 1988). Some countries have a system of constitutional law and judicial review of law not too dissimilar to that found in the United States. In addition, almost all the countries have well-developed systems of administrative law that play a major role in the control of the bureaucracy and in the redress of grievances by individual citizens. Finally, the European Community is having some of its greatest impact through the European Court of Justice, and lawmaking through legal action will play an increasing role in the future.

The powers accorded the courts in European countries appear more diverse than many other features of their governments. For example, for constitutional questions, at one end of the spectrum is the United Kingdom, where the legal system has little concept that an act of Parliament could be declared unconstitutional by the courts, although actions of local governments are often proclaimed beyond the law's scope. At the other end of the dimension is West Germany, which in its postwar constitution copied many of the ideas of judicial review from the United States. West Germany has a very well-developed Federal Constitutional Court, as well as *Land* courts, deciding on a variety of constitutional and legal issues (Kommers 1976). Some of those issues, such as the legality of Communist and neo-

Nazi political parties, have been extremely sensitive politically. In between might be found France and Italy, where the constitutional courts have been given only limited jurisdiction. In France, for example, the right of access to the court depends on a case being referred by political officials rather than aggrieved citizens, and in Italy the lower courts must recommend that a case be reviewed.

The legal systems of European courts also vary a great deal. Again at one end of the dimension would be found the common law of the United Kingdom (and for the most part Ireland). Common law depends on precedent and the accumulation of rulings by judges over the years to determine what the law means. Further, through this process various fundamental principles of law have been "discovered." Parliament can overturn the precedents of common law, but unless there is specific legislation, the principle of *stare decisis* ("let the decision stand") governs. At the other end of that dimension we would find France, Spain, Belgium, Italy, and several smaller countries with code-law legal systems, derived more or less directly from the *Code Napoleon* of 1804. The purpose of code law is to detail, as far as possible, what is legal and what is illegal and to specify legal relationships among individuals and organizations. The aim is to leave very little room for judicial interpretation of law and to enable citizens and the state to know their rights before they act. In between these two extreme models might be found Scandinavian law, which is more detailed than the common law but a good deal more flexible than code law. Within these broad categories each individual country has its own variations on these legal themes.

Another feature common in European legal systems is the separation of administrative law from the other parts of the legal system. Often separate courts deal with administrative matters, and a separate body of law defines the rights and duties of public servants and the appropriate manner in which to administer public policies. Unlike most common-law countries, in code-law nations administrative cases usually cannot be appealed into the regular court systems. Administrative courts provide citizens a well-developed mechanism for seeking redress against government and against individual members of the public bureaucracy. This body of law also details the procedures that must be followed in making secondary legislation and may provide for review of such laws by a judicial body, such as the Conseil d'Etat in France. Finally, in addition to the regular administrative law courts, there may be special courts dealing with certain policies, such as the labor and social courts in West Germany or tax courts in a number of countries. Interestingly, the increasing role of the public bureaucracy in policymaking has led legal scholars in the United Kingdom, a country without an administrative law system, to advocate its development (All Souls-Justice 1988).

The Fifth, Sixth, and Nth Branches of Government

The bureaucracy is sometimes described as the fourth branch of government. If that is the case, then most European countries also have additional branches, the majority of which have something to do with the economic activities of government. Since the time European governments began to become heavily involved with economic activities, they have attempted to find the appropriate balance between political control of nationalized industries (or whatever form government's involvement in the economy took) and the free play of market forces to ensure efficiency. As yet no one has claimed to have found the full and complete answer to this question, but governments have put into operation a number of solutions. Further, economic activities have not been the only subject of major organizational innovations attempting to strike a balance between political control and managerial discretion. Governments' involvement in major public services, such as health care and education, have also been treated in a number of different ways, again in attempts to balance political control, efficiency, and, in the case of education, intellectual and academic freedom.

The public corporation is the most common form of organization used to meet the need of government involvement in the economy. These corporations typically are made responsible to a ministry in government (frequently the ministry of industry or of finance) and are then allowed substantial freedom to engage in their economic pursuits. Public corporations may be required to borrow money through public sources as needed and to do their accounting in certain ways, but their accounts tend to be differentiated from the main public accounts. In addition, typically they are not subject to the same personnel policies as are general government organizations. While all these practices permit public corporations to respond to market forces, they may make the corporation *too* independent of government and its policy objectives (Anastassopoulos 1985; Feigenbaum 1985; Vernon 1984). On the other hand, however, the separation of corporations from the main body of government does allow government to hide some of the costs of its economic activities (Peters and Heisler 1983) and to disavow responsibility if anything goes wrong. This strategy is not always effective; after two disastrous train crashes in Paris in 1988, the French minister of transportation resigned, and British prime ministers have been held accountable for the effects of strikes in nationalized industries. While far from perfect, the current arrangements do permit flexibility, although at some expense in accountability and control.

If government wants to distance itself even more from economic activities, it can use mechanisms such as quasi-public corporations or buying shares in nominally private corporations. So, for example, the two large public holding companies in Italy, Istituto per la Ricostruzione Industriale (IRI) and Ente Nationale Idrocarburi (ENI) hold a large percentage of the stock (sometimes 100 percent) in a number of firms, although those firms are not technically nationalized. The same strategy is used by Statens Företagens AB in Sweden (Waara 1980), the National Enterprise Board in the United Kingdom, and similar bodies in most European countries. These quasi-governmental arrangements provide infusions of capital to firms that face short-term crises or that are new and attempting to develop. This strategy faces two contradictory risks. One is that the money will be used simply for "lemon socialism" to prop up declining industries, especially those with large, regionally concentrated labor forces whose unemployment would generate political problems. The opposite risk is that government will be seen as being too speculative in supporting new firms and as "gambling" with public money (Redwood 1984). Both of these risks are real, but either may be worth it for the political and economic benefits produced.

Governments in European countries also seek to manage other programs "hived off" from their main functions. Some countries managed the social insurance programs in this way. Although employed citizens must pay payroll taxes to support these programs just as if they were part of government, the organizations that pay out the funds are managed almost as if they were private. For example, in West Germany the *Krankenkasse* (sickness funds) that are the public health insurance program operate as if they were private. There are now approximately 1,600 of these funds and they operate in limited competition with one another. The social insurance funds in France, Belgium, and Italy all are outside of government, albeit under government regulation and supervision. The National Health Service (NHS) is also organized as a separate institution in the United Kingdom, although it is clear that it is a government program, and has been increasingly a source of public controversy. Although doctors are direct employees of their hospitals, general practitioners in the NHS maintain the status of contracted free professionals rather than government employees (Klein 1983).[9] Both groups attempt to maintain their clinical freedom in the face of potential government intrusions. The university systems in many European countries are almost entirely public but are managed through a quasi-autonomous body of some sort or another in an attempt to ensure academic freedom. In Scandinavia, the established Lutheran church is in many ways public, with priests, organists, and other workers receiving public paychecks, although it certainly maintains its independence on social issues.

Social programs are important for governments and often are managed through quasi-public organizations. Central banks determining monetary policy are certainly as important, and even they are often hived off from the main line of government accountability and granted great independence. Governments differ substantially in the degree of autonomy they permit their central banks, with some, such as the Bank of England, being under close and direct supervision by the sitting government. Other central banks, such as the Bundesbank in West Germany and the Banque Nationale Suisse in Switzerland, are extremely independent and can, if they wish, make monetary policy quite independent of the desires of government. Further, it appears that the more autonomous central banks have been more successful than the politicized banks in achieving such goals as low rates of inflation and a favorable balance of payments (Woolley 1977).

In short, a number of organizations in Europe have very tangential relationships with governmental policy and accountability, even though they receive all or part of their funds from government and are responsible for the implementation of public policies. In the case of some quasi-public bodies—the now-famous "Quangos" in Britain, for example (Barker 1982)—they may be responsible for making government policy. Further, as we will point out in our discussion of corporatist arrangements in policymaking and even in policy implementation (Chapter 6), the boundary between public and private organizations is very indistinct, and to some degree almost all social organizations have some public role.

Summary

Government in Western Europe is a very large and complex entity. In most instances the public sector is more significant than in North American countries, especially when measured in terms of taxation and expenditure. There are some important similarities among these governments in addition to their great size and involvement in economic affairs. The most important is that European governments are parliamentary democracies. In each of the systems, with France being in part an exception, the political executive is directly responsible to the legislature and depends on confidence from the legislature to remain in power. This makes the politics of policymaking very different from that in a presidential system such as the United States. In a parliamentary system, government is not constrained by the need to reach agreement among the branches of government and should be able to act decisively. The major problem is that if that decisiveness is used without deliberation or accountability, abuse or seriously misguided policies may ensue. The opportunity for the latter may be especially great when more ideological parties—of the Right or Left—are in office. However, the choice of governing systems is always a trade-off, and European democracies usually function effectively and responsibly with their parliamentary system. Possibilities of abuse do exist but are tempered by fundamental commitments to democratic and legal action.

As important as the parliamentary nature of European government is, it is also important to remember that a great deal of government activity occurs outside the marble halls associated with the formal institutions of government. In particular, a great deal of the policymaking activity of contemporary governments occurs in the public bureaucracy. Here policymaking is much less impressive visually but is perhaps more important in determining what actually happens in government. More often than not, government consists of the gradual accretion of rules and regulations through the bureaucracy rather than dramatic acts of passing legislation. Nationalized industries, banks, and quasi-public organizations also have their own important policymaking functions. And in addition to these organizations we have both the European level of government and the subnational governments within each country (see Chapter 2). European government remains parliamentary at its core, but that core is surrounded by a host of extremely busy people all making their own contributions to the smooth governance of society.

Notes

1. For example, for a short period prior to the 1979 election in Sweden, the Liberal party formed the government with only just over 11 percent of the seats in the *Riksdag*.

2. The Constitution of the Fifth Republic gives the president the power to issue decrees on his or her own with the force of law, to declare a state of emergency if he or she sees fit, and then to assume virtually total control of government, and the power to issue a budget if the parliament cannot agree to one.

3. It is often arranged, however, that if a minister must resign, his or her alternate will resign from the National Assembly, paving the way for the former minister's return.

4. This model is derived from Richard Rose, *The Problem of Party Government* (1974). See also Peters (1981; 1990) and Katz (1987).

5. While not so pronounced as in the United States where the thirty-second advertising spot is a major part of campaigning, short news items are still important in European campaigns.

6. Charles de Gaulle did want to have such a body to replace the French Senate. The failure of the French voters to accept his recommendations in a referendum led to his resignation as president in 1969. France does have a Social and Economic Council, as do the Netherlands and Norway, that serves almost as a third house of Parliament on some issues. At a lower level of government, the Bavarian State Senate also is a corporate body (Wolfe 1974).

7. The four large states of North Rhine-Westphalia, Lower Saxony, Bavaria, and Baden-Württemberg each receive five seats; the three medium-size states of Hesse, Rhineland-Palatinate, and Schleswig-Holstein receive four seats; and the three small states of Hamburg, Bremen, and the Saarland receive three seats. There have been four nonvoting members from West Berlin.

8. Even then, however, there may be real conflicts between the demands of the senior civil servants and the remainder of the public employees, especially over issues that affect the status of the service.

9. The proposed changes in the National Health Service during the Thatcher government may make it even more autonomous. At this writing the full implications of these changes have yet to be determined.

Chapter

4

CHANGING PUBLIC OPINION
AND POLITICS

Politics in the 1980s was marked by many stark contrasts between expectations and apparent realities. The period has been described as one of selfish quiescence, but it was also marked by mass demonstrations for peace and social justice and electoral successes by new political groups, such as "Green" parties. The period has been described by some commentators in terms of "liberal," postmaterialist values but has also been marked by political successes by "neoliberal" (conservative), and even extreme right-wing, political parties. The 1970s and 1980s marked the full flowering of the welfare state but were at the same time decades in which tax cheating and the appeal of antitax parties have increased dramatically. Further, despite the welfare state and general mass affluence, homelessness and social deprivation have also become more apparent in Europe. Politics is never simple or stable, but the complexities and inconsistencies of social and economic life in the late twentieth century make politics all the more difficult for observers and practitioners.

We have already pointed out that politics and policymaking do not occur in a vacuum, but rather are reflections of the social milieu within which they take place. In addition to a country's social structure, another significant aspect of that milieu is the constellation of attitudes held by the public about government and about what government should be doing. Government is conceptualized very differently in different societies, and words such as "government," "the state," and "law" carry with them somewhat different connotations in different societies (see, for example, Almond and

Verba 1963; Verba, Nie, and Kim 1978). This is true even within a relatively homogenous political and social area such as Western Europe, or even within the *presumably* extremely homogenous Scandinavian region (Elder, Thomas, and Arter 1983; Sartori 1987). Unless those attempting to govern understand the constraints those attitudes place upon their actions, they are likely to be unsuccessful. On the other hand, those popular attitudes—which constitute something called "political culture"—are not immutable. They change and are subject to being changed. Thus political leaders are at once constrained by their political culture and capable of shaping it. The genuine leaders in government are typically those individuals who can reshape the popular political culture to conform to their own ideas of what government is about and then implement policies consistent with those cultural changes in a manner that endures.

Although some changes in political attitudes and practices have affected almost all Europeans, other changes have been confined to a subset of nations. Among the more hopeful of the political changes in the late twentieth century has been the redemocratization of three major European countries—Greece, Portugal, and Spain (Featherstone and Katsoudas 1987; Gunther, Sani, and Shabad 1988). Democracy had been suspended in all three countries—in Greece for only about a decade but in Spain and Portugal for much longer. By 1990 all three countries have managed, however, to rebuild very viable democratic systems and to open their societies to full participation by most citizens. Although this transition has been aided by these countries' *relative* affluence, compared to many Third World nations facing similar challenges, it still represents a remarkable political achievement by the leaders and public of the three countries. Likewise, West Germany was rebuilt after World War II as a democratic regime and as an extremely successful capitalist economy. With that reconstruction came, although somewhat slowly, a fundamental shift in political values.

In addition to their ideas about government and its institutions, citizens also have differing ideas about their societies and the problems that exist within them. Few of the problems that citizens or analysts identify in society are truly objective; most require some social definition before they really can become social problems (see Schneider 1985; Schulman 1988). Conditions that are defined as problems also have to be identified as *public* problems before government is likely to act upon them. Thus for most of the history of European countries, poverty was not defined as a social problem and certainly not one that government could, or should, do anything about; that some people were poor was the merely will of God or the result of their own lack of moral fiber. Once poverty was redefined as a social problem and as the responsibility of government, programs were begun to address the issue. Likewise, inequality between men and women was for centuries regarded as God's law,[1] but when it was defined as undesirable and as a public problem, programs promoting and demanding equality were quickly initiated. Thus the range of acceptable action by the state is a function of the identification of social conditions as social problems and then their recognition as problems for the public sector to solve. But again, that range of recognition and conceptualization of problems is subject to change, and creative and effective political leaders are capable of altering significantly the parameters of acceptable government intervention.

In this chapter we will be looking at only a few aspects of political culture and political values in the European democracies. We have already alluded to several important value changes in Europe, such as the decline of nationalism. We will now discuss several basic political values, such as trust and participation and then proceed to look at two significant dimensions of value change that represent some of the most important changes in European politics in the postwar era. One is the shift of political cleavages away from the traditional concern with class and economic issues toward greater concern with the "postmaterialist" issues of peace, equality, participation, and environmental protection. During the 1960s and 1970s this change in values appeared to be unstoppable, but economic change and the maturation of a generation of young activists may have slowed if not stopped the juggernaut.

The second value change of importance is the declining faith of many citizens in the capacity of government to produce the type of society they want to live in, at least at what they consider an acceptable price. This declining faith in government has produced a rather widespread questioning of the legitimacy of "big government" and a range of attitudes and behaviors that have been altering the nature of politics (Douglas 1989). Even countries that had been very accepting of the welfare state, and all the taxes that went with it, are beginning to question whether a more privatized approach to social problems may not be superior. In addition to questioning the welfare state's efficacy, citizens are beginning to vote against it and to find ways to avoid its costs. These value changes may produce a very different version of European politics from the one that has been the standard of the postwar world. It may also be that this apparent juggernaut will have to be braked when the difficulties of performing some government tasks in the private sector and the more fundamental value of government and its services are understood.

European Political Culture

It is impossible to say that there is a European political culture. Although there do appear to be some common values concerning democracy, the welfare state, and perhaps a few other common areas, as many things divide Europeans culturally—including residents of the same country—as unite them. Some of these differences live in the twilight world of ethnic stereotypes, while others can be substantiated empirically. The differences in political culture that do exist among the European countries are, however, along common dimensions, so that we can make meaningful comparisons. In this section we will discuss several common aspects of political culture, show how these differ among European countries, and make some inferences about the influence of these differences on politics in the individual countries.

Participation

Western European governments, as democracies, require citizen participation. Europeans do vote more readily than do Americans, and Scandinavians at least tend to participate more in interest-group activities than do Americans. For other Europeans, political participation beyond mere voting appears to be a somewhat suspect behavior. In fact, there is some evidence that some Europeans do not view participation in any form of organized social activity as highly desirable. For example, Table 4.1 shows levels of participation in a variety of social organizations by Europeans and non-Europeans. French, Italian, and Spanish citizens are substantially less likely to participate in groups than are Scandinavians and other northern Europeans. These data are supported by those in Table 4.2 showing membership in labor unions. Northern Europeans are much more likely to belong to labor unions than are southern Europeans, despite relatively comparable levels of industrialization, and are among the most participatory peoples in the world.

It might be argued that membership in social organizations is not a particularly good indicator of the likelihood of participation in politics; the organizations to which people belong might be birdwatching associations. Participation in any activities outside the home, however, tends to be correlated with participation in more specifically political activities (Almond and Verba 1963), and these data tend to be substantiated by others about attitudes toward political participation (but see LaPalombara 1987). Further, the evidence about membership in labor unions—organizations highly relevant to political activity—tends to be correlated with general

TABLE 4.1

Membership in Social Organizations[a]

(percentage)

	Great Britain	Ireland	France	Belgium	W. Germany	Netherlands	Spain	Denmark	Italy
One or more	52	53	27	42	50	62	31	62	26
None	48	47	73	58	50	38	69	38	74

SOURCE: Based on data from the Leisure Development Center Survey, cited in E. H. Hastings and P. K. Hastings, eds., *Index to International Public Opinion, 1982–83* (Westport, CT: Greenwood, 1984).

[a]Charities, religious, political, professional, or environmental organizations, trade unions, and so on.

TABLE 4.2

Proportion of Economically Active Population (nonagricultural)
Who Are Members of Labor Unions

Sweden	85
Denmark	79
Belgium	75
Finland	75
Austria	58
Norway	55
United Kingdom	54
Ireland	52
Portugal	40
Netherlands	38
Italy	37
Switzerland	35
Spain	35
W. Germany	33
France	22

SOURCE: Based on data from S. Mielke, *Internationales Gewerkschaftshandbuch* (Opladen: Leske & Budrich, 1983).

levels of organizational membership. Finally, even the birdwatching association may be involved in politics by lobbying for environmental protection or tax breaks for binoculars.

Political Trust

A sense of political trust is associated with political participation. Citizens who do not believe that their government, or their fellow citizens, can be trusted are less likely to participate in politics than are those who consider the political world more benign. If they believe that government will deal with their demands fairly and equally, they are more likely to press those demands on government. Similarly, if they believe that their fellow citizens are very much like them and are not out to gain special advantage through the political process, citizens will be more likely to join with others to press their demands. Without some belief in their fellows, it is difficult for any citizen to accept an active role in the political process.

Again, there is substantial variation among Europeans in the extent to which they trust one another and their governments. When asked whether they could trust others, more than twice as many Danish respondents thought they could as did French respondents (Table 4.3). In general, people in the British Isles and northern Europe were more trusting than those in southern Europe, although Spanish respondents demonstrated a good deal more trust in others than might have been expected. For most southern European respondents, however, there appears to be little basis for cooperation with their fellow citizens, for political or other purposes.

The level of trust or confidence expressed in political institutions is a somewhat more complex phenomenon to decipher (Table 4.4). On the one hand, citizens in most European countries expressed substantially more confidence in governmental institutions than they did in private-sector ones. In all countries there was a great deal of confidence in the armed forces and the police, and only in Italy and West Germany was there more confidence in major companies and the press than in the civil service. On the other hand, however, in most countries less than half of the respondents expressed confidence in some of the major government institutions. Government may be more trustworthy than the private sector, but relatively few citizens feel confidence in any of the institutions of their society. This lack of confidence in social institutions may be related to the rejection of "big government" and the search for a more privatized vision of the world that characterized much of the 1980s.

Equality and Justice

Citizens in most European countries have a more egalitarian conception of the "good society" than would be true for Americans. Although the political events of the 1980s showed some renewed acceptance of the private market and capitalism as a means of allocating resources, this apparent value change must be understood in the context of a continuing commitment to the welfare state (but see Chapter 8). Even if the market is to have the first opportunity to make allocations among individuals, those allocations will still be corrected by a second round of taxation and expenditure policies that protect the weakest in society. Only in Britain—and perhaps not even there—has the governing party launched a comprehensive attack on the virtues of the welfare state.

The survey evidence to support this contention concerning a commitment to equality and the welfare state is limited. The evidence does show high levels of belief in the virtues of the welfare state and its underlying purposes of greater equality and protection against the vicissitudes of the free market. This commitment may not be, however, as strong in some countries as might have been expected by either the programs' defenders or

TABLE 4.3

Levels of Interpersonal Trust, 1983
(percentage)

Would you say that most people can be trusted, or that you can't be too careful in dealing with people?

	Great Britain	Ireland	France	Belgium	W. Germany	Netherlands	Spain	Denmark	Italy
Most can be trusted	43	40	22	25	26	38	32	46	25
Can't be too careful	54	56	71	63	58	49	61	44	72
Don't know	3	4	7	12	16	13	7	10	3

SOURCE: Based on data from the Leisure Development Center Survey, cited in E. H. Hastings and P. K. Hastings, eds., *Index to International Public Opinion, 1982–83* (Westport, CT: Greenwood, 1984).

TABLE 4.4

Level of Confidence in Public Institutions, 1983
(positive responses, in percentage)

	United States	Great Britain	Ireland	Japan	W. Germany	France	Italy	Spain
Police	76	86	86	67	71	64	68	63
Armed Forces	81	81	75	37	54	53	58	61
Legal System	51	66	57	68	67	55	43	48
Parliament/Congress	53	40	51	30	53	48	31	48
Civil Service	55	48	54	31	35	50	28	38
Major Companies	50	48	49	25	34	42	33	37
Press	49	29	44	52	33	31	46	31
Unions	33	26	36	29	36	36	28	31

SOURCE: Based on data from the Leisure Development Center Survey, cited in E. H. Hastings and P. K. Hastings, eds., *Index to International Public Opinion, 1982–83* (Westport, CT: Greenwood, 1984).

observers who note the very high levels of social expenditures, especially in the Scandinavian countries. As mentioned, there may be some cultural basis for the shift that has been occurring in political behavior and in the willingness of citizens to consider alternatives to government provision of social services.

Summary

We have presented a brief catalog of some of the basic political and social values found in Western European countries. It could be extended to cover a variety of other value orientations, for example, attitudes toward authority, that also have substantial political relevance. Yet it is probably more important to discuss some of the dynamics of political values in Europe. These dynamics appear to center around the importance of noneconomic values in politics and the proper role of government in the social and economic lives of its citizens. The latter issue is as old as politics itself, but the former issue potentially represents a significant shift from the issues that have been central to politics in most of the democratic period.

Still the Age of Postmaterialism?

One of the important characterizations of public opinion in Western Europe in the postwar period has been that it has been becoming "postmaterialist." That is, the average European citizen is argued to have become more satisfied with his or her material lot in life and to have become more willing to entertain other social and economic values that might be gained through the political system. It has also been argued that the bread-and-butter issues of jobs, economic growth, inflation, and the like are becoming superseded by concerns with peace, participation, and protection of the environment. In this vision of the new European politics, governing will become less about providing material goods through Keynesian economic management and the redistributive programs of the welfare state and more about fundamentally altering society, and even the international economic system, in order to promote peace and justice. This view of politics is very much a vision of the world that is in the process of becoming; the majority of Europeans remained solid materialists even during the height of their affluence. In most attitude surveys, fewer than one-third of all respondents endorsed postmaterialist values as central to their own concerns. However, there has been some change in the postmaterialist direction, and that change is especially evident among the young and the educated who are likely to be opinion leaders.

It has also been argued that the postmaterialist vision is no more than an idealistic one, and with the reintroduction of scarcity into European politics during the 1970s and the continuing concern about resource availability in the 1980s, economic issues are once again asserting themselves as the focal points of European politics. Even with the massive postwar economic growth, there are still poor people in Europe—even in the most developed welfare states. Likewise, there are now large numbers of long-term unemployed—even in economic success stories like West Germany—whom prosperity has bypassed. While most people appear to be doing very well in Europe, there are still those who have been left out of the prosperity, and it is argued that some European countries are becoming "two-thirds–one-third" societies. Two-thirds of the people appear very prosperous and see little need for redistributive social and economic programs, while one-third may be suffering in ways not imagined since the postwar reconstruction. The percentages in this description of society may be somewhat pessimistic, but all economic problems have not been solved and many people would like government programs to make the economic system meet their needs.

We should remember also that the two-thirds who presumably are doing well through the status quo in Western Europe may be threatened as well. The events of the 1970s and 1980s have demonstrated again how fragile economic growth and prosperity may be in industrialized economies. The economic downturn in the 1970s was a reminder of the past and of the business cycle that has afflicted capitalist economies. To that business cycle must be added concerns about the accelerating product cycle (Krasner 1978). That is, products move increasingly rapidly from original design and development in an industrialized country to production in newly industrializing or underdeveloped countries, with lower wage rates than the industrialized countries of Western Europe. Thus the future of European countries as industrial powers may be problematic, and that uncertainty places in question some of the economic security that might foster postmaterial values.

The Nature of Postmaterialism

The concept of postmaterialism in Western Europe was developed largely in the works of Ronald Inglehart (1977, 1979, 1981, 1984). Along with Jean-Jacques Rabier at the European Commission in Brussels, Inglehart

TABLE 4.5

Indicators of Postmaterialist Attitudes:
Percentage Agreement with Goals

	Materialist Goals			Postmaterialist Goals					
	G1	G2	G3	G4	G5	G6	G7	G8	G9
Belgium	52	19	10	18	17	11	17	15	7
Denmark	24	23	31	20	17	8	11	7	7
France	43	18	21	13	28	9	14	9	11
W. Germany	44	24	18	12	11	9	11	4	3
Ireland	44	29	16	20	8	15	6	5	3
Italy	41	31	17	9	14	11	9	3	5
Luxembourg	29	33	28	22	11	19	7	7	9
Netherlands	26	14	18	24	26	14	13	10	10
United Kingdom	50	29	11	15	12	15	11	6	5
United States	25	16	20	16	12	16	10	18	8

SOURCE: Reprinted, by permission of the publisher, from Ronald Inglehart, *The Silent Revolution: Changing Values and Political Styles Among Western Publics* (Princeton, NJ: Princeton Univ. Press, 1977). Copyright © 1977 Princeton University Press. Reprinted with permission of Princeton University Press.

G1	=	Fight Rising Prices	G6	=	More Say in Government
G2	=	Economic Growth	G7	=	Protect Free Speech
G3	=	Maintain Order	G8	=	More Beautiful Cities
G4	=	More Say on Job	G9	=	Ideas Count
G5	=	Less Impersonal Society			

conducted a series of surveys in Western Europe, asking people about what they thought the principal issues facing government were and what government should be doing. What Inglehart found was less concern than expected with material issues and an increasing concern with less tangible values, such as participation and equality. In these surveys, conducted initially in the mid-1960s and then repeated rather frequently with some of the same questions, Europeans appeared to be saying that they wanted to see a change in what governments were doing. They appeared to demand that some attention be given to the more difficult issues of building a just and peaceful society, in more than simply economic terms (see Table 4.5).

These postmaterialist attitudes toward government and policy were not distributed equally throughout the population. One of the major differences occurred among Europeans of different ages (See Table 4.6). In general, younger respondents were much more likely to give postmaterialist responses than were older ones. This is to be expected as the younger respondents would not have experienced the Great Depression, World War II, or even the period of economic readjustment following that war. Their world would have been one of great and consistently increasing affluence, and they could not be expected to assign great value to something that was merely a fact of their existence, rather than the miracle that mass affluence appeared to older Europeans. With the assured (at least psychologically) economic base, perhaps with the restlessness of youth, or through the rejection of the values of their parents, the younger Europeans began to think about the intangible benefits that governments were not providing. Especially prominent in their minds were the apparent inconsistencies between democratic ideals and the actual practice of large, bureaucratic governments in their countries. They were also aware of the apparent contradictions between norms of equality espoused by many political leaders (and even constitutions) and the continuing economic disparities in all industrialized countries.

The several European nations also differ in their degree of materialism and postmaterialism. As shown in Table 4.7, the smaller countries of Europe (with the exception of Denmark) tend to be more postmaterialist than the larger countries.[2] Although they are highly speculative, several factors might account for this finding. One is that these smaller countries

TABLE 4.6

Postmaterialism by Age (1976)
in Belgium, France, Germany, Italy, the Netherlands, and the United Kingdom[a]

Age Group	Materialist	Postmaterialist
15–24	25	20
25–34	29	16
35–44	35	11
45–54	39	8
55–64	47	6
65 +	52	5
AVERAGE	37	12

SOURCE: Ronald Inglehart, *The Silent Revolution: Changing Values and Political Styles Among Western Publics* (Princeton, NJ: Princeton Univ. Press, 1977). Copyright © 1977 Princeton University Press.

[a] Excludes mixed and indeterminate responses.

TABLE 4.7

Postmaterialism by Country, 1970–79[a]

Ten European Countries

	Materialist (percentage)	Postmaterialist (percentage)
Belgium	25	14
Denmark	41	7
France	35	12
W. Germany	42	8
Ireland	36	7
Italy	40	9
Luxembourg	35	13
Netherlands	31	13
Switzerland	31	12
United Kingdom	32	8

Six Countries Across Time

	1970	1973	1976	1979
Belgium				
Materialist	36	32	36	27
Postmaterialist	8	8	8	11
France				
Materialist	38	35	41	36
Postmaterialist	11	12	12	15
W. Germany				
Materialist	43	42	41	37
Postmaterialist	10	8	11	11
Italy				
Materialist	35	40	41	47
Postmaterialist	13	9	11	10
Netherlands				
Materialist	30	31	32	38
Postmaterialist	17	13	14	19
United Kingdom				
Materialist	36	32	36	27
Postmaterialist	8	8	8	11

SOURCE: Based on data from R. Inglehart, *The Silent Revolution: Changing Values and Political Styles Among Western Publics* (Princeton, NJ: Princeton Univ. Press, 1977), and R. Inglehart, "Post-Materialism in an Age of Insecurity," *American Political Science Review* 75 (1981):880–900.

[a] Excludes mixed and indeterminate responses.

are wealthier, on average, than some of the larger countries, such as Britain and Italy (and the smaller Ireland), and have been wealthier longer. Also, the Low Countries suffered extensive devastation in World War II and might be expected to search for more idealistic solutions to problems so that potential conflict could be averted; their small size would make more bellicose solutions impractical. Switzerland, being neutral, might share some of that sense of the need to create a more just international and domestic order. Also, the countries scoring the highest on postmaterialism have historically been deeply divided along noneconomic cleavages, such as language and religion. Therefore, citizens in these countries might understand better than most that all political conflicts do not arise from economic concerns, nor can they be solved solely by applying money. Hence, the creation of a more just and participatory society may appear a more natural political concern in ethnically divided societies than in societies where politics historically has been more class-based.

In addition, the socioeconomic and political characteristics of respondents appeared to affect rather significantly the degree to which they accept postmaterialist values. Education in particular was related to their willingness to transcend economic concerns and consider alternative uses for state power in changing the society (see Table 4.8). In every country surveyed, respondents with a university education or better were three or four times more likely to espouse postmaterialist values than were respondents with only a primary school education. Some economic effect seems apparent here—those with more education are also more affluent and perhaps less concerned about their own economic future. There was, however, a strong independent effect of education and its ability to open the individual's mind to a variety of alternative futures for the society.

Finally, those who identified themselves with the political Left also gave

TABLE 4.8

Postmaterialism by Education
in Belgium, France, Germany, Italy, the Netherlands, the United
Kingdom, and the United States

Value Orientation	Level of Education		
	Primary	Secondary	University
Postmaterialist	6.1	15.0	30.4
Materialist	93.9	85.0	69.6

SOURCE: Based on data from R. Inglehart, *The Silent Revolution: Changing Values and Political Styles Among Western Publics* (Princeton, NJ: Princeton Univ. Press, 1977).

more postmaterialist responses than did those who classified themselves as being on the political Right. This is in part because some of the items used to construct the scale for materialism also were concerned with law and order as well as strictly economic concerns, and conservatives would be expected to respond very strongly to a notion of order in society. However, those who were inclined toward the political Left seemed to see greater importance in the freedom and participation items in the postmaterialism scales than did those who called themselves political conservatives. This is somewhat paradoxical, given that many parties of the political Left have continued to press for redistributive economic policies and to place an emphasis on employment and other economic concerns of the working class. However, as we will be pointing out in the next chapter, the nature of the Left-Right dimension in politics is changing and even crumbling, so that we must be extremely careful about characterizing parties and their ideologies. The traditional Left parties may no longer speak for a significant segment of the population. New parties with new issues (Poguntke 1987) have captured at least a part of the Left in politics—Herbert Kitschelt (1989) refers to these parties as "left-libertarian"—and are pushing for more fundamental changes in society than most social democratic parties have contemplated for several decades.

Changes in Postmaterialism

As with so much else in European politics, the apparent shift toward postmaterial values has been slowing or even stopping since the mid-1970s. While society and politics in the 1980s were certainly different from what they were before the 1960s' burst of postmaterial values, much of the old concern with material issues has been retained and, to some extent, reinforced. The sources of that reinforcement should be obvious, with the continuing economic problems of many European countries making conventional bread-and-butter issues central to the minds of many citizens. Unemployment continued to run in the double digits in some European countries in the mid-1980s, and in some regions it was much higher (see Table 1.4, p. 7). Thus workers were uncertain about job availability; for them politics is still very much about employment, prices, and economic growth.

In addition to these hard economic facts, changes in popular culture have further slowed the advance of postmaterialist values. For whatever reasons, the 1960s and the early 1970s were a period of intense social and political ferment, in which young people were in the vanguard. For example, the antiwar movement in the United States and student movements in European universities were in the forefront of a number of the significant social and cultural changes at the time. Even in Eastern Europe, the spring of 1968 was a period of ferment and change. Although it now would be impossible to return to the more placid and conformist past, in most Western societies the 1980s were not a period of such ferment. As a consequence, the new generation is not being socialized politically to question the material values of their society. Gucci is now a more important cultural symbol than is Che, and the generation that came of age politically in the 1980s does not appear to have the same collective commitment to social change as did some earlier ones.

On the other hand, some very profound changes are occurring in European society that press toward even greater acceptance of postmaterial values. One is that even though there is high aggregate unemployment in a number of European countries, most of those who have remained employed are more affluent than ever. This is especially true because of the increasing number of two-income families. To some extent what the welfare state (see Chapter 8) was designed to guard against has been happening in Western Europe, with the richer (or at least the well off) getting richer and the poor remaining poor. Further, the majority of those who are doing well are doing so outside of manufacturing industries. They are earning their money in service and high-technology industries requiring higher education and permitting some differentiation from the traditional class-based organization of industry. There is greater equality in the workplace, so that even those who are "workers" may tend to think of themselves differently than they would had they been in traditional manufacturing industries. Further, even the traditional manufacturing industries have made some changes in managerial practices to promote greater participation and equality. Simple appeals to lower-paid workers as an industrial proletariat are unlikely to be successful, even if service workers earn less than they might have as industrial workers, or industrial workers are still employed in manual jobs.

In addition to changes in the occupational structure, advanced education is now more widely available in Europe than it ever has been (see Table 4.9). We have already seen that education is probably the most powerful factor associated with developing postmaterialist values. We cannot be sure how higher education produces this tendency. It could be by simply opening up people's minds ("expanding their consciousness") to a greater range of possibilities for the society; or perhaps because the university milieu during the 1960s and 1970s was associated with very fundamental challenges to traditional values. It does appear, however, that higher education, even though it creates economic and social elites, also tends to be associated with challenges to dominant social and cultural patterns.

TABLE 4.9

Increased Educational Attainment in Western Europe
(proportion of population 25 + with some postsecondary education)

	1961	1966	1971	1976	1981
Belgium	4.0		2.6		7.5
Finland	4.1		6.1		13.8
Greece	2.5		3.9		7.6
Ireland		4.5			7.9
Netherlands	1.3		7.2		–
Norway	1.9		6.6		11.9
Portugal	1.1		1.6		–
Spain	0.8		3.7		7.1
Sweden	–		8.3		15.4
United Kingdom	2.4			11.0	

SOURCE: UNESCO, *Statistical Yearbook* (Paris: UNESCO, annual).

Third, some real-world events have strengthened the environmental movement in Europe. That movement is one significant repository of the postmaterialist value structure and is perhaps the component with the greatest chance of spreading its message to the mass public. The nuclear accident at Chernobyl and its radioactive fallout all over Western Europe is the most obvious impact of human society on the environment, but there have been many other occurrences. People living in southern Germany, Switzerland, and Scandinavia can see the impact of acid rain daily. Chemical spills have killed millions of fish in the Rhine. The seal populations in the North Sea and the Baltic have been virtually exterminated by either pollution or a virus whose impact was accentuated by pollution. The list of horrors could be extended easily, but the fundamental point is that environmentalists need to do very little public education—the newspapers and television news do it for them almost every day. Although postmaterialism is a broader concept than simply the environment, the trade-off between environmental protection and economic growth is a central concern in that value system.

Other political events have assisted in the growth of the peace movement in Europe. Peace and especially nuclear disarmament have been components of the ensemble of issues that the postmaterialists have advocated since the 1960s, and there was a resurgence of activism in the 1980s. This agitation largely centered around the issue of siting American nuclear-tipped cruise and Pershing missiles in Europe. Although there were significant demonstrations in the Netherlands and West Germany, and smaller ones elsewhere, the most visible antinuclear agitation was in the United Kingdom. There the "Greenham Common Women," who camped for months at a proposed missile site, came to symbolize the antiwar movement and, to some extent, other postmaterial values (especially feminism). The success of other interest groups (especially short-lived *Bürgerinitiativen* in West Germany and the Netherlands) has demonstrated also that there was a political market for ideas outside the mainstream of the dominant parties and that nonconventional political activity can have an influence, even in political systems that appear bureaucratic and conservative.

The final factor affecting the development of postmaterialism in European politics is that the cohort of Europeans socialized during the 1960s and 1970s is beginning to come of age politically. They are beginning to assume significant leadership posts in their societies and governments, and even if they are not affiliated with political parties or movements that espouse "pure" postmaterialist values, their political behavior can still be expected to be influenced by their formative political experiences. Perhaps more important, however, political movements that do advocate the postmaterialist position have gained greater political prominence and responsibility. The most obvious of these are the "Green" parties that have gained seats in parliaments in at least four European countries and have also become forces to be contended with in many regional and local elections. The 1989 elections to the European Parliament demonstrated a growing appeal of the Greens all across Europe, even in the United Kingdom, which had been immune to their appeal. Although the Green in their title refers to environmentalism, these parties also have strong commitments to participatory politics and the whole range of other postmaterial political values (Hay and Haward 1988; Rudig 1988; Spretnak and Capra 1986).

In addition to the Greens, however, less visible political parties have programs advocating strengthened environmental protection, open government, and greater mass participation in government. For example, Britain's Social Democratic party, or, as it became, the Liberal and Democratic party, has sought to make government much more open and participatory and has made its own party structure far more participatory than the other parties (Pridham 1983; Rogaly 1988). Smaller parties with these participatory goals and commitments to "liberal values" have also begun in a number of European countries, but perhaps nowhere is the contrast more stark than in Britain, with its tradition of hierarchical governments and limited popular participation.

Perhaps somewhat oddly, some parties of the political Right have also espoused a populist perspective on participation by "the people." They have argued that the people want a more conservative, lower-cost, lower-tax, and less interventionist political system. In this view, it is the bureaucracy and the professional politicians who want to retain "big government," and to counteract those groups the people must be allowed to participate more directly. Mrs. Thatcher, for example, might be regarded as the first leader of the British Conservative party who could in any way be considered a populist. Her politics is based less on *noblesse oblige* than on appeals to a middle class and upper working class that has come to see its standard of living and position threatened by taxes and demands for greater economic equality coming from the Labour party (Jenkins 1988). The "Progress party" in Denmark and Norway has a similar populist appeal against bureaucracy and government.

In summary, a great deal has been made of value changes in Western Europe around the theme of postmaterialism. What one finds may depend on what one expected to find. If the observer expected to find business as usual, with class-based political parties and economically based issues at the center of politics, then the degree of postmaterialism that exists in Europe in the 1990s might be surprising. On the other hand, if a different observer expected to find the flower children of the 1960s in charge of government, he or she would be surprised to see the extent to which traditional economic issues remain a central concern of politics in Western Europe. That observer may have been even more surprised to see the extent to which economic issues have returned to even greater prominence with economic slowdowns. In short, the value changes that have occurred in the broad conception of politics and political issues in Europe are many and complex. They are also very different in different countries. The question of postmaterialism in Europe is by no means resolved; it is being acted out in the political arena every day.

Big Government

The other major area of attitudinal change in Western Europe has been in the conception citizens have of their government, and especially in their view of government and the existing parliamentary democracies as the best, or even an acceptable, means of addressing important social issues. During the 1960s and the early 1970s there was an overwhelming belief in the capacity of the public sector to reform and reshape society positively. Even in countries that had nominally conservative governments, there was a strong sense that government was a positive force for the improvement of society and the well-being of the populace. Gaullist France, Britain under Harold Macmillan and later Edward Heath, Germany under Konrad Adenauer and then Ludwig Erhard, all regarded government as a means for solving problems and for improving the material and social well-being of the population. Even in John F. Kennedy's America (presumably the country most opposed to big government) Camelot was to be publicly, not privately, managed, and the Great Society programs of Lyndon Johnson carried on a surge of interest in a more positive government.

A great deal has happened since the 1970s, much of it fueled by external economic shocks. Government had been willing to accept the credit when the economy functioned well, and it had then to be willing to accept the blame when it functioned poorly (Rose and Peters 1978). Many came to see outcomes such as "stagflation," which the orthodox economic theory of the time argued were probably impossible, as resulting from government "meddling" in the economy. Many citizens saw the dramatic reversal of their economic fortunes as not only the result of government mismanagement, but to a great degree a function of government being involved in the economy in the first place.

The disappointment and disillusionment with government went much deeper, however, than merely its (alleged) economic mismanagement. In the United States the war in Vietnam raised fundamental questions in some people's minds about the capacity of government, even in a democracy, to behave in a humane fashion. Other people questioned the capacity of democracies to make and implement defense policy. In other societies, not faced directly with an unpopular war, more mundane questions about the humanity and effectiveness of governments were raised. These were often directed toward the public bureaucracy, and included indictments of the social services and tax systems. Even in the Scandinavian countries, long thought to be both supportive of the welfare state and politically docile, there were vociferous complaints about taxes and the treatment of citizens by the bureaucracy; children's author Astrid Lindgren even wrote fairy tales about "big government." Some groups—for example, Parisian students in 1968—questioned the foundations of the societies within which they lived and the relationship of governments to the economic and social systems. All of these social movements raised questions about the role of government and the desirability of strong, centralized governments.

Indicators of Disaffection

We have now said that many citizens in Western Europe became disaffected with their governments and with "business as usual" as practiced in their nations' parliamentary democracies. This is an easy assertion to make,

TABLE 4.10

1970s' Attitudes Toward Public Services
(percentages)

| | Level of Government Spending | | | |
	Too High	Too Low	Just Right	Don't Know
Denmark	10	31	48	11
France	2	68	23	7
W. Germany	6	46	40	8
United Kingdom	20	36	35	9

| | Favor Cutting Taxes and Services | | |
	Yes	No	Don't Know
Denmark	37	60	3
France	25	55	20
W. Germany	29	62	9
United Kingdom	38	50	12

SOURCE: Based on data from R. M. Coughlin, *Ideology, Public Opinion, and Welfare Policy* (Berkeley, CA: Institute of International Studies, Univ. of California, 1980).

but there is also substantial empirical evidence to back it up. Some comes from responses to a variety of surveys conducted in Europe, many asking the same questions over time. Other pieces of evidence come from the manifest behavior of citizens, rather than merely their expressions of discontent. We would argue that this behavioral evidence, although somewhat less specific than the attitudinal evidence, is stronger because it indicates citizens' willingness to do more than simply say they dislike what is happening when they are asked; they appear willing to "put their money (or even their lives) where their mouth is." We will be using four indicators of the disaffection that citizens have about their government: attitudes, voting and the formation of parties, tax evasion, and the use of referenda to bypass parliament.

ATTITUDES. Political attitudes reflect the pictures people have in their minds of government and its proper role in their lives. At least in comparison to citizens in the United States, Europeans have been accepting of a strong, positive role for government in managing the economy and in ensuring at least a minimal standard of living for citizens through welfare-state programs (Coughlin 1979). As demonstrated in Table 4.10, if we take the mid-1970s as a baseline for attitudes toward government, Europeans have generally been supportive of government and its role in society. Like most people, they would generally prefer to pay fewer taxes and to retain more money for their private consumption preferences. They were not, however, resistant to government, even "big government." Further, they tended to think that the democratic political systems with which they were familiar functioned rather effectively and that those governments were, on the whole, desirable ways to organize political decision making in their countries.[3] During the postwar period they have shown relatively little interest in experimenting with different forms of government. When the institutional status quo is threatened, even those who might have been seen to be interested in fundamental change (the French Communists in 1968, for example) have rallied around the flag of the existing system.

As has been implied by some of the preceding discussion, a great deal has changed in the attitudes of Europeans toward government since the 1970s. In general, in the 1980s and early 1990s they demonstrate much less willingness to pay for the services that governments provide with their taxes and show some increased skepticism about the efficaciousness of existing regimes. These attitudes do not represent open rebellion against the status quo, but they do demonstrate some unquiet about the existing structures and policies. Later we will point out some behavioral manifestations of these attitudes; right now the attitudes themselves demonstrate what many Europeans have been thinking about government.

Interestingly, to some extent the attitudinal changes relative to "big government" appear to be the antithesis of many of the cultural changes implied by the "postmaterial" values just discussed. While the postmaterial values do stress individual participation in government, the rejection of government and some disavowal of the contemporary political system represent a rejection of government. Likewise, while postmaterial values reject economic growth and to a great degree individual avarice, individual citizens' reactions to government taxing and spending reflect their continuing concern with maintaining and expanding personal consumption. Of course, single individuals may not be expressing both views, and individuals may change their views over time, but there does appear to be some ambivalence about the role of the individual and how he or she relates to the economy and the polity.

The attitudes that many contemporary Europeans display toward government and the welfare state are well encapsulated in the phrase of "two cheers for the Welfare State" (Taylor-Gooby 1982). Several researchers in Britain (see especially Taylor-Gooby 1985; Whiteley 1981) have found that citizens support the programs of the welfare state in general, but demand better, privatized services for themselves. Survey respondents, for example, support the idea of the National Health Service and its equal access of medical care, but want private care for themselves and their families. This is to some degree a set of attitudes born out of affluence, as there are now options that did not exist at the end of World War II when much of the welfare state (at least in Britain) was created. This concern with personal advantages may also reflect basic changes in society, as the "enterprise culture" becomes more prevalent in Britain. The phenomenon may not be entirely British, however, as surveys in Scandinavia have pointed out (Hadenius 1986).

This specific rejection of government's taxing and spending activities appears repeated in some more generalized concern about existing governmental structures. In this instance the major question seems to be the change that has not happened, rather than any overt rejection of existing governmental institutions. An impartial observer might hypothesize that after four postwar decades of peace and prosperity, citizens might be increasingly pleased with their governments. They do not appear to be so; satisfaction with democratic institutions has been changing little, and in some countries (Belgium, Ireland, Luxembourg) there is evidence of a decline in satisfaction (Table 4.11). Other scholars (see Kaase 1988; Lawson and Merkl 1988) have discussed declining support for democratic institutions in European countries. This decline, or lack of increasing support, could reflect several factors. One would be a transfer of concern about spending and taxing to a general rejection of the governmental system. In addition, those committed to postmaterial values might consider existing political institutions as insufficiently authentic in providing opportunities for participation, since those available are few and indirect. Likewise, the increasing number of regional separatists may regard the existing national governments as illegitimate. For whatever reasons, however, the existing institutions of government do not appear to be increasing their political support as they once did, and as they might have been thought to do given the real success of government and the economic system.

POLITICAL PARTIES. Although much of the agitation against government in the 1960s and the 1970s came from the political Left, broadly conceived, the real beneficiaries appear to have been parties on the political Right. The late 1970s and early 1980s produced a series of political leaders who achieved office by running against the status quo and by promising real change—usually in a conservative direction. So, for example, in 1976 the Social Democrats in Sweden were thrown out of office, for the first time since 1935, by a coalition of bourgeois parties. Although such changes elsewhere were not as rare as in Sweden, the 1970s and 1980s have produced longer periods of bourgeois government control in Denmark, Norway, and especially the Netherlands than during most of the postwar period. Mrs. Thatcher was elected in the United Kingdom in 1979, survived two reelections, and has become the longest serving prime minister in modern British history. As perhaps the exception, but still a reaction to the Gaullist status quo ante, the Socialist François Mitterrand was elected as president of France in 1981.

In addition to the successes of the more traditional parties of the political Right, the period of reaction to government produced a number of new parties dedicated to even more fundamental public policy changes. Among the most famous of these is the Progress party in Denmark, headed by the flamboyant and controversial Mogens Glistrup. Glistrup advocated reducing the public budget virtually to zero. One of his more extreme (and attention-getting) proposals was reducing the defense budget to a figure sufficient only to pay for an answering machine saying "We capitulate" in several languages. Glistrup, who definitely practiced what he preached, was jailed for not paying his taxes, but his party has met with some success, receiving almost one vote in six in an election in the early 1970s. Other

TABLE 4.11

Satisfaction with Democratic Institutions, 1973–1988
(percentages)

	1973		1984		1988	
	VS	FS	VS	FS	VS	FS
Belgium	13	49	6	38	9	46
Denmark	7	38	20	48	17	57
France	4	37	4	36	5	46
W. Germany	5	39	12	59	13	64
Greece	–	–	19	41	14	37
Ireland	9	49	7	43	9	46
Italy	2	25	1	19	2	25
Luxembourg	16	36	11	53	14	56
Netherlands	8	44	6	48	8	53
Portugal	–	–	–	–	8	45
Spain	–	–	–	–	11	36
United Kingdom	7	37	11	49	10	47

SOURCE: Commission of the European Communities, *Eurobarometer* (Brussels: Commission of the EC, quarterly).
VS = very satisfied.
FS = fairly satisfied.

countries, such as Norway, have had copies of the Progress party, and in the 1989 elections the Norwegian party polled enough votes to become the third largest party in the *Storting* (Parliament).

The political Right has taken on a more ominous slant in some parts of Western Europe, and these movements represent an even more fundamental repudiation of political democracy and the liberal society. The most famous example of these rightist parties is Jean-Marie Le Pen in France and his *Front National*. This party is dedicated primarily to limiting the rights of immigrants in France, especially blacks and North Africans. The ultimate aim appears to be deportation of these immigrants (Mauco 1984). Although he was much less successful in the 1988 elections than predicted, Le Pen does represent a force of extreme conservatism that will have to be contended with for some years. The National Front in the United Kingdom has similar policies and aims (Taylor 1982), as do smaller anti-immigrant movements in other countries. Even liberal Sweden has had local political debates over whether to resettle any more immigrants in communities. Sjöbo, a small community in southern Sweden, passed a referendum refusing to accept immigrants being sent there by the central government (Webb 1988). While ethnically motivated, rather than being direct attacks on democracy and the welfare state, these movements do demonstrate substantial discontent with the manner in which European politics and society have been developing.

Whether directed at immigrants or at taxes, these various political parties and electoral movements of the extreme Right do demonstrate something of a decline in faith in government as it had been practiced in the postwar world. These right-wing parties clearly do not represent the postwar consensus favoring a mixed-economy, welfare state and a liberal and largely permissive social system. While it would be easy to say that the strength of that consensus was always overestimated, few manifest responses to it occurred before the 1970s and 1980s. Again, it would be too facile to lay blame for all this at the door of economic and energy problems, but those certainly did demonstrate the vulnerability of the economic system that had been created and perhaps the vulnerability of the associated political system.

TAX EVASION. Another behavioral indicator of citizens' disaffection with government is their willingness to evade taxation. Taxes are a legitimate claim that the state can make on the resources of individuals, and to some extent to deny that claim is to deny the legitimacy of the state (Ardant 1965). We have argued earlier that the principal legitimacy threat faced by contemporary political economies in Western Europe was not a violent overthrow by their people in a revolution but the quiet erosion of popular confidence and commitment. We labeled this change in values "political bankruptcy" (Rose and Peters 1978). Although the fiscal problems many governments have encountered may make real fiscal bankruptcy appear more possible, the dangers of metaphorical bankruptcy—the bankruptcy of authority—appear even greater. While a manifestation of fiscal problems—high tax rates—may generate some of the political bankruptcy, the erosion of the authority of the state appears to go substantially deeper.

The difficulty in looking at tax evasion as an indicator of the state of government is that reliable information about it is difficult to gain (Frey and Weck 1983). Given that the activity is illegal, most citizens are very reluctant to report evasion, and if they did they would tend to minimize its amount. Further, in their actual behavior, citizens would do everything possible to disguise their illegal actions so there would be no "paper trail" that could prove evasion. Despite those difficulties of measurement, some empirical evidence about the amount of tax evasion in several countries is available.

Some of it is survey evidence, in which citizens are asked about tax evasion. Again, given that they would be unlikely to report illegal activity, even if they were sure that the interviewer was not from the authorities, more indirect indicators must generally be used (but see, Frey 1979; Laurin 1986; Listhaug and Miller 1985; Pettenati 1979). One is to ask respondents whether they think tax evasion is a crime or, as one respondent said, whether it is merely a necessity of modern life (Vogel 1974). Some evidence indicates that those who report that they do not regard evasion as criminal would be more likely to engage in such behavior themselves (Lewis 1982, 161–77), given that the moral dimension of tax evasion appears to be a primary factor in preventing it. A second measure of real tax evasion is to ask citizens whether they believe their neighbors are engaging in it. Again, it is assumed that respondents would believe their neighbors are evading because they know they themselves are.

Some of the most direct evidence on tax evasion has been gained by Urban Laurin (1986) in his study of Swedish taxpayers. His respondents were willing to report their own behavior, and 30 percent said they had underreported income and 12 percent had overreported deductions. Allowing for some respondents who did both, about one-third of the Swedish population regularly evades taxes. And this occurs in a country that is considered extremely law-abiding and with a well-developed sense of public morality. The only limited longitudinal evidence available (see Table 4.12) points to increasing levels of uncivic behavior. Further, Laurin explains the behavior in collective choice terms. Citizens believe that everyone else is evading, so why shouldn't they? In short, some of the sense of community

TABLE 4.12

Changes in Attitudes to Tax Evasion in Sweden
(percentages)

	1968	1981
Tax Evasion Is Inconsiderate of One's Fellow Citizens		
Agree Strongly	62.5	51.0
Agree Somewhat	25.8	30.2
Disagree Somewhat	8.0	13.3
Strongly Disagree	1.7	3.1
Don't Know/No Answer	2.0	2.4
One Can Scarcely Complain If People Use All Available Opportunities for Tax Evasion		
Agree Strongly	7.6	15.4
Agree Somewhat	13.1	25.5
Disagree Somewhat	28.5	22.8
Strongly Disagree	46.7	33.2
Don't Know/No Answer	4.1	3.0
Penalties for Tax Evasion Are Not Severe Enough		
Agree Strongly	9.8	3.0
Agree Somewhat	14.7	6.6
Disagree Somewhat	37.6	30.4
Strongly Disagree	30.3	54.3
Don't Know/No Answer	7.7	5.8

SOURCE: Based on data from U. Laurin, *På Heder och Samvete* (Stockholm: P. A. Norstedts, 1986).

and trust among citizens that may be important in preserving the state has been eroding.

Other survey evidence indicates similar patterns of behavior and belief in other countries (see Hessing, Elffers, and Weigel 1986; International Labor Office 1987). Survey researchers Michael Johnston and Douglas Wood (1986), for example, found that about one-third of the British population does not believe that there is anything wrong with evading the value-added tax, and only about 3 percent see anything seriously wrong in doing so.

About two-thirds of the respondents said that they might do it themselves. Indeed there appears to be a rather pervasive belief that evading taxes is not immoral. To the extent that it is illegal, it is regarded as a very minor-league crime hardly worth a second notice. Citizens seem to feel that government has little or no legitimate claim on the resources of individuals and that therefore evasion is acceptable, so long as they are not caught. Fear of detection appears to be a more powerful deterrent than any moral claims of the state or of civil society (Spicer and Lundstedt 1976; Spicer and Thomas 1982). The popular attitude is clearly "catch me if you can."

In addition to the survey evidence, indirect indicators can also provide some idea of the level of tax evasion. One of these is how much cash money is circulating in an economy. If we assume that one reason for using cash for transactions, as opposed to safer methods such as checks or credit cards, is that there is no record of cash transactions for tax purposes, then the amount of money circulating in an economy can be an indicator of evasion (Cagan 1958; Feige 1979). There may be some national variations based on other economic variables—for example, the level of development of the banking and credit card industries—but taxation appears a central issue in the use of cash transactions. The ratio of currency to M_1 (a standard indicator of the total money supply) would then be a rough, but usable, indicator of tax evasion.

When this indicator of evasion is examined (see Table 4.13), several interesting patterns emerge. The first is that the ratio of cash to M_1 has been increasing in several societies, despite the tendency of modern economies to be fueled by plastic or electronic transactions. Apparently something is happening to make evasion more acceptable or more desirable. The second thing is that there are large differentials in the ratios in different countries, with some of the countries most famous for tax evasion—France and Italy (Gaudin and Schiray 1984; Mondari 1965)—having rather low ratios. Although the logic of this finding may be that if evasion is widely accepted one need not hide transactions, it also indicates that evasion is more widespread than some might like to believe. Tax evasion is not just a Mediterranean pastime but is common in almost all industrialized countries. The third interesting point in the table is that there appears to be an inverse relationship between apparent evasion of taxes and tax protest movements. Countries that have had significant tax protest parties and interest groups, such as Denmark, appear to have lower rates of evasion than do similar countries without such movements, such as Sweden. As Hirschman (1970) argued, citizens have the choices of "exit, voice and loyalty." When citizens choose "voice" through parties, they may be less likely to choose "exit" through tax evasion. As political scientists Ola

TABLE 4.13

Ratio of Cash in Circulation to M_1

	1975	1980	1985
Austria	.412	.493	.454
Belgium	.440	.451	.386
Denmark	.150	.149	.088
Finland	.257	.287	.228
France	.251	.215	.202
W. Germany	.332	.345	.330
Ireland	.390	.393	.429
Italy	.187	.146	.146
Netherlands	.307	.335	.306
Norway	.368	.413	.261
Portugal	.178	.327	.334
Spain	.267	.515	.489
Sweden	.654	.423	.487
Switzerland	.347	.370	.376
Turkey	.276	.302	.278
United Kingdom	.338	.330	.177

SOURCE: Based on data from the International Monetary Fund, *International Financial Statistics* (Washington, DC: International Monetary Fund, monthly).

Listhaug and Arthur Miller (1985) argue, tax evasion may be as much a political act of protest as an economic activity to enhance purchasing power.

Tax evasion is a difficult behavior to measure, and it may also have some inherent weaknesses as an indicator of the delegitimation of "big government" in Western European democracies. Interesting, however, is the extent to which tax evasion, and perhaps more the readily observed governmental concern about it, has varied in time with concern about the government's performance and legitimacy. It appears that tax evasion is becoming a greater concern for governments, if for no other reason than that more than ever governments need all the revenue they can possibly collect. Whether evasion has the deeper political meaning of delegitimation that we have ascribed to it here is subject to debate and analysis, but the level of evasion seems to indicate that governments do not have the moral claims on the resources of citizens that they might once have been able to enforce with little or no difficulty.

REFERENDA. We have noted earlier that European democracy has been representative and parliamentary. As usually practiced, this would mean that policy decisions would be made in Parliament or by the prime minister, with the public being involved only to the extent that they would vote on Parliament's decisions by voting at the next election. This representative democracy has begun to change to some extent, as more decisions have been referred directly to the public in referenda. While a huge volume of decisions are not so decided, especially when compared to the significant use of referenda in American state and local government, the use of referenda indicates either that governments do not feel confident about making decisions, or that the public wants to take decisions away from those usually held responsible for them.

In at least one country—France—the referendum has a clear constitutional basis. The Constitution of the Fifth Republic gives the president the right to call for a referendum for constitutional reforms under special circumstances, although Charles de Gaulle stretched that constitutional mandate substantially. He was very successful in appealing directly to the public on issues, such as Algeria, that might have produced immense difficulties within government. However, his failure to win approval of a referendum on the reform of the Senate in 1969, and his subsequent resignation from office, has made recent French presidents very reluctant to use the "enhanced" version of the referendum power.

Entry into the European Economic Community was the occasion for many countries to use the referendum. In the United Kingdom, this was the first use of a national referendum to advise Parliament or to make policy. Referenda on the issue were also held in Denmark and Ireland (in favor as in the United Kingdom), and in Norway (opposed). Referenda may have been used in part because the issue was so basic, involving to some degree an abrogation or redefinition of national sovereignty. Another reason, of course, is that it was a difficult and emotional issue, and elected politicians may have felt that they could only lose by making the decision themselves. This was especially true in Norway, where the EEC issue deeply divided the country and produced a political trauma that to some extent still lingers (Orvik 1975). For whatever reason, the EEC decisions have demonstrated the power of referenda as popular decision-making devices and as a means around parliamentary democracy.

In addition to entry into the Common Market, politicians have also referred to the people a variety of other issues that they felt were too hot to handle. These include some issues related to the modernization and secularization of predominantly Roman Catholic countries, such as divorce in Italy and Ireland. Other referenda have involved national reactions to an industrial and technological society, such as nuclear power in Sweden. Still others have concerned how best to cope with regional and ethnic differences within countries, such as self-government for Scotland and Wales within the United Kingdom. Referenda have also been used for advice on major foreign policy decisions, such as Spain's role in NATO. Finally, Switzerland has a long tradition of using referenda for policymaking, in part as a means of directly involving the public in government decisions in a potentially difficult society to govern (four languages, two religions, and a strong tradition of local autonomy). In short, referenda have been used when the public felt that representative democracy was not doing quite what it should and could, and when those representatives themselves were uncomfortable about their ability to make acceptable choices.

The NIMBY phenomenon (Not in My Back Yard) has also begun to spark a use of referenda in many European countries, although largely at a local rather than national level. This social movement, if something so decentralized and disorganized should be so called, is in itself a reaction to big government and to industrial society. Siting of controversial facilities, ranging from nuclear power plants to halfway houses for convicts and substance abusers, is always a difficult job and increasingly has been opposed by local groups who often want the facility in principle, just not in their neighborhood. In addition to other forms of political activity, these groups have used local referenda to demonstrate to those in government and business their opposition. In most instances these referenda have no binding powers but are useful means of demonstrating popular concern and disaffection with the actions of central government. They also to some extent represent postmaterialism in practice, because of the commitment to protecting the local environment and stopping developments such as nuclear power stations.

Summary

Europe and Europeans have been through a number of changes since World War II, and these changes are reflected in their attitudes toward government and the role of government in society. There have been some apparently contradictory shifts in attitudes, especially since the 1960s. On the one hand, many Europeans (especially younger ones) have come to see issues other than the successful management of the economy as central to the role of government. In particular, they demand improved protection of the environment, movement toward peace, greater equality (by class, gender, and race, if applicable), and enhanced opportunities for participation as central goals for government. Many of these Europeans do not consider that their current governments are doing particularly good jobs of reaching these "postmaterialist" goals.

On the other hand, other Europeans (or perhaps the same ones at different times) want greater economic growth, or at least they want to retain a larger share of what growth there is for their own consumption. They have come to reject, or at a minimum seriously question, many of the programs associated with the welfare state and the mixed economy that have been so successful in maintaining social harmony and individual well-being in the postwar period. They appear to want lower taxes, fewer programs (except perhaps the ones that directly benefit them), and a more laissez-faire approach to economic management. In short, they want to turn back the social and economic clock somewhat to a period of less government and greater personal economic freedom and initiative.

While somewhat disparate, these two lines of attitude change do have at least two points of similarity. One is that they are more individualistic than most social and political thinking has been in postwar, or even postdepression, Europe. Whether it is through participation in government or in making their own economic choices, Europeans appear to be extolling the rights of the individual and his or her capacity to make decisions about the future. This is true even in countries that do not appear to attach a great deal of importance to individual participation. Associated with the increased demand for participation has been some apparent delegitimation of government as the appropriate decision-making body in society. Again, this is not manifest rebellion in the streets but rather a quieter, more reasoned assertion of the limits of state power, whether in regard to peace protests or tax policy. Thus a new Europe may be a more individualistic and less statist collection of citizens and countries. The state will remain strong, almost certainly stronger than that found in the United States, but it has been reminded of its limits and of the willingness of citizens to engage in a variety of activities to limit its power.

Notes

1. It is not at all clear why God should have been getting such bad publicity in these discussions of public policy.

2. Later research showed substantial increases in the degree of postmaterialism among Danish respondents.

3. This was increasingly true of the population in West Germany, who had rather limited experience with democratic government, and that which they had had during the Weimar Republic was not positive. The economic successes that postwar Germany enjoyed appeared to reinforce the idea that democratic government worked (Baker, Dalton and Hildebrandt 1981).

Chapter

5

PARTIES AND VOTERS
DEALIGNMENT, REALIGNMENT,
OR WHAT?

Prior to the 1987 general elections in Britain, the possibility of a "hung parliament," a parliament in which no party had a majority and in which several smaller parties could hold the balance of power, was a topic of heated political discussion and numerous anxious editorials. In most of modern British political history, such an outcome had not been considered as a possibility. Across the Channel, the French had been experiencing several years of "cohabitation" (Duverger 1987) in which the presidency and the prime minister were of very different political tendencies. Farther north, in the fall of 1988 Swedish voters faced the possibility of returning a Parliament in which a "Red/Green" coalition of communists, ecologists, and the Center party held the balance of power between the two large voting blocs. In 1989 voters in neighboring Norway threatened to return a hung Parliament in which no logical coalition would be able to form a government. Although they are isolated events, all of which were resolved quite easily, these examples do illustrate the increasing volatility and diffusion of voting and of political parties in Western Europe. Voters appear much less predictable in their choice of party and in their choice of whether or not to vote, and new political parties have been forming with some rapidity. The stability of the party system, and the stable connections of groups of voters to parties, has come into some question, and political parties as a whole may have lost some of their important capacity to mediate between the mass public and the government.

Before public opinion can be translated into effective governmental action in a democratic political system, it is filtered and mediated through political parties and elections. That mediation, however, is far from a guarantee that the policies the public wants from its government will be those that are actually delivered. First, political parties must assemble platforms on the issues and choose candidates to compete for office, and these activities will almost certainly involve compromises about policy ideas. In addition, a voter may agree with one party on some issues and with several other parties on others, and he or she will have to convert all these preferences into a single vote. The voting system then further aggregates all these individual voting choices into a collective choice of parliamentarians, a process that may distort further voters' policy preferences. Once elected, parliamentarians often cannot be sure why they won. Which policy stances were decisive in the choices made by the voters, and on which ones did voters really disagree? In short, the democratic political process may be a very blunt instrument for allowing voters to choose governments, and even blunter as a means for them to choose policy.

The difficulties encountered in translating popular preferences into public policies in most Western European countries are different from those found in the United States or another two-party system. Some of these differences enhance the capacity of European voters to choose policy, while others diminish it. For example, most European political systems (major exceptions are Ireland, West Germany, and the United Kingdom in which there are effectively only two choices for governing party) are multiparty systems, which allow voters to consider a range of political parties and to select the one closer to them in a number of different policy areas. The correspondence between personal preferences and available party position may not be perfect, but it will probably be better than in a two-party system. In addition, proportional representation allows any political party that can mobilize any substantial support at all in the electorate to gain some representation in the legislature. Having the seats in Parliament, in turn, allows the parties to transmit voters' preferences directly into the policymaking process. Two-party systems, and the single-member district, plurality-voting systems that produce them, tend to restrict voter choice and to produce substantially less legislative diversity.

In addition to being more numerous than parties in the United States, political parties in Western European countries also tend to be more ideological. Even in the two-party (but increasingly multiparty) system of the United Kingdom, at least one political party (Labour) is substantially more ideological than any American party. While in two-party systems and single-member districts (Downs 1957) parties move toward the middle of the distribution of voters, in multiparty systems parties have an incentive to differentiate themselves from others in order to claim a share of the vote. This logic, along with the history of more ideological politics in continental Europe, tends to produce political parties with more distinctive stands on policy issues. Parties may also differentiate themselves along other dimensions. A number of parties, for example, represent voters with regional concerns, whether that regionalism is based on language, religion, culture, or simply geography. Again, unlike two-party systems, parties based on other than economic issues are capable, with proportional representation, of gaining seats in the Parliament and therefore bringing their particularistic viewpoints directly to bear on policymaking. The issues represented by these parties are often not commensurate with other socioeconomic values and cannot be solved by a different distribution of the public budget. The possibilities for compromise are therefore lessened, and the level of polarization among the parties may be more intense.

Yet in some ways a two-party system does allow for greater voter sovereignty over governments. When a voter in such a system goes to the polls, he or she knows that a vote that is cast is in effect a vote for a government to be formed by one party or the other. In a multiparty system, however, it is not always clear in advance what sort of government will be formed after the election is over. If there are a number of parties in the legislature, with none having a majority, the parties will have to bargain among themselves to form a coalition that can govern. Not only can this take weeks or even months, it can also produce some very strange political bedfellows. For example, in Finland, the coalitions formed during the mid-1980s were composed of Social Democrats and three or four other parties but excluded some seemingly more likely coalition partners. Also, some parties from the extreme Right or Left may not be deemed suitable coalition partners. If these extreme parties constitute a significant share of the members of Parliament, the options for forming governments are narrowed. Finally, coalition governments with numerous and diverse membership may be very weak, or even weaker minority governments may be formed; both of these outcomes will tend to limit the impacts of an election on public policies.

The aggregative decisions left to individual voters in a two-party system therefore must be made by party leaders after an election in a multiparty system. Those leaders must assemble a number of different party platforms and promises to form a government program sufficiently broad to satisfy all the parties needed to form a government. This aggregation is effective as long as the party leaders have the trust of the citizens who voted for the party, but may be disruptive to democratic norms if they do not. Voters must be confident that their interests will not be sacrificed to the career interests of politicians who want to become ministers.

In fairness, not all multiparty systems are as fluid as just implied. In Sweden, for example, it is clear to voters that there are two possible coalitions—one of the Social Democrats and the Left-Party Communists, and another of the three major bourgeois parties.[1] Voters may move their votes around within the two blocs without disturbing the essential nature of the coalition that would be formed after the election. The dynamics here are essentially two-party, although the choices allowed to voters are more like multiparty systems. This "moderate multiparty" system (Sartori 1966, 1976) is an effective compromise, with some of the virtues of both systems.

The other virtue that two-party systems have for policymaking is that the parties are almost inherently ones of compromise and accommodation. Parties in a two-party system tend to be characterized by a wide range of opinion within a single party (witness the range of ideas and members in the Labour party in Britain [Hatfield 1978; Wainwright 1988; Whiteley 1983]). The members have been forced to make some compromises among themselves simply to survive as political organizations. The pragmatism and the ability to compromise are substantial virtues for policymakers. Few policy decisions are so unambiguous that multiple viewpoints cannot be brought to bear on them, and few significant social problems are readily soluble by simple, ideological solutions. The political art of compromise, which may be absent from ideological political parties and leaders, often is a central ingredient in making government function smoothly and efficiently. A Swedish politician once described his nation as a land "plagued" by compromise, but the alternative plagues may well be more dangerous to a democracy.

This chapter will discuss political parties and voting in Western Europe. This is a huge task to undertake in a single chapter, or even in a single book, but we plan to describe the fundamental features of the socioeconomic environment that engenders parties, some characteristics of the parties themselves, and finally something of the changes that parties and party systems appear to be undergoing. In particular, we will be concerned with the alleged dealignment and realignment of European voters and parties. In Chapter 4 we pointed out that economic issues have lost some of their capacity to excite and mobilize the citizens of European nations, and with that loss has come some declining interest in political parties that were based primarily on socioeconomic class (Dalton 1988, Dalton, Flanagan, and Beck 1984). This voter discontent is a particular problem for Left parties, but has been apparent for parties of the Right also.

The shift away from established political parties has opened two possibilities. The first—realignment—is that citizens will seek to give their political allegiance to different types of political parties, representing different cleavages in society. Some of the new parties may, in fact, represent very old breaks (for example, regional parties) in society, while others such as the Greens may reflect newer ones. The second option—dealignment—is that citizens will give less and less enduring allegiance to any political party. Voters may participate in politics both by floating among the existing parties and relying on interest groups—especially single-issue "flash" groups. In many countries these interest groups seem more successful than the party system in producing effective action and promise to be a continuing feature of political life. Their existence means, however, that many citizens will reduce their levels of participation until a single particular issue mobilizes them to join an interest group. Either of these two major options for party systems will change something of the nature of politics in Western Europe and will present some fundamental challenges to the systems of governing.

Social Cleavages and Political Parties

Political parties and political competition arise from competing interests in a society. These competing interests, in turn, reflect cleavages within the society that have relevance for public policy. Many societies in Western Europe have histories of deep and divisive socioeconomic cleavages; in almost all there has been violence and loss of life—and in several civil wars—based on these divisions. Further, in most countries these historical cleavages persist into the 1990s. Their manifestations are rarely as bloody as they once were, but many may become more violent. Governing a European country therefore means coping with a number of cleavages and the associated tensions, and politics also means reflecting the aspirations of numerous different social groups. This makes European politics much more complex than the simple characterization of class-based politics could ever permit.

The Historical Roots of Cleavage

One way to understand the development of political cleavages in Western European countries is to think of a series of three revolutions or movements that swept the continent, each producing massive political repercussions that are still being felt today. These three "revolutions" can be assigned to historical periods, but all are also ongoing events. To some extent, the issues on which these upheavals were based have never been resolved, and the politics of most European countries is still oriented around one or more of these massive social changes.

The first of these movements was the Protestant Reformation, beginning in the late sixteenth century. While some sort of accommodation was reached in the Peace of Westphalia of 1648, to date it is still being fought over (politically and physically) in some parts of Europe—Northern Ireland, for example. The termination of the Thirty Years War in 1648, and the redrawing of national boundaries that has continued since that time, has left some countries religiously homogenous and others deeply divided by religion. As shown in Table 5.1, the Scandinavian countries are almost entirely Protestant, and countries such as Spain, Italy, Ireland, and Portugal are almost entirely Roman Catholic. In other countries, especially the Netherlands and the United Kingdom, religion has been and continues to be a central political issue (Lijphart 1977; Rose 1971). The general secularization of all industrialized societies has to a large degree mitigated the influence of this cleavage (van Mierlo 1986; van Putten 1982), although the

TABLE 5.1

Religious Variations in Western Europe in Percentages

	Roman Catholic	Protestant	Other/None
Austria	89	7	4
Belgium	93	1	6
Denmark	1	97	2
Finland	–	96	4
France	82	2	14
W. Germany	45	51	4
Greece	1	–	99
Ireland	94	5	1
Italy	91	–	9
Netherlands	40	38	22
Norway	–	99	1
Portugal	94	–	6
Spain	100	–	–
Sweden	–	99	1
Switzerland	43	44	13
United Kingdom	9	62	29

SOURCE: Based on data from C. L. Taylor and M. Hudson, *World Handbook of Political and Social Indicators,* 2d ed. (New Haven, CT: Yale Univ. Press, 1972).

dozens of deaths from sectarian violence in Northern Ireland in an average year would appear to give the lie to that facile statement.

The second revolution to sweep over Europe was a nationalist one. One common figure with which to associate this revolution was Napoléon Bonaparte in France, although in Britain the process of nation-building may have taken place earlier, and in some countries, such as Italy and Germany, it did not occur until much later in the nineteenth century. In Spain and other countries the process continues today as central governments attempt to create loyalty and control in regionalist and nationalist areas, and those regionalist forces strive for greater autonomy or full independence (Lijphart et al. 1987). Early national integration, as in the case of Scotland into the United Kingdom, is no guarantee that nationalist sentiments will not persist (Furniss 1984). Even when a country is nominally well integrated, as is Norway, elements on the periphery may still consider themselves different and want to maintain their own values and culture (Oystese 1980; Rokkan 1966). Table 5.2 gives some information on the extent of regionalist divisions in European nations based on language, culture, or simply on geography. These regional sentiments might not all be politically relevant, but most are, and governments must find ways to govern while still accommodating the demands from these component parts of their nations (see Chapter 2).

The third revolution to pass through Europe was the industrial revolution, bringing with it the familiar politics based on social class and economic wealth. Again, however, this revolution is far from complete, and several countries are now contending with socioeconomic changes experienced by Britain and Belgium in the 1830s, France and Germany in the 1870s and 1880s, and Scandinavia around the turn of the century (Kuhnle 1975; Lafferty 1971). Even within countries that have nominally industrialized, there are pockets of more traditional primary economies—agriculture, forestry, fishing—that claim special status and want to protect their own ways of life. These economic claims are often closely related to the cultural claims just mentioned. Further, while some countries or some regions are experiencing the industrial revolution for the first time, other countries or regions are going through a transformation to a "postindustrial" economy based more on knowledge and information than on physical production (Bell 1973; Touraine 1971). The full socioeconomic and political ramifications of that change have yet to be explored (but see Huntington 1974), but it may constitute another wave that fundamentally transforms social and economic life.

While some regions of industrialized countries benefit from the spread of knowledge-based industries, others are being deindustrialized as foreign

TABLE 5.2

Fragmentation of Western European Societies

	Taylor and Hudson[a]	Stephens[a]	Composite[b]
Austria	0.13	0.02	48.7
Belgium	0.55	0.50	50.0
Denmark	0.05	0.00	47.0
Finland	0.16	0.13	47.4
France	0.26	0.40	53.3
W. Germany	0.02	0.00	49.9
Greece	0.10	0.09	56.0
Ireland	0.04	0.37	47.8
Italy	0.04	0.10	51.3
Netherlands	0.10	0.06	49.7
Norway	0.04	0.00	41.8
Portugal	0.01	0.00	58.2
Spain	0.44	0.39	51.0
Sweden	0.08	0.00	41.0
Switzerland	0.50	0.52	61.9
United Kingdom	0.32	0.03	45.0

SOURCE: Based on data from C. L. Taylor and M. Hudson, *World Handbook of Political and Social Indicators,* 2d ed. (New Haven, CT: Yale Univ. Press, 1972); M. Stephens, *Linguistic Minorities in Western Europe* (Llandysul: Gomer Press, 1976); and J.-E. Lane and S. Ersson, *Politics and Society in Western Europe* (London: Sage, 1987).

[a] The indices range from 0.0 to 1.0; the closer to 1.0, the more heterogeneous the country. These data refer only to ethnolinguistic fragmentation and do not include effects of migration.
[b] Broad index including religious, ethnic, and class cleavages. The larger the number, the more fragmented the society.

competition forces the shutdown of traditional heavy manufacturing industries. Table 5.3 gives some information about politics based on the industrial revolution, with the proportion of the labor force who are members of trade unions and those who are still employed in the primary economy. The economic cleavages in European countries are, however, somewhat more complex and dynamic than any one table could illustrate adequately. For example, unionization is occurring more among white-collar, public-sector employees rather than among blue-collar, private-sector employees. This is changing the nature of the union movement, as well as the nature of labor and social democratic parties.

The information presented in the first three tables demonstrates that most European countries have multiple political cleavages. Some reinforce each other, as when a disproportionate share of cultural separatists are also farmers and fishermen. Others, however, are cross-cutting and may minimize the capacity of any single cleavage to divide the country deeply. Further, we need to understand that these cleavages may themselves not be distributed equally throughout a country; the politically meaningful division between Protestant and Catholic in the United Kingdom is confined largely to Ulster and several of the large cities in Great Britain, and most areas in Belgium outside Brussels are monoglot. Even with the several social cleavages in Switzerland, most communes are quite homogenous. Table 5.3 gives some indication of the overall levels of social fragmentation in European countries, but even that does not speak to the geographical distribution of cleavages and of politically relevant tensions that may exist

TABLE 5.3

Socioeconomic Cleavages

	Agricultural[a] Employment	Industrial[b] Employment	Unionization[c]	Urbanization[d]
Austria	2	40	58	29
Belgium	3	30	75	21
Denmark	8	26	79	37
Finland	12	33	75	23
France	8	32	22	17
W. Germany	6	40	33	33
Greece	29	28	30	18
Ireland	16	36	52	19
Italy	12	34	37	28
Luxembourg	4	35	–	–
Netherlands	5	27	38	26
Norway	9	40	55	18
Portugal	24	37	40	12
Spain	18	32	35	42
Sweden	5	30	85	27
Switzerland	7	39	35	15
United Kingdom	3	32	54	36

SOURCE: Based on data from ILO (annual); S. Mielke, *Internationales Gewerkschaftshandbuch* (Opladen: Leske & Budrich, 1983); and UN (annual).

[a] Percentage of economically active population employed in primary economy.
[b] Percentage of economically active population employed in secondary economy.
[c] Percentage of economically active population belonging to unions.
[d] Percentage of population in cities of 100,000 or more.

within different parts of a country. Taken as a whole, however, countries such as Switzerland and Belgium are substantially more heterogeneous than countries such as Sweden and Ireland. These socioeconomic differences often are translated into substantial differences in the politics of these countries.

Electoral Systems and Political Parties

Social cleavages and divisions can always manifest themselves through violence, mass demonstrations, or particularistic interest-group activity. To be most effective in democratic politics, however, these cleavages must be converted into political parties that attempt to present the social group's viewpoint directly in the legislature or in the political executive. If a particularistic political party can gain some share of power in a country, it has a real opportunity to make its voice heard. This representation, in turn, will enhance the social group's political power and efficacy. In some instances group consciousness results from political activity and political success rather than being the foundation of that political action.

Political systems are designed to be more or less conducive to the formation of political parties and to the capacity of those parties to gain seats in the legislature. Even when premised clearly on democratic norms, an electoral system can make it difficult for small parties to gain seats in the legislature and hence can make it difficult for particularistic issues ever to gain a place on the public agenda. One electoral system, the single-member plurality voting systems found in the United States, the United Kingdom, West Germany,[2] and for a while in France in a slightly modified form, tends to disadvantage smaller parties by forcing politics toward a two-party model. Proportional representation schemes, on the other hand, allow smaller parties to gain a foothold in Parliament, often with only quite a small share of the total vote.

The single-member district, simple-plurality system of voting awards the single seat available in each electoral district to the candidate who receives the most votes. Coming in second or third in this system means the same as coming in forty-second—there is no representation from that constituency. Thus a party may do quite well all around the country but receive very few seats in the legislature. For example, in the 1987 British elections, the Social Democratic-Liberal Alliance ran candidates in every constituency and received over 22 percent of the popular vote, but received only twenty-two seats (3.4 percent) in parliament. Alliance candidates came in second in 275 constituencies and were often very close to the winner, but this electoral strength did not produce any additional seats for them. The single-member district system tends to advantage two large political parties that can compete throughout the country. The major exception to this generalization is that parties with a strong regional concentration of votes may be able to do reasonably well. The Scottish National Party, for example, was able to gain three seats with many fewer votes than the Alliance because all their votes were concentrated in Scotland. As well as reducing the number of parties represented in parliament, the plurality voting system tends to enhance the probability that a single party will receive a majority of seats in the parliament and will be able to form a strong government on its own.

The several varieties of proportional representation,[3] on the other hand, enable small parties to gain representation in parliament. In these systems each constituency has more than one seat, and these seats are divided among the parties roughly in proportion to their percentages of the votes. Some countries, such as Sweden and Denmark, also retain a pool of seats at the national level to ensure that the final distribution of seats in the legislature very closely mirrors the distribution of votes by the population. To many people proportional representation does appear more democratic, but, as pointed out earlier, the number of parties it generates sometimes makes it difficult to form a workable coalition to govern. Some countries reduce this problem by requiring that a party win a certain percentage of total votes (5 percent in West Germany or 4 percent in Sweden) before receiving any seats.[4] More radical proportional representation systems with a very low threshold for representation, as in the Netherlands where the entire nation functions as a single constituency and an electoral quota to gain a seat of less than 1 percent, may produce a substantial number of parties in parliament. In the mid-1980s, for example, Belgium had thirteen parties in parliament and the Netherlands had twelve.

Clearly, all Western European countries are more multiparty than is the United States or Canada. Even Britain, which employs the same plurality voting systems as the North American countries, now has what is in effect a multiparty system. This appearance of multipartyism would be somewhat diminished if the three parties gaining seats from Northern Ireland and reflecting the tortured history of that province were removed. Even on the island of Great Britain, however, in 1987 five parties (counting the then Alliance as one) were able to gain seats in Parliament—two being regionally concentrated in Wales and Scotland. Germany, with a hybrid electoral system of half single-member districts and half proportional representation with a high (5 percent) threshold of representation, has parliamentary representation from only four parties (counting the Christian Democratic Union/Christian Social Union [CDU/CSU] as one). France has had a version of single-member districts, although with two rounds of balloting, during much of the Fifth Republic, and this has reduced somewhat party system fragmentation. Somewhat in contrast to expectation, Greece, which has a proportional representation system, has only three parties in its parliament after the most recent election, and the party system has been tending toward bipolarity. Although the impact of electoral systems is by no means as clear and dramatic as has been hypothesized (Duverger 1964; Taagepera and Grofman 1985), there is some relationship between proportional representation and the direct representation of societal cleavages. If those cleavages are sufficiently intense, however, they will apparently find some avenue for gaining political representation.

Party Systems

We will now combine the analysis of social cleavages and electoral systems and determine just what types of party systems they produce in Western European countries. By party systems, we refer to the number of parties regularly competing for, and gaining, office and the manner in which they interact (Daalder 1984). While the characteristics of individual parties are important, to a great degree they are influenced by the party system within which they exist. Any political party that does not behave appropriately for the party system within which it is embedded is unlikely to have much success, either in gaining votes from the electorate or in influencing policy should any of its candidates be elected to parliament. However, it appears more likely that third and fourth parties will form in nominally two-party systems than it is that multiparty systems will become two-party systems (the previous example of Greece notwithstanding).

The analysis of party systems has taken a number of twists and turns but has been oriented around the distinction between two-party and multiparty systems (Duverger 1964; Sartori 1976). As indicated, there really are no real two-party systems in the larger European countries; perhaps the only major representatives of that breed in the developed world are found in the United States and New Zealand. However, as Giovanni Sartori (1976) has pointed out very effectively, not all multiparty systems are the same (see Table 5.4). He made the distinction between what he called "moderate multi-party" systems and "extreme multi-party" systems. In the former, although there may be a number of parties competing for seats, the dynamics are bipolar, so that there are in effect two logical coalitions or groups of parties competing. In such a system, the parties are really divided along a single-issue dimension (but see Sinnott 1984). For example, in Sweden

TABLE 5.4

Types of European Party Systems

	Poles	Polarity	Drives
Two Party	2	None	Centripetal
Moderate Multiparty	2	Limited	Centripetal
Extreme Multiparty	3+	Extreme	Centrifugal

SOURCE: Adapted from G. Sartori, "European Political Parties: The Case of Polarized Pluralism," in *Political Parties and Political Development,* ed. J. LaPalombara and M. Weiner (Princeton, NJ: Princeton Univ. Press, 1966), 138.

there are really two blocs divided along an economic dimension, with one bloc (Social Democrats and Communists) representing primarily the working classes and the other bloc (Moderates, Liberals, and Center) representing primarily the bourgeois. Further, in a moderate multiparty system, the politics between the two blocs is not intense or sharply polarized, and there is some capacity for compromise solutions. We have already used Sweden as an example of this type of party system, and the model also fits the other Scandinavian countries (although perhaps not as well). In Norway, for example, the interjection of religious and regional issues makes the divisions among the parties more complex and the number of possible coalition partners greater.

The extreme multiparty system is more like the stereotype of multiparty politics sometimes offered as a contrast to the presumed civility of two-party politics. In such an extreme system, there are a number of parties divided along various issue dimensions—frequently involving religious, ethnic, and regional issues as well as economic class. Further, the divisions among the parties tend to be more intense, and the possibilities for compromise on issues are minimal. Such a model to some extent describes Italian politics for most of the postwar period, or French politics prior to the formation of the Fifth Republic (Luethy 1955). In both countries there has been the usual Left-Right split on economic issues, but to that must be added several other cleavages. One is clericalism and the issue of the role of the Roman Catholic church in secular affairs, such as education. Another is the very existence of the state itself, with parties of the Left (communists) and Right (neofascists and monarchists in Italy, early versions of Gaullism and the Poujadists in France) at times challenging the very nature of the existing regime. Finally, both have small but significant ethnic and regional cleavages. In such a setting, politics becomes not so much a question of compromise but one of changing coalition partners to cope with specific policy problems (MacRae 1967; Pasquino 1980). Government still functions in these countries (LaPalombara 1987), but in ways not readily understood by observers more attuned to the subdued dynamics of two-party or moderate multiparty political systems.

The differences in party systems tend to be associated with variations in the organization and behavior of the political parties that comprise them. Most fundamentally, the goals of parties in the two systems tend to be different. In a two-party system, the parties' major goal is to win the election and to govern, and as a consequence ideologies and issue stances tend to be flexible. As economist Anthony Downs (1957) has argued, parties in this type of system select policies in order to win elections rather than vice versa. They are also "parties of maneuver," attempting to find the best policy positions on which to fight the next election. Because of the need to be flexible and able to maneuver quickly, these political parties must travel light. Their ideological baggage is kept light; they tend to be pragmatic about most issues. They also tend to be elite or "caucus," parties, which manage internal affairs in the legislature rather than in the mass party, and have a relatively small mass membership compared to their voting strength. The British Conservative party, which continues to behave as if it were in a two-party system, has only approximately 1.2 million formal members but collected almost 13.8 million votes in the 1987 elections. If there were more mass members with a greater voice in party management and the development of policy stances, maneuvering would be much more difficult.

Political parties in extreme multiparty systems, and to some extent even those in moderate ones, tend to be quite different from those in two-party systems. In the first place, they are "parties of position" rather than of maneuver, and stake out relatively stable positions on central policy issues. These positions are often based on a comprehensive ideology, but may also be products of their own organizational histories. Although parties in extreme multiparty systems want to do well in elections, winning may be a subordinate goal to that of remaining true to party values and ideals. Such parties also tend to be mass ones, and attempt to develop mass memberships and, in some cases, to structure their members' political life. There are real differences among parties even within the same country, and these tendencies usually are not as pronounced in parties in moderate multiparty systems as in more extreme systems.

A better idea of the dynamics of parties in these two types of systems can be gained by examining Figures 5.1a and 5.1b. This figure assumes that voters in a country are distributed along a single Left–Right ideological

FIGURE 5.1

Hypothetical Distribution of Voters

a. Two-Party or Moderate Multiparty System

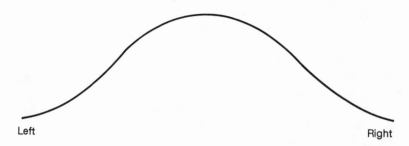

Left   Right

b. Extreme Multiparty System

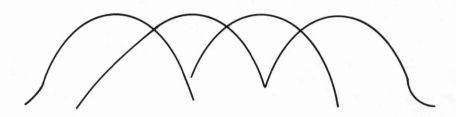

continuum. We have already pointed out that politics in most European countries is far from this simple, but the fundamental logic remains the same even if multiple continua are included. In Figure 5.1a, we assume a two-party system and a unimodal distribution of voters. Parties here have an incentive to move toward the center to capture more votes, to compromise, and to become less differentiated on ideological and issue grounds. In Figure 5.1b, on the other hand, there are a number of separate nodes of voters, and if the electoral system is conducive (or perhaps even if it is not), separate parties can form to occupy each node. In such a distribution of voters, political parties have little or no incentive to move toward one another (there is a large valley with few voters between the "hills" with the voters). Hence the parties should stake out a position serving one of the nodes of voters and defend that position. While this will mean that the chances of any single party winning a majority in an election are very slim, neither will any party lose its support.

The differences in party systems and in electoral strategies of parties may explain some of the variation in voter turnout in various countries. In a two-party system, if there are many voters with views situated away from the center of the distribution, they are likely to feel as if they have no option that really matches their preferences. Even voters who ideologically are near the center of the distribution may feel that the choices between the parties are not sufficient to warrant the effort required to vote (Riker and Ordeshook 1973). On the other hand, voters in multiparty systems are likely to have the opportunity to vote for a party that very closely reflects their preferences, and consequently they should feel that their votes will be more efficacious.

In summary, party systems are to some degree a product of the cleavages in society that divide people politically. If the society is divided along a number of dimensions, it will be difficult for the party system to be anything but multiparty; there may be too many differences to be contained effectively in a simple two-party system. Even if these tendencies toward multipartyism already exist, they may be reinforced by the electoral system. A single-member district plurality system usually will push politics toward a two-party model, but the electoral system may not be sufficient in itself to overcome basic cleavages, as has happened in contemporary Britain. Multipartyism need not, however, imply unmanageability. Moderate multiparty systems are almost as stable as the quasi-two-party systems, such as West Germany and the United Kingdom. Further, more extreme versions of multiparty systems appear to provide governance for their societies and have adapted over time to become rather more like more moderate multiparty systems.

Types of Parties

Although each political party will have a distinctive history and a distinctive set of ideals, certain types of parties tend to appear in most European countries. Further, these "families" of parties themselves coalesce in the European Parliament (Lodge 1986; Pridham and Pridham 1979). Thus they discern substantial affinity among their own roots and their own programs. Although we could certainly hone our classifications more finely and produce more classes of parties (see for example, Beyme 1985; Lane and Ersson 1987), we will briefly discuss the six principal categories of political parties that play major roles in the politics of contemporary Western Europe.

Conservative Parties

If we begin on the political Right, the first large group of parties we encounter we will label "conservatives." They wear this label in many countries, as in Britain, but they also go under a number of other banners such as Fine Gael in Ireland and the "Moderates" in Sweden. As shown in Table 5.5, almost every Western Europe country has a party that fits into this group. The largest number of them bear the word Christian in their titles. The prevalence of "Christian" is indicative in part of the parties' anticommunist positions as well as formal or informal linkages to the church in Roman Catholic countries. In general, these parties represent socioeconomic and cultural conservatism and have deep historical roots. For most of the postwar period conservative parties were a component of the consensus in favor of the mixed-economy welfare state, but in the 1980s they weakened their commitment to the welfare state and became increasingly antistate and pro-market. They were also, on average, very successful during that decade and formed the government, or were part of

TABLE 5.5

Conservative Parties

Austria	Austrian People's Party (ÖVP)
Belgium	Christian Social Party (PSC/CVP)
Denmark	Conservative People's Party (KF)
Finland	Conservative Party (KOK)
France	Republican Party (PR)
	Rally for the Republic (RPR)
W. Germany	Christian Democratic Union/Christian Social Union (CDU/CSU)
Greece	New Democracy (ND)
Ireland	United Ireland (Fine Gael)
Italy	Christian Democratic (DC)
Netherlands	Reformed Political Party (GVP)
	Christian Democratic Appeal (CDA)
Norway	"Upper" (Høyre)
Portugal	Social Democratic Center (CDS)
Spain	Popular Alliance (AP)
	Union of the Democratic Center (UCD)
Sweden	Moderate Unity (MS)
Switzerland	Christian Democratic People's Party (CDV)
United Kingdom	Conservative and Unionist Party (CUP)

the governing coalition, in nearly half of the European countries as of September 1989.

Despite their recent political successes, in several countries the conservatives are in danger of becoming outflanked on the Right. One dimension of this "flanking" is along economic issues, and this is quite evident in Denmark and Norway—hardly pillars of conservatism—where the "Progress" party (*Fremskridspartiet*) has made significant electoral gains. The Progress party in both countries is a radical antitax and antistate party, seeking to impose drastic cuts in the size of the public budget and in public employment. At one point the Progress party was the second largest single party in the Danish parliament, and in the election of September 1989 it came in a close third in the Norwegian elections. The Progress party in Norway also has been successful in local elections, being in governing coalitions in Oslo and several other major towns. Blessed with entertaining leaders, the several manifestations of this party have been able to make an impact in high-tax countries with their simple message of tax reduction, debureaucratization, and privatization.

The other dimension along which conservative parties run the risk of being outflanked is immigration and race. At times parties on the radical Right of European politics are alleged to emulate the platform and ideals of the Nazi party, although in most cases immigrants (especially from Africa and Asia) have largely replaced Jews as the scapegoats. The *Front National* in France, led by Jean-Marie Le Pen, is a prime example of such a party. It opposes further immigration into France and would like to find ways to send many Africans back from whence they came. These views are rationalized in terms of nationalism, protecting jobs for "real" Frenchmen, and preserving French culture. Although his views are repugnant to many people inside and outside France, Le Pen caused a substantial scare in the 1988 campaign for the presidency and received over 14 percent of the vote on the first ballot. France is not alone, however, in having parties like this; the National Front in Britain, the MSI in Italy, and *Fuerza Nacional* in Spain (among others), and the Flemish Bloc (at the local level) in Belgium are similar. The surprisingly strong showing of the right-wing, anti-immigrant Republican party in West Berlin elections in January 1989 demonstrated just how widespread support for anti-immigrant parties has become. West Berlin had a clear Christian Democratic majority prior to that election and was generally considered among the most tolerant places in Europe. The electoral success in West Berlin was followed by equally large votes in several other *Land* elections, indicating that the Republican party may be able to produce more than isolated support.

Liberal Parties

Moving to the Left (but not too far), one encounters the liberal parties, which appear in a number of guises. They appear as the "People's party," the "Free Democrats," the "Left," and as the plain "Liberal party," among other titles. These are nineteenth-century liberal parties, believing in the virtues of the free market but also in greater religious, social, and political freedom than conservative parties were willing to advocate. Liberal parties were crucial to the formation of the welfare states (Ashford 1986; Verney 1957) in the early twentieth century in several European countries, but have since been outflanked on the left by labor and social democratic parties. In most countries the liberals have been reduced to small parties, often regionally concentrated. Despite their small size, these parties have been important coalition partners for larger ones, especially in West Germany, where the Free Democrats have been a partner in most governments. Liberals share some values with both of their larger ideological neighbors—conservatives and social democrats—and therefore are able to serve as coalition partners for either.

Although Liberal parties may make ready coalition partners in a number of countries, this may not be a sufficient base for maintaining a political party. Their ability to bridge the gap between major ideological camps may be uncomfortable, especially in more ideologically oriented, multiparty political systems. As a consequence, Liberal parties have been attempting to present some clearer image of themselves to voters, oriented to some extent around the concept of "freedom." However, there the Liberal parties have had their appeal weakened by right-wing parties like Progress. In short, Liberal parties are having some difficulty in finding an appropriate electoral niche for themselves.

The Center

In France, a collection of parties operating between the Conservatives and the Socialists were once referred to as the "swamp of the center." Other analysts have argued that there is no such thing as a center in politics (Duverger 1964), even though center parties may exist (Daalder 1984). Center parties do indeed exist and to some extent have been flourishing in several European countries. In some countries these parties bear the title "Center" (Sweden, Finland, Denmark),[5] while in others their centrist politics tends to identify them. Some may bear such older titles as "Radical" or "Republican" but now essentially function as center parties.

Center parties have several different lineages. Some arose out of the conflict between church and state in the late nineteenth and early twentieth centuries, and the center in several countries has been split along clerical and anticlerical lines, or along religious lines where religion is a political issue. Center parties also have an agrarian background, especially in Scandinavia, and in several instances the name was changed from "Agrarian" to "Center" to attempt to appeal to nonrural voters. This change also reflects some modernization of the party's policy stances, of its advocacy of ecology, and its growing appeal to white-collar workers. In other cases the center is actually very much like the Liberal parties just described. What makes these parties "Center," besides their names, is that they tend to straddle the fence on socioeconomic issues, being more free market than social democrats and labor but more accepting of state intervention in economy and society than conservatives or most liberals. As have the liberals, center parties have been frequent and excellent coalition partners in many countries. They often have the advantage, however, of having a stable base of rural voters on which to build in an election.

Social Democracy

Again, several different labels are applied to social-democratic parties, but it is clear that there is some commonality of principle and style among

TABLE 5.6
"Left-Libertarian" Political Parties

Austria	Greens
Belgium	Agalev (Dutch)
	Ecolo (French)
Denmark	Socialist People's Party
Finland	Greens
France	Ecologists
W. Germany	Greens
Iceland	Women's Party
Italy	Radicals
Luxembourg	Green Alternative
Netherlands	Green Progressive Accord
Norway	Socialist People's Party
Sweden	Left Communist Party Center
Switzerland	Greens Progressive Organization
United Kingdom	Greens

SOURCE: Based on data from H. Kitscheldt, *The Logic of Party Formation: Ecological Parties in Belgium and West Germany* (Ithaca, NY: Cornell Univ. Press, 1989).

them. The most common titles are "Social Democratic" and "Labor," titles that go a long way toward describing the parties' nature. First, these are parties of the political Left that have been important in the extension and, where they existed at the time, the initial adoption of the mixed-economy welfare state. Social democratic parties may espouse broadly socialist principles but are certainly not revolutionary or antisystem in their politics; they are indeed democratic. Further, in most of Western Europe, these tend to be the parties of organized labor, and trade unions are often officially affiliated with the party. In many cases these parties began as labor movements outside of government and politics and only later became political parties.

In many European countries social democratic parties have become the natural parties of government. In Scandinavia, for example, the period of bourgeois governments during the late 1970s and early 1980s was the exception rather than the rule. These periods of rule have made most social democratic parties more pragmatic than ideological in their styles, although ideology is still used at election time to mobilize the faithful. This pragmatism also has produced a number of splinter groups—either within the party or organized as separate ones—that advocate what they consider the "true" meaning of socialism, an interpretation that is usually somewhat to the left of that of the larger social democratic parties. Further, the pro-system stance of these parties has made relationships with the communist parties in their countries often very difficult, and what might appear to be natural allies have at times been bitter political enemies.

Communist Parties

Finally on the conventional Left–Right continuum of political parties we encounter the communist parties of Western Europe (Waller and Fennema 1988). Almost all European countries now have a communist party, and a number have several expressing different interpretations (Marxist, Maoist, and so on) of communism. As of the mid-1980s, ten Western European countries had at least one communist in Parliament, and in France the communists were for a three-year period part of the coalition that formed the cabinet and supplied several government ministers. An amalgamation of communist parties in Finland, the SKDL, also has been part of governing coalitions several times, indicating in part Finland's need to be sensitive to the Soviet Union even in its domestic politics but also the nation's long history of rural radicalism. The communists are also represented in the European Parliament, with 41 (mostly from France and Italy) of the 434 seats.

Over time communist parties in Western Europe have become parties almost like all others in democratic countries. Most are now described as "Euro-communist," indicating that they are European (democratic) first and communist second. Although they maintain some of the rhetoric and trappings of a revolutionary party, no communist party in Europe could really be described as revolutionary or Stalinist any longer (although the French party held to some of its old beliefs for quite a long time), and most now are more oriented toward the domestic politics of their own country than toward Moscow.[6] Although the voting patterns for communist parties are complex, we need to remember that in many instances these are not urban, industrial parties of revolution but rather rural, agricultural, or intellectual parties of protest (Allardt 1964; Blackmer and Tarrow 1975). With the general modernization of socioeconomic and political life in Western Europe and the development of new parties of protest ("Greens," and so on), communist appeal has waned in many countries. In elections taking place around 1975 they received an average of 7.8 percent of the vote across Europe, but in elections around 1985 they received only 5.9 percent of the vote—a drop of almost 25 percent.[7] Similar losses of voting strength afflict the larger communist parties in France and Italy, and the Italian party has dropped the hammer and sickle from its emblem to appear more modern. Although clearly not simply another political party, the differences between communists and the rest appear to be diminishing. This movement is, of course, assisted by reforms and democratization within the Soviet Union and other Eastern European countries.

Others

The final group of parties we will mention is a very loose group indeed. Although it includes a number of different types of parties, the most important for our discussion are two groups: those that are oriented around regional issues and those that are oriented toward the "New Politics." As we have pointed out, regionalism is far from a new political issue in Europe, but in a number of countries the issue had been subsumed under conventional Left–Right politics. For example, Scotland and Wales voted heavily for Labour, and to some extent for the Liberals, because of the concentration of working-class voters in these two parts of the country and the historical connection of the Liberals to regional issues, such as Welsh disestablishment (Wald 1983). Only in the early 1970s did regionalism reemerge in the shape of regional political parties. By the late 1980s at least eight European countries had political parties in Parliament reflecting regional (including religious and language) sentiments.

The New Politics is oriented around specific social and political issues, rather than around primordial sentiments, such as language and religion, that have shaped the Old Politics (Poguntke 1987). The most important of these parties have been the Greens, or ecologists. As the name implies, parties of this type are strongly environmentalist, but they also stress other values associated with postmaterialism, such as peace, equality, and participation (Rudig 1988). Although they have won seats in several European parliaments, the Greens have been most successful in West Germany, where they received over 8 percent of the vote in the 1987 elections. The Social Democrats in Britain, at least prior to their split in 1987, were somewhat similar to the Greens (especially on issues of participation), although almost entirely lacking in the flamboyance associated with Green politics (Buerklin 1981, 1985). Another interesting party expressing values of this type are the Women's List in Iceland, which was able to win over 5 percent of the vote in elections during the 1980s and received representation in the *Althingi,* or Parliament. The Greens and their allies in the Rainbow Group have also done well in European elections and, in 1989, won forty-eight seats in the European Parliament (up from forty-one in 1984).

While they are interesting to voters and analysts alike, the parties built on the New Politics have proven to be somewhat unstable and unreliable once in Parliament, in part because they do not "play the game" of lawmaking. These new parties also are built on a fluid and even more unreliable electoral base (Dalton 1988); consequently, they have not had the influence over policy that some observers had initially expected. The major impact of the Greens may be through forcing the traditional parties to consider their own stances on the environment, social justice, and perhaps on other issues, such as nuclear weapons, in order to appeal to Green voters. This is especially true given that these voters are disproportionately young, affluent, and educated, and may be expected to be the future opinion leaders of Western Europe.

PARTIES IN THE EUROPEAN PARLIAMENT. We have mentioned already that political parties have begun to coalesce across national boundaries and to form groups involving members from all countries in the European Community. There have been some movements toward joint campaign activities across national boundaries, and popular politicians from one country have made appearances (in a few instances disastrously) in other countries. For the most part, however, the European parties are very loose groupings that exist within the European Parliament more clearly than outside.

There are currently nine party groups in the European Parliament (Table

5.7). The political groups on the Left, such as the Socialists and Communists, are very well known in the member nations. The groups in the center
and Right are, however, more particular to the European setting. The
largest group on the Right is the European People's Party, which actually
are Christian Democrats, plus Fine Gael from Ireland. Other groups on the
Right are the European Right, the European Democratic Alliance, European Democrats, and the Liberals and Democrats.[8] Finally, there is the
Rainbow Group composed largely of Greens and their allies, plus a few
independents. Although these party groups as yet have little effect on
national politics, they do constitute a possible foundation for strictly European politics. As noted, it is important that the politics of the European
Parliament is organized around the parties rather than around the nation-
states from which the members are elected. This implies that the nation is
not the major issue dividing Europeans politically.

Summary

This brief catalog of Western European parties has not done justice to the
special nature and history of each political party that exists, but it has
demonstrated some of the diversity and complexity of the party systems.
These parties represent something of the long political history of Europe,
with a veneer of new parties and new issues laid over old parties and old
issues. The older parties have found ways to survive many years, even when
it might have been thought that their usefulness had passed (for example,
Liberals in Britain or Republicans in Italy). The party systems are still
undergoing change, and scholars as well as practical politicians disagree
over just how fundamental is the realignment of European politics. We will
now turn to a more direct analysis of these changes and their implications
for future European politics and government.

Dealignment and Realignment

We began this chapter with a very brief discussion of the phenomena of
change in European voting behavior and political party systems. What has
transpired between that brief mention and this point was all background
for a discussion of the changes, whether real and enduring or only
ephemeral, that have come to dominate discussions of mass politics in
Europe. The categories of change that have been mentioned are somewhat
different, although they both stem from a common cause. That cause is
disaffection with and weakening of allegiance to the major political parties

TABLE 5.7

Membership in Party Groups in the European Parliament by Country, 1989

	Communists	Socialists	Rainbow Group	Independents	European People's Party	Liberals	European Democratic Alliance	European Democratic Group	European Right
Belgium	–	8	4	–	7	4	–	–	1
Denmark	1	4	4	–	2	3	–	2	–
France	7	22	9	–	7	13	13	–	10
W. Germany	–	31	8	–	32	4	–	–	6
Greece	4	9	–	1	10	–	–	–	–
Ireland	–	1	1	1	4	2	6	–	–
Italy	22	14	7	2	28	4	–	–	4
Luxembourg	–	2	–	–	3	1	–	–	–
Netherlands	–	8	2	2	10	3	–	–	–
Portugal	3	8	1	–	3	9	–	–	–
Spain	4	27	3	8	17	1	–	–	–
United Kingdom	–	46	–	2	–	–	1	32	–
TOTAL	41	180	39	16	123	44	20	34	21

*Numbers refer to number of seats in EP; parties are listed in order from left to right.

in Western Europe, and to a greater extent in other developed democracies as well. This disaffection can manifest itself in three ways: in more rapid swings among existing parties by voters, by the development of new parties that will capture the issues and the social cleavages that the older parties appear incapable of accommodating, or by indifference toward partisan politics manifested through abstention from voting. None of these changes bodes well for the future of the existing political party systems.

The major political parties in Europe—comprising mostly the first five categories of parties just described—have not, of course, vanished, nor are they likely to do so any time soon. They may, however, face a period of declining electoral fortunes and, if the prophets of realignment are correct, some real eventual danger of being supplanted by new parties. A realignment would not be new, as major partisan realignments occurred around the beginning of this century and again (although to a lesser extent) at the end of World War II. But after three decades of great economic expansion and political stability, the changes implied by realignment appear very threatening to many Europeans—not least the elective politicians whose career prospects may be diminished. The current constellation of parties has come to represent stability and dependability, and a movement away from that party system may be very unsettling.

Evidence of Change

The concepts of dealignment and realignment are somewhat ambiguous and potentially difficult to measure (see Dalton, Flanagan, and Beck 1984). The two terms each could mean several things, and the different interpretations of the concepts may not mean the same thing. For example, dealignment could imply that individual voters are no longer loyal to parties (especially the "major" parties likely to form governments) but do remain active politically, or it may imply that the citizens are less likely to be voters at all. Evidence for these varying interpretations would therefore include data about the voting swings among parties, changes (especially decreases) in partisan identification, and election turnouts. We will now examine some evidence about each of these possible interpretations.

PARTY VOTING. The most direct approach for examining the alleged dealignment of voters in Western Europe is to look at the voting for political parties. This can be done in two ways. One is to look at the percentage of vote going to the major parties—those parties likely to be able to form a government, or that historically have been partners in coalition governments. In many countries the various multiparty systems and the wide

TABLE 5.8

Changes in Two-Party Share of Vote in Two-Party Dominant Systems

	1950s	1960s	1970s	1980s
Austria	81.6	83.6	85.5	84.4
Germany	78.0	85.8	85.1	85.1
Ireland	74.1	79.1	81.2	82.4
United Kingdom	95.4	88.6	80.0	71.6

range of coalition partners makes such an assessment difficult if not impossible. Therefore, we will concentrate on a few countries in this section, and extend the analysis to other countries in subsequent sections.

Table 5.8 gives some summary voting statistics for four European countries where (possibly with some stretching) we could identify the major parties from which there would be dealignment. Only in Britain could there be said to be any significant movement away from the dominant parties. There the two-party percentage of the vote has been declining over the years, as nationalist parties and then the Alliance parties (Liberal and Social Democratic[9]) began to capture larger shares of the votes. In the other countries the percentages going to the major parties have remained virtually unchanged. This does not take into account, however, the decline of a few dominant parties, such as the Socialist party in Austria and Fianna Fail in Ireland, but these parties lost votes in part to other likely government parties. These findings do not imply that the other four-party systems have been completely stable. In most cases there has been some shifting about in strength among the major parties, and some shifting of votes—with some parties being created and others dying—among the "minor" parties. These voting statistics do, however, indicate that no massive shift away from the parties of government has yet taken place. Other evidence on the psychological attachment of citizens to political parties may not be as sanguine for those parties.

A second, and more comprehensive, way to examine shifts in party systems is to look at the overall volatility of voting for parties. Volatility here is measured as the sum of the absolute values of change of percentage of votes for all parties from election to election (Budge 1982; Pedersen 1983). Of course, the signed values of these changes will always add to zero, but the sum of the absolute values (divided by 2 to make it vary between 0 and 100) gives a good measure of the extent of shifting among parties in elections. This does not say what segment of the voting population is the source of that change. The shifting could be the result of a number of new voters choosing new parties, or it could be regular voters becoming disenchanted with the options being offered them by the current party system, or changing parties because of changing personal economic circumstances. Determining the source of all the individual changes would require extremely extensive survey research, but the aggregate measure of volatility does illustrate some important overall changes in the political party system.

As shown in Table 5.9, the volatility of voting has been increasing across time, and it increased especially rapidly from the late 1970s to the 1980s. The figures for the 1980s were almost 50 percent higher than those for the early 1960s, and the change appears to be accelerating. Although not shown, there is substantial variation among countries in volatility and in the change therein. Volatility is somewhat greater in multiparty systems, where the numerous options among the parties give voters the opportunity to select gradations of opinion and platform—voters may be offered several brands of socialist, conservative, and center parties. The *changes* in volatility, however, appear to be greatest in two-party (or those close to two-party) systems, which are now coming to look more like multiparty systems. One could look at these data and argue that the important finding is 90 percent stability rather than almost 10 percent change between elections (Mair 1984). Even with that more conservative perspective, there does appear to be significant flux in European party systems indicative of some realignment among or dealignment from all parties.

PARTISAN IDENTIFICATION. As intimated, there has been a marked decline in the attachment of voters to political parties. In almost all European countries for which we have data, the proportion of "strong partisans" among the voting population has been declining (Table 5.10). The decline

TABLE 5.9

Aggregate Electoral Volatility in Western Europe[a]

	1960–64	1965–69	1970–74	1975–79	1980–84	1985–87
Average Volatility	6.5	7.4	8.8	8.3	9.4	9.6

SOURCE: Based on data from P. Mair, "Party Politics in Contemporary Europe: A Challenge to Party?" *West European Politics* 7 (1984): 170–84; M. N. Pederson, "Changing Patterns of Electoral Volatility in European Party Systems, 1948–77," in *Western European Party Systems,* ed. H. Daalder and P. Mair (London: Sage, 1983); 1985–87 calculated from T. T. Mackie, "General Elections in Western Nations," *European Journal for Political Research,* annual.

[a] Excluding Greece, Luxembourg, Portugal, and Spain.

TABLE 5.10

Changes in Partisanship
(percentage reporting strongest level of party identification)[a]

	1975	1977	1979	1982	1985
Belgium	8	13	8	9	9
Denmark	19	17	19	13	13
France	9	11	9	9	5
W. Germany	11	12	7	12	8
Ireland	2	2	10	9	6
Italy	15	12	20	19	15
Luxembourg	12	12	13	7	12
Netherlands	12	17	11	12	9
United Kingdom	3	2	11	9	9

SOURCE: Based on data from *Eurobarometer,* quarterly; and R. S. Katz, "Measuring Party Identification with Eurobarometer Data: A Warning Note," *West European Politics* 8 (1985):104–8.

[a] Autumn of each year; changes in question wording may have produced some variations, but they would tend to be in the *positive* direction, not the generally negative direction found here.

has been especially marked in the United Kingdom, Ireland, and West Germany, but appears to be present also in other countries (Mair 1984; but see Katz 1985). This decline in partisanship is important for several reasons. One is that, as existing political parties become less capable of exciting voters, the voters become more subject to mobilization and change by other political groups and movements. This increased change ultimately may destabilize political systems, although the stability of most contemporary European countries makes this threat rather remote.[10] Further, for the individual citizen, the absence of a stable partisan allegiance makes the voting choice more difficult and may lead to abstention rather than voting. Increasing levels of abstentions will, in turn, contribute to an increased dealignment in the party system. Abstentions may become especially pronounced as young people are not socialized into a political party early and therefore may never develop an interest in politics or the habit of voting. Despite the numerous criticisms of partisan politics, political parties do play an important role in democracies, and their weakness may imply the weakness of democratic politics in general.

In addition to the reduction in the overall levels of voter identification with political parties, the connection among traditional socioeconomic cleavages, partisan identification, and voting also appeared weaker during the 1980s than it had previously. Political party allegiances have traditionally been anchored in social class, or in ethnic divisions, that are enduring features of society and politics. A part of dealignment has been that party affiliations increasingly are oriented around issues or more transient features of society. Political parties therefore may lose their utility as long-term political organizers and as shapers of future political generations. This too opens the way for greater political diversity, which, although not undesirable in itself, does make political life and governing more unpredictable and hence more problematic for citizens and politicians alike.

THE DECLINE OF CLASS VOTING. In addition to overall dealignment and declining partisanship, some more specific decline in the linkage of political parties and social classes or other socioeconomic groups is apparent. Social democratic, communist, and labor parties are no longer the parties of the working classes, in part because these classes have begun to vote more readily for other parties. Some may be ethnic and regional parties, as in the late 1988 by-election victory of the Scottish National Party in Govan, an overwhelmingly working-class district of Glasgow in which Labour had received almost 65 percent of the vote in the 1987 general election. Further, class lines blur because of large-scale structural economic changes, and as the working classes become more bourgeois, they (by objective standards) may be more willing to vote for middle-class parties. In the future, whether people work in the public or the private sector may be as important as what they do in determining which party they will vote for (Andersen 1984; Blais, Blake, and Dion, forthcoming; Worre 1980).

As working-class voters move away from their traditional parties, the parties they left behind may attempt to appeal to different types of voters, such as middle-class service workers and intellectuals. The political Left has always attracted its share of such voters, but the appeal appears to have intensified as some types of service workers become the *Lumpenproletariat* of the postindustrial era. Finally, the development of new political parties— the Left-Libertarians described earlier—expressing different meanings for the political Left also blurs the class dimension of politics and diminishes the extent to which politics is about economic rather than other issues (see Chapter 4). Although these appear to be the directions in which politics is moving in Western Europe, loosening its class basis to some extent loosens a solid anchor for political behavior that appeals to abstract ideals or specific issues cannot replace (Dalton 1988). This may mean that politics will be much more fluid and unpredictable than it has been in the past.

The delinkage of politics from the traditional class basis has been most evident in the United Kingdom (Rose and McAllister 1986; Särlvik and Crewe 1983) but has had some manifestations in most industrialized countries (Van der Eijk and Niemoller 1983). In Britain, which had been perhaps the country with the closest connections between class and voting behavior, the ability of social class to predict voting behavior has been declining. Although some analysts continue to argue for its utility (Heath, Jowell, and Curtice 1985; but see Crewe 1986), and others argue for a redefinition of the meaning of class in the late twentieth century (Dunleavy 1979), both the analyses of social scientists and the real-world inroads of the Thatcherite Conservatives make it clear that class politics is moribund if not dead. Although he attempts a number of possible explanations, Mark Franklin's (1985) detailed analysis remains inconclusive, although it documents very thoroughly the relative effects of changing social structure and partisanship. Politics in Britain is no longer as predictable as it once was, and even the simple-plurality electoral system appears incapable of controlling tendencies toward creating new parties and expressing new sentiments through the political process. What remains to be seen is if, over time, these changes will also produce greater instability in governments, and if Britain will become (after Mrs. Thatcher leaves office, perhaps) more like multiparty European countries with coalition governments.

TURNOUT. Although figures for election turnouts may not give direct evidence about dealignment or realignment of party systems, they can indicate any general waxing or waning of interest in politics among the population. A decline in turnout may indicate that the existing political parties, likely to win the elections and to form governments, are not capable of exciting the potential voters sufficiently to get them to vote. This decline, in turn, may indicate that those parties may not be supplying the public what it desires in the way of public policies. In addition, if voters do not have sufficient interest in the existing political parties, they may be easier to mobilize for new political parties (ranging from the Greens to the National Front) or for interest groups that have come to serve some of the same functions as parties. This declining popular interest in existing political parties has been especially evident in the United States, but is also something of an issue in other industrialized countries.

The evidence presented in Table 5.11 indicates that there indeed has been a declining turnout of voters in most Western European countries. In over two-thirds, fewer voters turned out for elections in the 1980s than they had (on average) in the preceding three decades, and a similar number showed lower turnout in the 1980s than in the 1970s. In several of the countries interest in politics (as expressed by voting) has on average declined in each successive decade since the 1950s. Some decline in turnout is evident even for Belgium, which nominally has compulsory voting. This declining turnout is all the more significant because of increased levels of education and affluence, characteristics usually associated with greater interest in politics and with higher levels of political participation. In short, something appears to be happening in European politics to make it less appealing to voters. While it might be argued that this is a positive change—more political parties are deemed capable of governing even by nonadherents so that losing an election would be less serious—the signs are generally regarded as being more ominous.

SUMMARY. The evidence just presented has not been completely uniform, but what appears is a general picture of decline in the existing party systems

TABLE 5.11

Changes in Turnout[a] in Elections

	1950s	1960s	1970s	1980s
Austria	94.4	92.9	92.9	90.1
Belgium	88.2	86.2	85.7	86.5
Denmark	81.5	87.1	85.5	85.5
Finland	86.0	84.7	77.9	75.4
France	74.5	74.8	80.5	69.9
W. Germany	83.7	84.7	90.2	85.9
Greece[b]	75.4	81.5	89.3	80.6
Iceland	89.2	89.6	88.2	87.4
Ireland	73.6	73.5	75.6	74.4
Italy	90.3	89.6	89.2	84.3
Luxembourg	87.6	84.2	84.0	83.4
Netherlands	93.0	92.5	83.0	84.2
Norway	78.4	82.5	81.6	82.9
Portugal			84.0	73.2
Spain			71.4	74.1
Sweden	77.6	85.5	90.1	89.7
Switzerland	67.5	62.9	52.7	47.4
United Kingdom	80.3	76.4	74.9	74.0

SOURCE: Based on data from T. T. Mackie and R. Rose, *International Almanac of Electoral History* (New York: Facts on File, 1982); and T. T. Mackie, "General Elections in Western Nations," *European Journal for Political Research*, annual.

[a] Valid votes cast as percentage of electorate.
[b] Elections suspended from 1964 to 1974.

of Western Europe. Potential voters seem to have less interest in politics, at least as practiced by the major political parties, and a declining proportion of eligible citizens choose to go to the polls. Further, the voters who do choose to vote are more volatile, so that parties can no longer depend on stable legions of adherents who will vote for their party in almost any election. Finally, the parties are no longer linked closely with social classes or other stable socioeconomic groups and hence there is not the stable base for parties to build on; the issues that form the basis of most new political parties appear to have more fleeting attachments for voters, and the parties may come and go very quickly.

These findings do not mean that all is lost for democracy in Western Europe. Some analysts would argue, in fact, that these changes have enhanced democracy. Rather than having to depend on large, stable (and perhaps bureaucratic and ossified) political parties, citizens now have several options for expressing themselves politically. A number of newer, small political parties operate almost as interest groups, carrying specialized political and policy messages to the Parliament. Interest groups—especially short-lived ones oriented around particular issues—exist that are able to get things done politically without resorting to electoral politics. Finally, citizens themselves are more capable, because of increased education and prior participation in political life, of working through the political system (especially the public bureaucracy) to get things done. In short, although parliamentary democracy and electoral politics are still the dominant political models in Europe, they have been changed and must now accommodate more informal politics operating around their borders.

Conclusions

The changes in politics that we have outlined in this chapter are likely to continue and perhaps even accelerate. Citizens will be even better educated, on average, in the future and should feel greater political efficacy in dealing with government and its bureaucracy. Further, the increasing complexity of policy issues, and of social and economic life in general, may make conventional politics and political parties less suited for their resolution. There may be greater dependence on the bureaucracy and the courts for policymaking, and with that a greater emphasis on the role of interest groups rather than political parties as the most appropriate instruments of citizen participation. In addition, policy issues looming over the horizon in industrialized countries, such as environmental degradation, global warming, and public deficits to name but a few, may require something other than politics as usual for successful policymaking. It is not clear whether the "old" political parties and their traditional modes of conducting business in parliaments will be best suited for dealing with these issues. In particular, the "catchall" political parties that have developed in Europe, and that have been considered a sign of modernization there, may be outmoded as complex policy issues require more specialized and intense participation.

The movement toward greater European unification may also place some strain on political parties and their ways of doing business. Each year more important decisions will be made in Brussels and Strasbourg, and despite the development of Europe-wide party groups, this aspect of politics is still the weakest on the European stage—even weaker than Europe-wide interest groups. Therefore, politics in the European Community may also be more bureaucratic and more concerned with the participatory role of interest groups than of political parties. The parties will continue to exist, and voters appear likely to continue to cast the bulk of their votes for parties that have been in existence for years if not centuries. The meaning of the voting, and its real impact on the policies and programs that affect the everyday lives of Europeans, may, however, be very different.

Notes

1. The three bourgeois parties in Sweden are Moderate Unity (conservatives), the People's Party (Liberals), and the Center. In the past the Center was a coalition partner of the Social Democrats. It tends to be somewhat differentiated from the other two parties by its stands on ecology (strongly in favor) and nuclear power (opposed).

2. In West Germany, half of the members of the *Bundestag* are elected from single-member districts by plurality voting and the other half are elected by proportional representation from *Land* lists.

3. There are three types of proportional representation in use in Western Europe: D'Hondt, St. Lague, and the Single Transferable Vote (Ireland).

4. The threshold value in West Germany was set comparatively high in an attempt to prevent small extremist parties from gaining any parliamentary representation. This was a direct reaction to the history of the Weimar Republic (1919–1933) and the rise of the Nazi party. The Constitutional Court was given the right to ban the participation of nondemocratic political parties for the same reason.

5. The name itself can sometimes be misleading. The Center party in the Netherlands is actually on the extreme right.

6. The Soviet Union's *glasnost* and *perestroika* may diminish any need of European communists to attempt to take cues from Moscow.

7. These differences are, of course, influenced by political conditions and issues in each country, but the trend is interesting even with the caveats that must be made.

8. If nothing else, the names of these groups indicate that democracy is still a positive symbol in European political life.

9. After the 1987 election the Alliance re-formed into two different parties, with the majority of the SDP and the Liberals forming the Liberal and Social Democrats, while the remaining members of the SDP loyal to Dr. David Owen became the Social Democrats.

10. In the 1988 Swedish elections, for example, it was feared that the "Greens" would receive enough seats to prevent the Social Democrats from forming their usual alliance with the Left-Party Communists, and thereby a political crisis would ensue. This did not happen, but the possibility did create a sense of instability.

Chapter

6

STILL THE CENTURY OF CORPORATISM?

The title of this chapter was first used by Phillipe Schmitter (1974) over a decade and a half ago. He used it to address the apparent emergence of a pattern of close interrelationships between interest groups and government in a number of industrialized societies, especially those in Western Europe. Schmitter borrowed this title from a much earlier (1934) manuscript by Mihail Manoïlesco, who argued that the twentieth century would be one in which politics would be dominated by interest groups and their intimate connections with government policymaking. We have already seen that political parties appear to be losing a substantial amount of their capacity to mobilize and excite citizens politically. Because of this, interest groups have been permitted a somewhat greater scope for influence than would have been possible previously. In fact, the public role of interest groups now has been enhanced to the point where the distinctions between state and society have become blurred. Although most citizens and many scholars believe that a boundary between state and society characterizes liberal societies, the two sectors have become so closely merged by a gradual "osmosis" that they are almost indistinguishable (Kraemer 1955). During the 1960s and most of the 1970s, it appeared as if the answer to the question by Manoïlesco and Schmitter was almost certainly affirmative.

In addition to attempting to describe the evolution of politics in Western industrial societies, there is a strong normative component in the work of students of corporatism. Not only was corporatism what *was happening,* apparently it was also what *should happen.* Some of this writing thinly disguised the belief that corporate structures for interest intermediation were capable of promoting economic growth without significant conflict among business, labor, and the government. The models of Scandinavia and West Germany were advanced to policymakers in Britain and the United States as examples of how to deal successfully with economic tensions in society (although writing from a different intellectual tradition, see Shonfield 1965, 199–201). Much of the literature on corporatism was hopeful about the future of industrialized democracies and their ability to manage any social and economic conflicts through corporate bargaining and structured interest intermediation.

Much has changed, however, since the late 1970s. Perhaps the most important consideration that has changed is the level of economic growth; the concepts of scarcity and uncertainty have been reintroduced into the European political economy (Rose and Peters 1978; see Chapter 1). With scarcity has come the need to make hard redistributive decisions among groups in society, a type of decision that corporatist bargaining systems seem to find difficult (Gourevitch 1986). It is easy to make policy decisions when they imply only differential levels of new benefits to groups; it is much more difficult when gains for one group imply actual losses for other groups of citizens. In those instances, when choices are frequently "zero-sum" (Thurow 1980), the right to participate often becomes the right to veto decisions that would affect your own group adversely. And with economic uncertainty comes an unwillingness to make decisions that will create binding future commitments, including perhaps commitments to participation. Given that corporatism is premised on an ability to make binding commitments, that system of governing becomes difficult to manage effectively with stagnant or declining resources.

The other factor that has changed in many European countries is the development of a number of single-interest groups organized around other than economic issues. Again, we have already pointed out that political and social values have been changing since the 1960s and that there is increased (even if not dominant) concern with issues other than bread-and-butter economic ones. Issues of peace, justice, the environment, greater equality for women, and the like have all become major political issues for many people in Western European countries (see Chapter 4). Although similar "attitude groups" have existed for decades in Western Europe, these groups and their issues have gained special political prominence in the late twentieth century. Most corporatist solutions, however, remain based primarily on economic interests, especially tripartite bargaining among business, labor, and government (Wilensky and Turner 1987). Corporate pluralist arrangements in the Scandinavian countries (Rokkan 1966) tend to permit participation by a broader array of interest groups, but even those arrangements appear predicated largely upon economic interests and the resolution of potential economic conflicts. Thus, to the extent that politics becomes oriented around noneconomic issues, corporatist solutions to the problem of interest intermediation are likely to be less effective. This is even more true given that many of these attitude groups come together to address one very specific issue—the siting of one nuclear plant or one missile base—and then dissolve. Corporatism, on the other hand, demands some stability to be able to enforce deals that are made between government and interests.

It may well be that the close association of interest groups and government implied by corporatism will not be effective when noneconomic groups are involved. Economic group members have something very tangible to gain directly from membership in their union or their business group (Moe 1980; Olson 1965); people may join ecology groups only because of a shared attitude. As a consequence, members of an attitude group may leave the organization more readily than members of an economic group. If the mass membership of an ecology, peace, or another attitude group does not approve of what the leadership is doing, they lose nothing by leaving to form another group, or simply leaving the movement entirely. In fact, they would probably lose psychologically by remaining members of a group with which they disagreed. The leadership of an economic group can bargain with somewhat greater certainty that he or she can deliver the support of the mass membership for a deal with government than can the leader of an attitude group. Further, government can also be more confident that a binding deal has been struck if an economic group is involved rather than an attitude group.

Another important characteristic that differentiates bargaining with economic interest rather than attitude groups is the stakes involved. With economic groups, the bargaining is usually just over money. As money is almost infinitely divisible and somewhat expandable, bargaining can usually produce some acceptable outcomes. Bargaining with attitude groups, however, frequently involves haggling over political and moral values, or what economist Fred Hirsch (1976) calls "positional goods." Those values are at once more absolute and less divisible. Therefore, no amount of bargaining may be successful in getting someone to change his or her mind or accept a "deal"; the very notion of a deal over moral values would be repugnant to many essential participants in a bargain. Thus economic issues may always be able to be resolved, even if it takes the infusion of new economic resources, while moral claims on government have no such simple solutions.

The Nature of Corporatist Politics

To this point we have been discussing "corporatism" as if we were quite certain of what the word meant. Although the term has been subject to numerous interpretations and subtle nuances of meaning in the literature, Schmitter's (1974, 93–94) definition remains the one most commonly used. He defined corporatism as:

> . . . a system of interest representation in which the constituent units are organized into a limited number of singular, compulsory, noncompetitive, hierarchically ordered and functionally differentiated categories, recognized or licensed (if not created) by the state and granted a deliberate representational monopoly within their respective categories in exchange for observing certain controls on their selection of leaders and articulation of demands and supports.

This is a long and complex definition, and several of its component parts merit some additional discussion.

The first point requiring discussion is the very strictly defined number and type of interest groups involved in a corporatist system. To be successful, Schmitter argues, a corporatist system can recognize only a few interest groups, each representing and controlling a major component of the economic system (labor, agriculture, and so on). These organizations would be *Spitzenverbande,* or peak organizations. There may be, for example, many labor unions in the society, but when it comes time to bargain with government, all those unions must be amalgamated into one (or perhaps a few if carefully differentiated) peak organizations. These peak organizations themselves should be hierarchical, so that the leadership can speak for the mass membership and not be opposed internally after an agreement has been reached with government and other peak organizations.

A second important component of this definition is the role played by the state in the recognition, licensure, and even formation of interest groups. There would be less need for such hierarchical arrangements among interest groups if there were no state with which to bargain. Thus in a corporatist arrangement economic bargaining is tripartite, with government having its own interests to defend and playing an active role, rather than being just an impartial mediator between business and labor (Benjamin and Duvall 1985). Governments in European democracies have assumed the responsibility of managing their economies, and with that responsibility comes a strong political interest in making the economies function well. As noted, it is in the state's interest to limit the number of groups with which it must bargain and to be able to strike binding agreements with those groups. Given its authoritative position and its legal powers, the state can decide whom it will recognize as the legitimate representative organizations for policymaking purposes. It can thus pick and choose among interest groups to find those with which it can bargain most successfully. Those groups must, in turn, be able to deliver the agreement of their mass membership once a deal is made, and must be willing to bargain with some sense of the collective good in mind. If those interest groups do not already exist, government can assist in their creation (Lehmbruch 1979). Thus in this arrangement interest groups and the state have a close and almost symbiotic relationship (but see Peters 1989a, 157–63).

The final important part of the definition follows from the remark concerning symbiosis. Both sides in this corporatist arrangement must sacrifice a portion of their autonomy if the arrangement is to survive and succeed. The loss of autonomy is greatest for the interest group because, as the definition of corporatism stipulates, it must give up some of its bargaining latitude in exchange for continued access to decision making (see also Heisler with Kvavik 1974). In particular, even if the interest group does not like the outcome of a particular round of negotiations with government, it must accept it with little or no public protest in order to retain its position as the central organization in that functional area. Bargaining in corporatism is repetitive, and being a player may be as important as winning every round. What the interest group loses on one round it may expect to gain in the long run through having continued guaranteed access. The state, on the other hand, gives up a smaller portion of its autonomy by granting that guaranteed access and consultation. The government of the day may still have to act, at times, as it sees fit, but it must also expect to have to bargain and to permit interest groups to participate somewhat in most decisions. Further, if the corporatist system is to be successful over time, interest groups must also expect to have some real influence over decisions; without that influence the groups have little reason to remain involved in the process. Thus, although both parties gain by a corporatist arrangement, both are bound by it as well.

In addition to his general definition of corporatism, Schmitter (1974, 103) distinguishes between "state corporatism" and "societal corporatism." In the instance of state corporatism, the impetus for the formation of interest groups and for their linkage to the state emanates from the state itself. While this form of corporatism is rather uncommon in Western Europe, government clearly has taken the lead in attempting to get some policy sectors in some countries, such as Spain and Italy, organized. Further, if the sector is organized but with multiple and competing groups, the state may encourage the formation of a single group to represent the sector. The contemporary role of the European Community in fostering interest groups across the whole community is to some extent a version of state corporatism (Daltrop 1986, 100–104). Such corporatism also characterized, in part, pre-democratic Spain (Anderson, 1970), in which the labor syndicates allowed to exist by the Franco regime were very much linked directly to that regime, and largely fostered by it.[1]

Societal corporatism has been much more characteristic of contemporary Western Europe. In this version of the corporatist arrangement, interest groups are formed autonomously and spontaneously, and precede their relationship with the state. Only when it becomes clear that both sides of the potential arrangement have something to gain by formalizing their connections does anything approaching the corporatist pattern emerge. It is important to note, however, that once the corporatist bargain is struck, the interest groups do enter a quasi-public status because of their close, and possibly official, relationship with government. While the bargain may be somewhat Faustian, it is still one from which the interest group and its members will benefit, although at the expense of some potential autonomy and room for bargaining. Also, in the "societal" version of the corporatist relationship, the necessity for peak organizations may be relaxed somewhat to allow for more open bargaining, as has happened in Italy (Regini 1982). The term neocorporatism is also used at times regarding corporate politics in contemporary Europe (see Table 6.1). This is in part to differentiate corporatism as it is now practiced—largely societal corporatism—from earlier, state-directed models such as those found in Franco's Spain and Mussolini's Italy (Bortolotto 1934).

In addition to Schmitter's two categories of corporatism, at least three other versions or variants have been discussed in the literature on Western European politics. First, German political sociologist Lehmbruch (1982) developed the concept of "liberal corporatism," which emphasizes the importance of two-stage bargaining over policy. Initially there would be bargaining among the interest groups themselves, usually within specific sectors. Thus, prior to negotiating with government, labor unions would meet to discuss what they collectively want and can accept from the negotiations. Then negotiations between the interest groups and government would occur. The first stage may extend sufficiently far as to have potentially competing interests (labor and business) discuss issues prior to becoming involved in their negotiations with government. This conception of corporatism recognizes the multiplicity of interests that may exist within a single economic sector in a modern economy; unions in manufacturing industries may have little in common with public service unions, for example. It also recognizes, however, the need of government to bargain with a limited number of interest groups, and the need of those groups to make binding deals for the entire economic sector. In this version of corporatism, the need for a formal "peak organization" is relaxed, but the functional need to generate a common bargaining position for each economic sector is not.

Another concept, closely related to liberal corporatism, is "corporate pluralism" (Heisler 1979; Rokkan 1966). This term refers to arrangements quite similar to societal corporatism, but in which there is not as close a connection between the state and the interest groups as in a fully developed corporatist policymaking. Interest groups in corporate pluralism do have some legitimate role to play in representing their demands to government, and usually in implementing public policies, but they also retain greater autonomy of action. Therefore, the system combines some of the characteristics of corporatism with some of those of pluralism. Interest-group participation in government in the Scandinavian countries tends to be corporate pluralistic. There are strong norms of widespread democratic participation, with any possible conflicts arising within the open bargaining system being mitigated by the equally strong norms of consensus that have permeated much of Scandinavian policymaking (but see Michiletti, forthcoming).

The final term to note is "mesocorporatism" (Cawson 1985). Most conceptions of corporatism are directed toward central government and the upper echelons thereof, and involve broad bargaining across sectors about economic issues. Yet arrangements very much like corporatism also exist at lower levels within government. Some may exist in subnational governments, especially given the increasing importance of regional governments in Western Europe, and particularly in making economic policy (Keating and Jones 1985; Perez-Diaz 1984). In these mesocorporatist arrangements, the interactions may not be the tripartite bargaining that typically characterizes corporatism at the national level. Rather, only one interest may really be affected by the public policies and organizations in question; only one important industry may exist in a region. What does remain of the general corporatist model, however, is a close connection between government and the organized interests.

Although we have by now spent a good deal of time looking at alternative definitions and concepts, we should not lose sight of the fundamental characteristic of corporatist politics and policymaking undergirding this discussion. At root, corporatist politics is supposed to be doing two things for government: co-opting interests in the society and improving the objective quality of the decisions made by government. To co-opt interest groups, regularized interactions between governments and these groups have developed, or at least did develop. Rather than sporadic lobbying or demonstrations, interest groups have been made a significant and legitimate component of the process of governing. Interest groups have accepted this institutionalized arrangement at the price of some loss of autonomy. Such losses have not been unilateral, however, and governments also have had to sacrifice some autonomy to gain greater certainty and less manifest opposition to their decisions. Governments have had to agree to let interest groups have their say about policy and, at least in principle, to have some real influence over the decisions that are made.

A second purpose central to all corporatist arrangements is their role in managing the political economy. With their acceptance of Keynesian economics, the governments of the industrialized democracies accepted the role of managing their economies (Stewart 1971). In so doing, they also accepted the necessity of dealing with organized economic groups that can facilitate or hinder economic management. If labor demands high wage increases and is willing to strike for them, or if business leaders demand high profits and are willing to depress wages or lay off workers to get them, then government economic policies may be in trouble. Corporatism is an institutionalized mechanism for addressing the concerns of those powerful economic groups and of enabling governments to produce economic plans and policies that have some chance of implementation. Interest groups are also major repositories of information and expertise, and governments can ignore their advice only at the risk of making serious mistakes. Government policy is effective only when it is implemented, and corporatism makes that implementation more certain and less painful.

All the various forms of corporate arrangements just discussed share these common features, which have become extremely important for understanding the manner in which contemporary government is conducted in Western Europe. If we do not understand the central position allotted to interest groups in economic policy, and to a great extent in most other policy sectors as well, we will not be able to understand the policy outcomes. The question that remains, however, is whether corporatism is now a *sufficient* (while probably still *necessary*) approach to understanding the conduct of government in Western Europe.

This question is especially great when the concept of corporatism is stretched to cover political systems, and perhaps policy issues, for which it is not really appropriate. The concept could be strained to the point of being meaningless by attempting to explain everything about interest intermediation in industrialized societies (see Jordan 1981). So, for example, there has been an academic debate over whether France is a corporatist political system (see Keeler 1981; Wilson 1983). While corporatism provides a useful intellectual model against which to compare the real world, it is perhaps more important to understand how interest groups function in France than to make any arbitrary decision about whether the nation can be forced into the corporatist mold. Much the same would be true of Spain and its *pactos sociales,* social pacts at the regional level, which have some corporatist elements but lack several others (Perez-Diaz 1987; Roca 1987). Is Spain corporatist, and does it matter? We must always remember that corporatism is not a test that a country must pass in order to be modern or European, but rather an approach to imposing some intellectual order on an otherwise confusing political world.

It is also important to remember that corporatism can be thought of as a continuous rather than simply a nominal category. That is, countries can be more or less corporatist in the manner in which interest groups interact with government. For example, Table 6.1 classifies twelve European countries based on their degree of corporatism (Schmitter 1981; von Beyme 1981). Not only do some countries sometimes described as having corporatist politics come out rather low on this scale, such as Switzerland, but there is substantial variation between the two components—centralization

TABLE 6.1

Degree of Neocorporatism in Twelve European Countries

	Monopoly of Associations	Centralization of Organizations	Total
Austria	1[a]	3	1
Norway	5	1.5	2
Denmark	8	1.5	4
Sweden	5	4.5	4
Finland	5	4.5	4
Netherlands	2	9	6
Belgium	3	9	7
W. Germany	9	6	8
Switzerland	7	14	9
France	10	14	13
United Kingdom	13	12	14
Italy	13	14	15

SOURCE: From Klaus von Beyme, "Der liberale Körporatismus als Mittel gegen die Unregierbarkeit," *Neokörporatismus,* ed. U. von Alemann (Frankfurt: Campus, 1981), p. 139. With permission of the publisher, Campus Verlag, Frankfurt/New York.

[a] "1" = maximum.

and monopolization—of the index. Thus, again, we should not be too quick to make judgments about the existence of corporatism, but we are better advised to attempt to understand some particular patterns of inter-mediation.

Finally, it should be noted that corporatism may be an explanation for European politics that is locked in time as well as space. Even for countries that displayed clear corporatist patterns during the 1960s and 1970s, there appear to have been major shifts away from these forms of decision making. First, economic change required governments to be less generous in grant-ing access to policymaking because many difficult redistributive decisions had to be made. The incentive for interest groups to be involved in decision making was also reduced, given that much of what was being distributed was costs rather than benefits, and the group leaders ran the risk of losing their legitimacy with group members. Further, the nature of the interest-group universe and some of the issues being addressed by government changed, and problems that could not be solved with money, and in which business and labor were not central actors, became important in politics. We will need to assess the extent to which corporatism continues to be the important feature of European politics that it clearly once was.

The Institutions of Consultation

Leaving aside questions about which of the several descriptions of corpo-ratism is the most valid, whether corporatist arrangements retain the power over policy they had, whether they are likely to persist, and whether one country or another is corporatist, we can still examine the institutional structures that have been developed to accommodate group interests in Western Europe. These intermediation structures can and do function without the existence of a full-fledged corporatist arrangement. The institu-tions used to accommodate interest groups in Western Europe are designed primarily to ascertain the groups' ideas about policy prior to its being enacted, but sometimes the groups themselves are used to implement the public policies that affect them directly. Implementation of this sort is used commonly when the interest groups possess specialized, usually individual-level information that government could duplicate only at great cost.

Institutions for Processing Inputs

Governments have developed a variety of mechanisms for consulting interest groups in their societies and for considering their opinions before final decisions are reached. In none of these mechanisms are groups guaranteed to be victorious, especially when many possibly conflicting groups are being consulted on the same issue. What the groups are guaranteed, however, is that they will be heard. Further, in many European societies, as Norwegian political sociologist Stein Rokkan (1966) once wrote, "votes count but resources decide"; in other words, the ability of interest groups to mobilize and participate may count more for public policies than formal electoral politics. The following are the principal means of accommodating interests, arrayed along a continuum roughly related to the degree of formalization of the process of inclusion.

SOCIAL AND ECONOMIC COUNCILS. One means of including interest groups in policy deliberations is to create institutions, which some analysts have likened to third houses of Parliament, that include interest-group representatives. Like the corporatist senates discussed earlier, representation in these institutions is on the basis of social and economic interest rather than geography. The two major examples of these bodies are the Social and Economic Council in the Netherlands (*Sociaal Economische Raad*, Wassenberg 1982) and the Economic and Social Council in France (*Conseil Economique et Social*, Hayward 1966). Both of these bodies draw rather broadly from the spectrum of interest groups, while concentrating on business and labor. Involving labor has been especially important in France because conservative Gaullists needed to integrate the unions into the governing apparatus. This was seen as one means of creating harmony rather than conflict in economic policy, and has not diminished after a Socialist was elected president. The social and economic councils in both countries have significant influence, even if they have little formal power beyond the right to be consulted on economic and social issues. In both cases, the council recommendations are taken very seriously. The Dutch council has a virtual veto, especially if the vote is unanimous on an issue. There is a similar type of social and economic council in Norway (*Økonomiske Samordningsrad*), but it lacks the direct integration into the decision-making process that characterizes the French and Dutch examples.

Although not exactly the same things, parliamentary or royal commissions may serve some of the same functions as social and economic councils. The principal difference is that the commissions are appointed to consider specific problems, often with the purpose of generating their own legislation rather than reacting to the government's legislative suggestions. Once they have finished their deliberations on that specific policy question, the commission goes out of existence, although other commissions will be considering other pieces of legislation. The power of commissions is most entrenched in Sweden, although they are also used extensively in the other Nordic countries (Ståhlberg and Sjöblom 1989). In Sweden commissions *(Statens offentliga utredningar)* have been used to consider almost all significant new legislation. In most cases the commissions are composed of civil servants plus a significant number of interest-group representatives. Historically operating by reaching consensus before announcing a decision (Meijer 1969), these commissions ensure that interest-group demands are thoroughly ventilated and accommodated. This may result in a very slow legislative process, but there is not likely to be significant opposition once decisions are announced. The norms of consensus and deliberate consideration appear to be relaxing, however, as the demands on government for decision making increase and the representation on commissions is extended to more groups.

Royal commissions in Britain and parliamentary commissions in other countries (Van Putten 1982) have many of the same functions as do commissions in Sweden. The role of interest groups, however, is less pronounced in most other countries, and hence the co-optive potential is also less. In Britain, for example, interest groups are involved primarily in providing evidence to the commissions rather than in providing members. The decision-making norms are not as consensual—in Britain or other non-Nordic countries—so that decisions likely to provoke significant political controversy may emerge from the commissions. Further, the commissions also often lack the time and money to do their own research and hence may produce less usable results. While still important for ventilating ideas and generating advice, commissions, lacking the ability really to co-opt interest groups, may not be able to substitute for other corporatist policymaking arrangements as a mechanism for managing potential political conflict.

ADVISORY COMMITTEES. The economic and social councils are freestanding bodies that include a variety of different interests and that discuss a variety of different policies. Although they lack the scope of economic and social councils, commissions also operate at a very high government plane. Almost all countries have advisory boards and committees connected with their policymaking departments. As the name implies, these bodies have the task of advising the ministries on policy. Rarely would their advice be binding, but a negative recommendation on a proposed policy would have to be taken seriously. In addition, the power of these advisory committees is often limited by their inability to determine their own agendas and the need to respond to the proposals presented to them by the ministries. This restriction, of course, limits their potential impact on policy and their utility as co-optive institutions.

Although they have the common task of advising ministries, advisory committees may differ along a number of dimensions. For example, some advisory committees are relatively broad and include a range of interests (as in the "corporate pluralist" Scandinavian countries), while others have a much narrower range of representation (Johansen and Kristensen 1982). Some advisory committees may include civil servants as representatives of other departments with which a policy must be coordinated, while other committees may be limited strictly to organized interests from the society. Including officials from other government organizations can smooth potential future problems of policy implementation, but it also allows a very powerful institutional pressure group to have a voice that may drown out the ideas of societal interests. Finally, in some cases the ministries may be required to consult formally with their advisory committees, while in others such consultation is voluntary. In all these cases, however, there is a mechanism that interests can use to exercise some direct influence over policy. And, just as in the more formalized corporatist arrangements discussed earlier, this can also be a mechanism for co-opting interest groups into accepting and supporting any decisions that are made after they have put forward their opinions.

The politics of advice is a big business in Western European governments. Although at times some effort has been made to keep the exact number of advisory structures, and their expenses, out of the public eye, the numbers run into the hundreds, and even thousands, in many countries. Some idea of the magnitude of advisory structures in several countries is offered in Table 6.2. As expected, these structures are very common in the Scandinavian countries. What is less expected is the large number of advisory committees in France, which indicates that even in countries not normally considered corporatist, government feels the need for advice and assistance from interest groups.

These advisory bodies are not spread evenly across policy areas. Agriculture and fishing appear to have a disproportionate share of the groups, and the social services and labor policy are also large-scale consumers of advice. On the other hand, policy concerns such as defense and taxation, which are often thought of as central to the state (Rose 1976), may have few if any advisory committees (Elvander 1972). The distribution of advisory committees among policy areas points out that in addition to their nominal function of advising, these bodies also have a strong legitimation and co-

TABLE 6.2

Number of Advisory Bodies in Government

Denmark	668
France	1,400
W. Germany	400
Netherlands	368 +
Norway	1,000
Sweden	519
United Kingdom	1,561

SOURCE: Data for Denmark are from Johansen and Kristensen (1982). Data for France are from Weber (1968). Data for West Germany are from Johnson (1983), 108. Data for the Netherlands are from Wettenschappelijke Raad voor het Regeringsbeleid (1977). Data for Norway are from Olsen (1966). Data for Sweden are from Meijer (1969); for a different view, see Ruin (1974) and Hadenius (1978). Data for the United Kingdom are from Her Majesty's Stationery Office (1980), 1.

optation function. While those political functions are perhaps less important for "defining functions," where legitimacy is assumed, they are crucial for governments' social and economic functions.

It is important also to get some idea of the types of representatives that sit on the advisory committees and the extent to which representation is apportioned among various interests in the society. Table 6.3 presents data on the distribution of representatives in three countries in the 1970s. Predictably, labor, business, and agriculture make up the bulk of the representatives, with business interests tending to be somewhat more represented than labor—especially in Denmark and Switzerland. This seeming imbalance is accentuated, at least in Switzerland, by the tendency of labor to have one individual serve on many commissions and committees, and thus be unable to participate as effectively as he or she might (Germann 1981, 1985). The individuals who participate in advisory committees tend to be well educated and capable but run the risk of being overextended in meeting the enormous needs of contemporary governments for advice and legitimation.

PETITIONS. An even less direct, although not necessarily less effective, manner in which interest groups can influence policy decisions is through formal petitions or *remisser,* the Scandinavian term. When a Scandinavian ministry wants to enact new legislation or issue new administrative regulations, it may be required to notify interested groups and request their opinions and advice. This procedure goes much farther than administrative law requirements in the United States, for example, because in addition to publishing a general notice of intent to legislate and then awaiting comments, the ministry must contact the interest groups directly—perhaps several times. Interest-group responses become a part of the legislative record and are transmitted along with the legislation as it is considered further. Although the practice has become more open and has expanded substantially, governments still have some latitude in deciding which groups should receive which *remisser*. In general, economic organizations, especially producers groups, receive many more petitions than do attitude groups (Egeberg 1981).

Again, the petition system does not guarantee interest-group success, but it establishes a set of statements on the record that politicians can ignore at their peril. The *remiss* system is not, however, as co-optive as are other mechanisms already discussed, because the interest groups do not directly bargain over a policy but merely present their views formally. If those views are ignored, the groups may feel justified in carrying on their political campaign through other means. This lack of co-optation may be especially important in Scandinavian countries because of the openness of government and the ability of interested parties to see just what information was used when policy decisions were made. If the evidence presented does not appear to conform to the government's decision, the interested parties will know it and are likely to protest.

Although not as formal as the *remiss* system, other European political systems do require interest-group consultation about certain policies. In Britain, for example, ministries may be required to consult with the affected interests prior to the issuing of statutory instruments (a form of secondary

TABLE 6.3

Memberships on Advisory Committees (as percentage of total)

	Denmark	Norway	Switzerland[a]
Labor	14.6	41.5	15.4
Business	30.0	41.0	29.9
Agricultural	12.3	7.2	11.5
Other	43.1	10.3	43.2
TOTAL	100.0	100.0	100.0

SOURCE: Based on data from L. N. Johansen and O. P. Kristensen (1982); J. P. Olsen (1988); and R. E. Germann (1981).

[a] Excludes representatives of subnational governments.

legislation). Here, however, the pattern of consultation may be extremely narrow, so that only groups friendly to the general pattern of policy in the ministry are likely to be consulted. Consumer interests are rarely consulted on anything other than strictly consumer issues. Yet consultation and negotiation are important components of policymaking in Britain (Jordan and Richardson 1982). The one exception to the general rule of narrow consultation is the public inquiry, which is broadly open to anyone who signs up to appear before the inquiry or to offer additional evidence. Although its nominal task may be very specific, the public inquiry in Britain can speak to much broader policy issues. For example, a public inquiry into the Sellafield nuclear accident in the 1950s has become an ongoing forum for general discussion of nuclear power and nuclear safety (Macgill 1987).

Implementation

Besides being used to make policy suggestions to governments, interest groups may also be used to implement public policies. The logic of using them for this task is much the same as including them at the formulation stage of policymaking. First, the expertise possessed by the group can be acquired at a very low cost. Attempting to duplicate that store of information would be difficult and expensive. In addition, this is yet another means of co-opting the group and making it as responsible for a decision as is the government itself. Thus allowing interest groups to implement policy may be a convenient means of "blame avoidance" (Weaver 1986). It allows government to eschew responsibility for most of what happens in the policy area and to deflect criticism to the friends and neighbors of those who might feel themselves wronged by decisions.

Certain types of public policies are particularly amenable to implementation through the affected interest groups. First, there are public decisions that require extraordinarily high levels of information and competence and that have the potential to impinge upon the definition of a profession. Thus a number of professions—most notably medicine and law—are usually given the right to define standards of practice for government and to enforce those standards through licensure and disciplinary programs. A closely related justification for interest-group implementation is that governments in democratic countries may not want to intrude into decisions that are thought to affect basic freedoms. They may therefore allow universities and other research institutions substantial self-regulation rather than be seen as trampling on intellectual freedom. A third category of decision suitable for implementation by the affected groups is one that requires a great deal of individual-level information. Thus farmers or fishermen in an area have intimate knowledge of local conditions and can perhaps make better decisions about allotments among individuals than can government, even decentralized government field staffs that should know local conditions. Finally, government may give noneconomic groups the right to implement policies affecting their culture and traditions for fear of creating more harm than good through norms of uniformity, or simple lack of understanding of that culture. In short, a good deal of what government does is amenable to using the affected parties as inexpensive but effective agents of implementation.

Threats to Corporatism

The corporatist pattern appears to be a very sensible way of organizing political life in complex economic and social systems. It permits extensive and authoritative bargaining among interests, and should enable governments to make decisions that are at once effective and relatively uncontested at the implementation stage. These decisions may not always be popular, but the manner in which they are made binds the participants not to oppose them (see also Heisler with Kvavik 1974). Further, by involving the affected interests and receiving their advice, decisions may be of higher quality than those that might be imposed by a more remote and less participatory government. With all these advantages, why does it seem that corporatism is losing some of its appeal and that European countries are becoming less corporatist? The answers to that apparently simple question are multiple and related to a number of interconnected social, economic, and political factors.

Economic Change

The first and probably central factor that must be considered in the apparent decline of corporatism is that the economies of most Western European countries have changed significantly in several ways and are likely to continue to change rapidly. The most important components of these changes for corporate politics are that economic growth is no longer as rapid and as predictable as it once was and that under international pressures, the structure of European economies has been shifting away from manufacturing and toward service industries. Both of these changes make corporatism likely to be a less effective tool for managing the political economy in the 1990s than it was in the 1960s, the 1970s, or even the 1980s.

First, corporatism is a system that is very adept at sharing the wealth and sharing economic success. When that success is less certain and there may be only blame to share, partnership in a stable bargaining arrangement loses some of its appeal. For government, having close links with pressure groups may make reaching redistributive decisions about allocations among socioeconomic sectors or industries even more difficult. This is particularly true if there are microeconomic issues—such as which firms in which regions of the country are to be closed—rather than broad macroeconomic issues on the bargaining table. Corporatism may do well in making decisions balancing pressures toward inflation, unemployment, and/or tax increases but will do less well in making decisions about where to utilize new industrial capital, or research and development funds, if government wishes to enhance economic growth. First, microeconomic issues will split the *Spitzenverbande* into their component parts, based on which industries (and therefore which unions) would win and which would lose. If the "liberal corporatism" model is assumed to be in operation, the first-stage bargaining among interests would be virtually impossible. Governments do not want to break the existing corporatist arrangements that may be useful in the future, but they also must promote overall economic growth. In addition, in corporatism only those interests that already exist will be represented at a bargaining table, whereas promoting economic growth may require fostering industries that do not yet exist or that may be too small to be significant bargainers. Corporatism may be quite suitable for "bailing out losers," but it is unlikely to be able to "pick winners" (Eliasson and Ysander 1981; Peters 1988), and that type of future-oriented decision making now may be required for effective economic policy.

Interest groups also have a diminished incentive to be a part of a corporatist arrangement if all they can do is distribute bad news to their members. Interest-group leaders will find it difficult to maintain members' support if they are perceived as being ineffective in extracting positive benefits from government. The mass membership may also feel that they would have a greater impact on policy by going outside any symbiotic arrangement with government and thereby regaining their rights to protest decisions. While the rank-and-file may not be able to gain anything concrete by exercising their right to protest, at least they will not have abdicated the right to try.

The slowing of economic growth in Western economies is often attributed to the shift from an industrial economy to a service economy. Most service industries do not have the potential for growth through capital investment and extension of markets that most manufacturing industries do. For our purposes, however, the shift to service industries may have another effect. On average, a smaller percentage of service workers tend to unionize than do workers in manufacturing industries. With a smaller percentage of the work force organized, any bargaining between government and the unions will apply to less of the work force and hence is likely to be less effective in managing the economy. Thus governments may have to develop other means for regulating, or at least influencing, the economic behavior of the labor force.

Also associated with the slower economic growth of many European countries is the internationalization of their economies. Historically these countries have had more open economies than the United States, but they have become even more open to international trade (see Table 6.4). With the increasing importance of such trade, the government is less able to control its own economy. Foreign governments, or even private citizens in foreign countries, may make the really important decisions for the domestic economy. In such a setting, attempting to bargain internally over prices, wages, and employment makes little sense and may be counterproductive. The real need in the internationalized economy is to be able to react quickly to rapid external changes and adjust internal markets and industries to meet those conditions. Corporatist arrangements may only slow down that adjustment by requiring consultation and side payments to those who lose.[2] Thus strategies that were effective in regulating the economy when production and heavy industry were the major concerns may become unproductive and self-defeating when the need is for adjustment and flexibility.

Mancur Olson (1982) has advanced some similar arguments concerning the impact of groups on economic growth. Olson argued, based to a large extent on his famous earlier work on voluntary organizations (Olson 1965), that group membership is rather pointless unless that membership extracts for the individual private goods that could not otherwise have been obtained. Therefore interest groups have as their purpose to extract differential benefits from the political system and engage in something of a Hobbesian *bellum omnia contra omnes* ("war of all against all") to wrest their benefits from government. His vision of the group-oriented political system was one of competition among a number of small groups, with consequent economic inefficiencies. One component of his solution was the development of "encompassing groups" that would mitigate the conflict among smaller groups within their own structures.

The reader by this time should see the similarity between the notion of the encompassing group and the *Spitzenverbande* as well as corporate arrangements in general. Corporate bargaining first limits the number of

TABLE 6.4

Trade as a Percentage of Gross Domestic Product, 1988

	Exports	Imports
Austria	35.4	34.5
Belgium	68.4	65.5
Denmark	32.7	29.7
Finland	25.2	24.8
France	21.5	21.4
W. Germany	32.4	26.7
Greece	24.2	30.4
Ireland	63.5	54.2
Italy	18.1	18.3
Netherlands	50.5	54.5
Norway	38.9	36.6
Portugal	33.5	40.4
Spain	19.5	20.7
Sweden	32.4	30.3
Switzerland	36.3	36.0
United Kingdom	23.3	27.1
United States	8.9	11.1

SOURCE: International Monetary Fund, *International Financial Statistics* (Washington, D.C.: International Monetary Fund, monthly).

groups participating in policy decisions to some degree and then brings them together as something of a "supergroup" encompassing all major economic segments of the society. If we accept this analogy then, in Olson's logic, corporatism should be related to economic growth, whereas we have argued that it appears to be inversely related to more rapid economic growth. The difference is to some extent the conception of the nature of the economy and also variations in the perceived nature of group competition in democratic politics (see also Mueller 1983). Although Olson uses the term distributional coalition, he does not deal directly with the effects of corporate bargaining and appears to exclude that structural arrangement from his model.

We believe that the impact of corporatism on economic growth is especially important in an internationalized and high-technology environment. Here the encompassing nature of the bargaining does indeed slow the process of adjustment to changing markets and make rapid response to external forces more problematic. Successful reaction to an internationalized economy requires one of two alternative political economies. One would be a state that has substantial bureaucratic power over economic policy and can direct resources toward perceived opportunities. Examples would be Japan (Johnson 1982), some of the newly industrializing countries, and perhaps France (Adams and Stoffäes 1986). The other would be a highly decentralized political economy allowing firms, and perhaps especially small ones, to make their own adjustments. The corporatist model appears to lie between these two models and may have outlived some of its utility.

Political Change

As well as undergoing significant economic change, the countries of Western Europe have undergone rapid and equally significant political change, some of which we have already documented. The most important for our purposes here is the shift away from accepting government as necessarily the central allocator of values in the economy. While the acceptance of the Keynesian model of economic management was crucial to the initial adoption of the corporatist model for interest intermediation, the decline of that school of economic thought—in practical even more than intellectual terms—has led to a questioning of the need and desirability of corporatism. In essence, if the free market is assumed to do a better job of allocating resources than any system involving government, then choosing among ways to relate economic interests to government is pointless (Bonnett 1985). The bargaining and public planning implied by the corporatist model have become ideologically unacceptable to a large segment of the governing elite in such countries as Britain. There corporatism is an epithet used to dismiss arrangements that potentially conflict with the operations of a free market (and an active if conservative government).

Corporatism, even if disassociated from ideology, may impose costs on government that some people would consider unacceptable. It has been argued, for example, that corporatism is related to the phenomenon of "ungovernability" that is said to characterize contemporary democracies (Dogan and Pelassy 1987; Schmitter 1981). As noted earlier concerning reactions to rapid economic change, corporatism implies a degree of bargaining, negotiation, and consensus-building that many participating in government would find unacceptable. This negative perception appears to be especially pronounced when corporatism is exported from societies with consensual norms (Scandinavia, and to some extent Austria and Switzerland) to societies with much more adversarial political norms such as the United Kingdom and France (Allardt 1984). Thus the early hopefulness of scholars of corporatism may not have been justified when their gospel was spread beyond its original borders.

Of course, all governments have not accepted the market as the allocative device; but even in those governments that retain a stronger bias in favor of a public role in policy, the "exhaustion of economic ideas" has led to some disinterest in corporatist solutions. In addition, the ideological style of governing that has come to characterize many political systems makes corporatist bargaining increasingly irrelevant. If governments know what they want to do and are willing to use all the powers at their disposal to produce action even if there is vocal political opposition (Peters 1988), then there is relatively little over which to bargain. In this setting, neither the quiescence of groups nor their stock of policy-relevant information is particularly valuable. Here even more than in most political environments, interest groups are perceived as the representatives of particularistic interests, while the government assumes that it represents "the public interest." This dismissal of interest groups is somewhat true of all ideological governments, but especially for parties of the Right.[3]

We should also remember that in many countries political issues have changed as much as have the ideological composition of governments (see Chapter 4). Although the return to ideological governments has placed economic issues again to some extent on the center stage, politics has come to encompass a number of issues, not all of which may be addressed by corporatist bargaining. The issues, even the economic ones, popularized by Green parties and similar New Politics movements are not accommodated easily into corporatist bargaining. This means that in order to be effective, governments must be able to deal with a variety of issues, not just the central question of economic management. Thus somewhat paradoxically, corporatism came to full flower in some Western European countries at about the time that it was beginning to become less relevant to an increasing proportion of the politically active population. In something similar to Downs's (1972) concept of the issue-attention cycle, governments were able to solve a problem—or at least devise a good institutional solution for one—at about the time that the problem itself was being supplanted, or augmented, by other problems and issues.

An increased concern with participation formed a major component of the change in political concerns in many Western democracies. In the 1970s and into the 1980s, participation came to mean mass participation approaching direct democracy. Not surprisingly, mechanisms of direct democracy began to be used in Europe to a much greater extent than previously. In such a world, the structured intermediation of participation implied by corporatism was increasingly unacceptable. Many citizens, even those with strong commitments to labor unions or other groups, were unwilling to abdicate their participatory rights to the leadership of the organization. Academic critics (Jessop, 1978; Panitch, 1979, 1980) pointed out this weakness in the corporatist model. In addition, corporatist bargainers began to have difficulty in delivering their members' commitments to the government.

We must be careful to remember, however, that just because the century of corporatism may be coming to an end, interest groups will not vanish or lose their importance in governing. Oddly enough, they may become *more* important. If the public sector has taken a vow of poverty, or had such a vow imposed upon it, governments will be able to make and implement fewer effective policies on their own. If we assume that there is still a public interest in having these services delivered or in having a function regulated, then the interest group(s) involved may be given a grant of authority to do so. The increase of "private interest government" (Streeck and Schmitter 1985), or more generally volunteerism, is a major indicator of the move to use the private sector increasingly to fulfill a policy role once fulfilled by the state. Instead of directly participating in making government policy, the new role for interest groups may be extracting some government resources for their own programs.

As noted earlier, the use of private parties to perform governmental tasks is hardly a new phenomenon. Several things do appear to have changed, however, in the way in which the groups are used. One is that some of the functions that were once high politics for the state, and handled through tripartite bargaining, may now be given to the groups themselves. The state then abdicates its role as mediator between interests whose powers may be asymmetric and also loses its ability to press autonomously for its own interests, or for the "public interest." Going along with this, the ideologies of many governments place a moral value on not becoming involved in many issues, especially economic ones. These governments have a willingness to grant power with relatively little responsibility or authority. Third-party government (Kettl 1987; Salamon 1981a) may be a very cheap way of conducting business in a strictly economic sense, but it may be very expensive from the perspective of accountability and responsible democratic government. While the United States has become accustomed to those grants of power (Hollingsworth and Lindberg 1985) over the years, most European countries have not, and the end of corporatism may signal a very different style of government.

Corporatism and Consociationalism

Economic interest groups are major political actors, but they do not represent all the interests in European societies. We have already noted in Chapters 2 and 5 that a variety of regional and ethnic interests have become more important in the 1970s and 1980s and that European societies are divided as much or more along these cleavages as by any economic differences. Corporatism is primarily a system for coping with economic issues. It appears ill suited for processing the nonbargainable demands that many ethnic and regional interests are making upon the state. Therefore, Western European states have developed other mechanisms for coping with these demands—mechanisms that bear some resemblance to corporatism but depend more on traditional political institutions, such as parties, legislatures, and cabinets for their implementation.

Consociational democracy is the term usually applied to the means for accommodating ethnic interests in European countries (Lijphart 1968; Steiner and Dorff 1980, 1981). The fundamental logic of consociational democracy is that societies that are deeply divided along ethnic lines will find policymaking through normal mass politics difficult or impossible. Therefore, a system of policymaking that can insulate government from pressures while still accommodating to them, is necessary for stability. In a

FIGURE 6.1

Consociational Democracy

		ELITE		
Elite A		Elite B		Elite C
Mass A		Mass B		Mass C

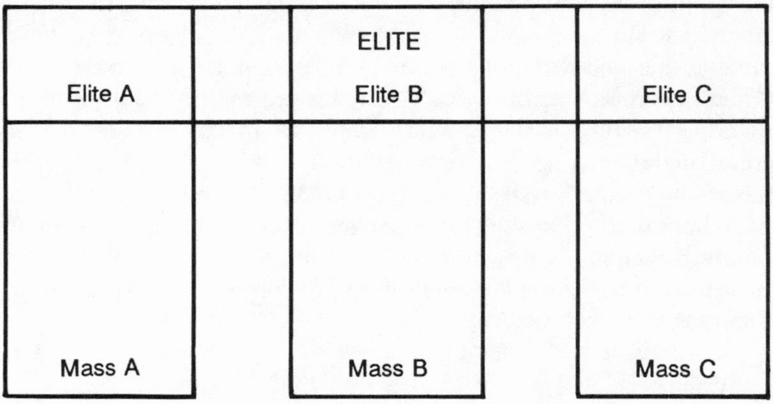

consociational system there is a vertical integration (see Figure 6.1) within the various ethnic communities; elites and masses in each community are closely tied, and the mass trusts the political elite that represents them. At the same time, there is a great deal of integration and mutual trust among the political elite (party leaders and other politicians) itself, regardless of individual partisan or ethnic affiliations. Mass politics in a consociational system can be conducted in a charged atmosphere or even without reference to the other ethnic communities (Lorwin 1966), but once the political elite meets to govern it can do so in an accommodative bargaining fashion. After decisions are reached, the elite has to be able to maintain sufficient confidence of its mass membership to "sell" the policies and to gain acquiescence if not enthusiastic acceptance.

To be effective, consociationalism depends on several conditions, most of which are psychological or attitudinal. The first is trust between elites and masses, which the elite must develop and maintain over time by not making agreements that stray too far from the wishes of the masses. Likewise, there must be agreement among the elite that the preservation of a stable democracy is more important than which segment of the society wins or loses each particular policy issue. From this basic agreement (more tacit than explicit) arises mutual trust and a bargaining style of accommodation. This form of politics has been successful for some time in the Netherlands, Switzerland, and to some extent Belgium and Austria.[4] As secularization and homogenization have lessened some of the tensions and the integration within each of the communities, consociationalism has, however, become a less dominant political feature in these countries.

There are some interesting parallels between corporatism and consociational democracy. Both depend on private negotiations among elites and the ability of those elites to sell any agreements reached to the mass memberships later. Both depend on segmenting the society and institutionalizing that segmentation. Further, both systems imply bargaining and something approaching consensus before a policy can be accepted. In short, many analysts consider both corporatism and consociational democracy less than democratic, yet both have been necessary (or at least sufficient) to manage what might otherwise have been extremely fractious political situations. Where the two arrangements differ is in the types of interests being accommodated and the use of political parties, rather than interest groups, as the means of expressing demands in the consociational solution. In some mesocorporatist arrangements, however, where the actors are regional, consociationalism and corporatism may be more similar than they are different.

Summary and Conclusion

Just as corporatism has come to influence significantly policymaking in Western Europe, so too theories of corporatism have come to influence greatly the analysis of Western Europe politics. While these structured interactions are extremely important, and have served as a useful antidote to the pluralist biases of many scholars, we must remember that they do not constitute the entirety of political life in European democracies. Furthermore, they do not even constitute the entirety of the interaction between state and society. As noted earlier, it would be easy to stretch the idea of corporatism to cover everything that occurs in the relationship between state and society and in the process make the term meaningless (see Migdal 1988). Instead, we should be cognizant of the limitations as well as the utility of corporatist models for politics in Europe.

One obvious weakness in these models is the concentration of structural relationships as an explanatory factor. A number of less structured patterns of interactions have arisen in European countries. We have also pointed out the number of structured interactions that do not meet the criteria of singularity and hierarchy. In short, interest groups in most democratic countries have found any number of ways of pressing their cases on government and do not depend on the formalism implied in many of these models. So, for example, interest groups may have close ties with individual legislators, or even sponsor them. They would not necessarily depend on a formal meeting to try to change policies. Thus understanding the influence of interest groups on policy may require a much broader knowledge of their interactions with government.

In addition, the corporatist model is relatively static in its assumptions and its outlook concerning the manner in which European politics functions. It appears locked into a particular time and space, and not adaptable to changing economic and political conditions (Nedelman and Meier 1982). We have detailed some of those changing conditions, and the change is likely to continue, or even accelerate. We would anticipate that in the future, European economic interest groups, both in their strictly economic roles and in their interactions with national governments, will be less visible than they have been. The necessity of interacting with the global political economy, including the European Economic Community, may require the assertion of a dominant state interest in some economic policies even if that should conflict with the demands of significant interest groups. At one time those policies might have been bargained out, but now they may have to be determined somewhat more singlemindedly. Oddly enough, just when many political leaders and citizens question the capacity of the state to make effective policy judgments about economic policy, the nature of the economic environment may mandate a more central role for the state.

Finally, as we have pointed out, economic policymaking and interests may be only a portion of the many concerns that affect the modern European state. As much as balancing the several economic interests, or even class interests (Panitch 1980), that exist within a single country, governments may be as involved in balancing the numerous regional and ethnic interests. Consociationalism may be as important as corporatism in maintaining the state and in making it an effective institution within the society. In addition, governments must balance the numerous attitude and single-issue groups that increasingly are pressing their demands on the public sector. Many governments have produced consociational solutions to accommodate the demands of ethnic and regional interests. Those ethnic demands, being phrased in absolute terms, may be more difficult to accommodate than the demands arising in corporatist bargaining, phrased as they usually are in financial and therefore highly divisible terms. In short, the issues covered by corporate bargaining may be only a part of the agenda for action in a contemporary political system. Corporatism, therefore, is at best a necessary but certainly not a sufficient condition for effective state management in the late twentieth century.

This may still be a century of corporatism. Corporate arrangements of all types—societal, meso, or whatever—continue to be important for the conduct of the public sector. Unfortunately for our analytic comfort, however, these arrangements may tell only a part of the story. A variety of interest groups are involved with government in numerous ways, and corporatism is only one method of interest intermediation. The difficult question may not be whether this is still the century of corporatism, but of what else is it also still the century.

Notes

1. It is unclear the extent to which Spain would fulfill the "requirements" for corporatism after its transition to democracy. See, for example, Roca (1987) and Perez-Diaz (1987).

2. Some writers have made this argument for West Germany's relative lack of success in adjusting to the changing world economy. The tightly linked system was very effective during growth (see Hall 1986) but has been less effective on the downside of change (see Marsh 1987).

3. These parties, of course, also have a free-market ideology that will make them accept the market rather than any set of politicized groups as the true representative of the public interest.

4. Consociationalism was successful for a time in even the troubled world of Lebanese politics and has been advocated as a solution for the problems of Northern Ireland.

Chapter

7

GOVERNING IN THE MIDST OF ECONOMIC CHANGE

The 1970s and 1980s were an era of real or perceived fiscal difficulty for most West European governments. Talk of cutting budgets, cutting public employment, and perhaps above all cutting taxes dominated political life. These financial difficulties for the public sector were in a part a function of the uncertainty of future economic growth, following several decades of sustained and rapid growth (Rose and Peters 1978). Although economic growth in the mid- and late 1980s was more sustained and somewhat greater than in the decade immediately after the oil crisis of 1973, a nagging uncertainty remained in the minds of many policymakers (see Chapter 1). The absence of an accepted economic dogma to guide decision making after the collapse of Keynesianism accentuated that practical uncertainty. Monetarism, "supply-side," and neo-Keynesian approaches were all advocated and showed some glimmers of success, but none was able to capture a consensus as Keynesian management once had.

Nations' fiscal difficulties also were a function of continuing government commitments to fund social programs begun in the 1950s and 1960s (or even 1930s). Demographic changes, inflation, and political pressures for enhanced benefits made these entitlement programs more expensive. These increasing program costs became even more uncontrollable by the indexation of benefits to meet increases in prices and/or wages (Weaver 1988). The costs of these social programs led many in and out of government to question the advisability of their continuation. The desire to eliminate social programs may actually be more deep-seated and ideological for many policymakers, but financial problems provided a useful justification. In the language of the time, governments were "overloaded" (Rose 1978), with too many responsibilities and inadequate resources to meet all their commitments. We will discuss some of the specific problems with those social programs, and possible responses, in the following chapter. Here, however, those programs serve only as the backdrop to changes in the machinery of government itself.

Finally, after the initial financial shocks around the times of the oil crises, governments' apparent fiscal distress was generated as much by ideological changes and citizens' backlash against taxation as by real economic conditions.[1] As just noted, economic growth is more problematic in the 1990s than it was in the late 1950s and 1960s, but continues to occur, and for most European countries it appears likely to get stronger. The unpredictability of economic growth that plagued the 1970s appears to have been reduced, and growth is predictable if not always large. However, whether in California, Denmark, Wellington, or wherever, groups have mobilized to lower or at least stabilize taxes and thereby have been able—wittingly or unwittingly—to place fiscal pressures on government.

The "era of retrenchment" has been (and continues to be) more than just simple demands for government to spend less money or employ fewer people. In several European countries it has been associated with a more sweeping indictment of government as usual and an attempt to impose an alternative ideological vision on government. While these new ideologues have been largely from the political Right, there is at least one major example of a reformer from the Left—François Mitterrand in France. Further, although most political leaders of this era have not had ideologies in the sense of an integrated and coherent vision of state and society (Shils 1968), they do have a set of beliefs about government. Those leaders have been able to communicate their ideas to their fellow citizens and have had the tenacity to place their ideas into practice to an almost unprecedented degree (Jones 1988; Kavanagh 1987; Netherlands Scientific Council for Government Policy 1983). This set of political beliefs at the elite level has successfully permeated mass thinking about government in many countries. The notion of an "enterprise culture" in Britain is an obvious example. Mrs. Thatcher has advocated that the British do what they can by themselves before turning to government. Many citizens in Western Europe no longer seem first to look to government to solve societal problems. Rather, they seem to feel "overloaded." The era of retrenchment and the leaders it has spawned have produced a major cultural change concerning government, and governing has come to mean coping with this cultural change as much as coping with more tangible factors, such as inadequate money and personnel. In the words of George Downs and Patrick Larkey (1986), the public sector has now moved "from hubris to helplessness."

Although retrenchment is usually discussed as a fiscal concept, it has numerous managerial and leadership ramifications as well. In the first place, some of the reasons behind the perceived need for budgetary retrenchment are managerial. Governments are usually discussed as "bureaucratic," bumbling, inefficient, and poorly managed (and those are the more polite terms used). Many critics see government's fiscal problems arising as much from the inefficiency of its own internal management practices as from any external fiscal pressures (see, for example, Savas 1982; for a contrary view see Goodsell 1985). These critics propose the private sector as the proper exemplar of good management for government (Downs and Larkey 1986, 23–58). Evidence of corruption—whether in the management of the Property Services Agency in Britain or in the defense sector in Sweden or wherever—only adds to the appearance of poor public-sector management (Doig 1984; Rose-Ackerman 1978). In the United States the phrase "fraud, waste, and abuse" has come to encapsulate a general feeling that many of government's financial problems can be laid at its own doorstep and that something must be done to make government work better.

In addition to the managerial causes (again real or perceived) of government's financial problems, popular pressures to reduce taxes usually have not been accompanied by concomitant pressures to reduce services. Numerous surveys of citizens in European countries and in other industrialized democracies have indicated just that; they want benefits but they do not want to pay taxes (Hadenius 1986; Sears and Citrin 1982; Taylor-Gooby 1985). Do more with less is now a common demand placed on managers in the public sector, and in the 1980s those managers (and their nominal political superiors) developed a number of mechanisms for coping with the difficult financial realities of government (Dror 1986, 51–72). In some instances the responses were mere budgetary changes and gimmicks (Tarschys 1985); some changed little more than the style of presentation without any real impact on levels of public expenditure. Other responses fell under the general rubric of "cutback management" (Levine 1978, 1980) and involved the micromanagement of organizations as they responded to declining resources and probably also declining personnel figures. Other responses involved large-scale changes in the manner in which government is organized and managed. At one time or another, almost all governments of European democracies attempted all three types of reform (Ingraham and Peters 1988), with varying degrees of success.

The new ideologues and their demands for management in turn required some rethinking of the role of political executives and the role of the career civil service in European countries. The role of political leaders who follow the current crop of leaders to political office may require even more careful rethinking. The rules of the governing game have been changed, in some cases fundamentally. The changes primarily tilt the playing surface in the direction of the politicians' end of the field and enhance their capacity to score policy goals. The politicians' end of the field is occupied, however, almost entirely by political executives, and parliaments still face difficulty in becoming major players. Subsequent governmental leaders may be able to learn and build an even greater capacity to get things done with their own resources, or they may want to return to a managerial system giving greater responsibility to the career civil service. If indeed times are tough, it may pay to minimize responsibility for what happens and attempt to place the blame elsewhere—on the career civil service, for example. Whatever their desires, those future political leaders will have to understand and react to the managerial and policy developments of the past decade.

This chapter will elaborate on the general theme of governments' reactions to fiscal problems and the problems produced by many citizens' image of poor management and general incompetence in government. Given many contemporary politicians' emphasis on the role of the "executive establishment," we will focus on efforts to change aspects of that establishment. We will examine the "reforms" that have been undertaken to cope with policy overload, with special attention to those affecting executive leadership in both the politics and the civil service. Many of these reforms have involved rather minor tinkering with structures of government, or with the processes for policy implementation (for a general critique of piecemeal reforms, see Gormley 1987). However, some of the most profound changes in management in the public sector have been occurring in the relationships between political executives and their career civil servants. These changes appear to go a long way toward defining the emerging nature of executive leadership.

Attempting to Cope with Retrenchment

Governments have adopted a number of strategies to deal with their problems in the era of retrenchment. Here we will attempt to catalog and briefly describe those coping strategies, ranging from very mundane tinkering to fundamental reorientations of the public sector. These reforms will be a backdrop for subsequent attempts to address the future of governance in Western European societies. The economic challenges posed by economic slowdowns and the need to retrench combine with the strains on the nation-state described in Chapter 2 to produce a problematic future for many governing systems. We do not expect the governments of nation-states to vanish or be the object of popular revolutions. The less dramatic, but equally troubling, real future of European governments may be the increasing indifference of their citizens, as they become more irrelevant as a source of governance. To some degree the irrelevance can be seen not only in the development of authority in different levels of government, but also in the growth of alternatives to the public sector. Privatization became a buzzword for coping with the problems of government in the 1980s, and numerous alternatives to government provision of services are being developed. In this chapter we will discuss more the "reform" of government management and organization as a solution to its problems, with privatizing government's economic functions a major (but not sole) component thereof (Ascher 1987; Henig, Hamnett, and Feigenbaum 1988). Chapter 8 will then discuss changes in the welfare-state programs so central to the functioning of contemporary governments, and some alternatives that are being tried.

Content of Reforms

One way to classify government attempts to cope with the need to retrench is to look at the content of those reforms. What were the problems in government diagnosed as sufficiently serious to need "treatment"? What were the natures of the interventions that were used? While far from unambiguous, we can think of these coping strategies in four basic content categories: budgetary, structural, procedural, and relational (see also Ingraham and Peters 1988).

BUDGETARY REFORMS. The simplest category of reform contains attempts on the part of governments to change the manner in which their spending plans are constructed, or the type of analysis or thinking that goes into the formulation of the public budget. As can be seen in Table 7.1, this alteration or manipulation of the budgetary process has been approached in several ways (see also Schick 1988; Tarschys 1985). Furthermore, to a greater or lesser extent, all the budgetary methods developed to cope with the problems of retrenchment appear to have had some successes, although usually less dramatic ones than their advocates promised.

The successes achieved by many contemporary budget reforms actually have been greater than most previous attempts at budgetary reform, such as PPBS, RCB, and the like, in part because the goals of the recent reforms have been more modest. While many strategies for budgetary reform in the

TABLE 7.1

Types of Reorganization and Reform

	Targets			
	Budgetary	*Structural*	*Procedural*	*Relational*
Load shedding	Privatization	Privatization	Deregulation	Politicization
Snakes and Ladders	Subnational Responsibility	Decentralization	——	Task Forces
Automaticity	Gramm-Rudman-Hollings	Japanese Personnel	Paperwork Reduction	——
Priority Setting	PPBS	——	Planning	Priorities and Planning
Squeezing	Main Alternative	Grace Commission	Grace Commission	——
Management	FMI/Next Steps	Quangoization	MBO	FMI/Next Steps

PPBS = Planning-Programming Budgeting Systems
FMI = Financial Management Initiative
MBO = Management by Objectives

1960s and early 1970s had something approaching comprehensive rationality as a goal, most contemporary reforms have had simpler intentions, such as merely reducing the volume of public expenditure (Peters 1989a, chap. 7). Hence strategies such as the "main alternative" for the Swedish budget (Ericksson 1983), which is simply beginning annual budget discussions around a 2 percent reduction of the previous appropriations, have very tidy and attainable goals—to force the agency delivering the service to be at least 2 percent more efficient. In some instances budgetary reforms in the 1980s were required to undo some of the work of earlier reforms based on rationality. For example, in Britain imposing simple cash limits on the budget was a response to the control difficulties stemming from the volume budgeting system introduced in the 1970s (Hogwood 1988, 131–39).

The budgetary reforms of the 1980s were not entirely without analytic content. However, even reforms with greater analytic content—such as the "reconsideration" initiatives in the Netherlands (Van Nispen, 1988)—had as a fundamental goal the reduction of public expenditures rather than the more grandiose goals of achieving some optimum allocation among competing purposes. The initiatives in the Netherlands select a few programs for extensive review (and perhaps budget reduction) each year. Unlike Programme Analysis and Review (PAR) formerly used in the United Kingdom, the goals are more budgetary than broadly evaluative. In the case of budgetary reform at least, the hubris associated with reform may be gone, but there is no sense of helplessness.

STRUCTURAL REFORMS. As the name implies, structural changes have involved transformations of the organizational framework that provides government services. These changes range from the simple jiggling and poking of the structure that is common in any era, faced with retrenchment or not (Peters and Hogwood, forthcoming), to very fundamental changes in the institutional fabric that provides public services. It is by no means uncommon to think that if government organization is correct, then those institutions will actually function smoothly. Unfortunately, however, despite its frequent use, structural reorganizations are really not very well understood either by those who implement them or by students of government (Campbell and Peters 1988; Leemans 1976; Pollitt 1984). As a consequence, reorganizations frequently do not meet the goals—especially those of enhanced efficiency (Salamon 1981b)—that have been set for them and often produce more disillusionment and disappointment than significant change in the way government works. Several types of structural reforms have been implemented, including *moving boxes, load shedding,* and *local government reorganization.*

The simplest structural changes are simply *moving around the boxes* that constitute the structures of government departments, or creating new components and/or destroying old ones. This is more or less easy to do in European countries, depending on at least two factors. The first of these is the formal powers granted to the prime minister, or the cabinet as a whole, to make changes in government structures. In some cases—for example, Switzerland—constitutional or legal principles severely constrain these powers. In other countries executives have very broad powers to reorganize. For example, in West Germany, the chancellor is given almost a carte blanche to reorganize government, while in the United Kingdom an "Order in Council" issued by the Privy Council Office in the name of the queen (but actually an action by the government) is all that is needed.

The second factor influencing the ability of the government to reorganize at will is its structure beneath the departmental or ministerial level. At one extreme is Sweden (and to a somewhat lesser extent Finland), where the boards are as much (or perhaps more) public law bodies with lives of their own as are the ministries. Next along a continuum of formality come France (Darbel and Schnapper 1969, 1972) and Norway (Laegreid and Roness 1983), which have well-articulated agency structures beneath the ministry level but the structures are more readily changed than in Sweden. At the far end of this continuum is the United Kingdom, with a somewhat indefinite structure beneath the ministries and a great ease of change for that structure (Peters and Hogwood, forthcoming). Despite the presence of this continuum, in all countries there has been some movement toward a more decentralized agency structure. In some, as in the United Kingdom, there is an attempt to decentralize almost all government departments to "agencies" (Kemp, 1990). In other countries, the moves are just for parts of government that appear to require special flexibility and a mission orientation (Timsit 1987).

Among the most fundamental structural changes tried have been the *shedding of public burdens* through privatization and deregulation. Even when programs have been retained in government, there has been a tendency to hive them off into smaller, presumably more accountable and mission-oriented organizations and to reduce the relative power and authority of the mainline departments. This has been seen, in among other examples, in the formation of *administrations de mission* in France and Belgium (Rigaud and Delcros 1984; Timsit 1987), *Projektgruppen* in West Germany (Lepper 1983), and in the proposed creation of mission-oriented agencies by the reform called "Next Steps" in the United Kingdom (Jenkins, Caines, and Jackson 1988). A number of efforts at decentralizing government have been made to promote efficiency, accountability, and a host of other political values by involving other levels of government (Peters 1989b). One common reaction to the perceived inability of existing government structures to deliver the goods in a manner that most people would desire seems to be to attempt to alter the existing service-delivery structures. This is hardly a new response to the problem, but the extent to which old reforms continue to become new problems remains interesting.

Another important structural change that has occurred in almost all European countries during the 1970s and into the 1980s was the *reorganization of local government* (Gunlicks 1981). As is often the case, the term reorganization has taken on a number of meanings, but there are several common features. The most noticeable has been the consolidation of local governments (see Table 7.2). In some cases by a factor of as much as ten to one, local governments have been made larger and presumably thereby more efficient. While there may be some question about the efficiency argument for larger units (Newton 1977; Strömberg and Westerståhl 1984; Westerståhl 1971), increased local government size has usually been associated with some increased responsibility for service production.

Along with increasing the size of local governments, many countries also created an intermediate level of government. Regional governments have been in place for some time in federal systems, such as West Germany and Austria, and in some unitary countries, such as Sweden and Denmark. However, as a part of devolution of power away from the center (at least as a

TABLE 7.2

Reduction in Number of Local Government Units

Number of Units

	1951	1982	Percentage Change
Belgium (commune)	2,670	596	78
France (commune)	37,983	36,391	4
West Germany (Gemeinden)	24,500	8,510	65
Netherlands (municipalities)	1,014	820	19
Norway (municipalities)	746	454	39
Sweden (kommun)	2,500	279	89
United Kingdom (districts)	c. 1,500	484	c. 68

policy goal), a number of countries created new intermediate governments (Keating 1988). In France and Italy these bodies have been given powers formerly held by the central government, while in the United Kingdom powers held by the local government have been divided among the two tiers of subnational government, with few new powers added. Again, it was thought that some programs could be delivered more efficiently in very large catchment areas. Transportation and physical planning, for example, need to cover large areas if they are to be effective. While some critics believe these reorganizations just add another level of government, with associated costs and bureaucracy, in general they have been popular and seem to have improved the quality of some public services.

We should not be terribly sanguine about the capacity of structural reforms to produce many tangible improvements in public-sector performance. These reforms do have two advantages, however. First, they give the appearance of action in dealing with problems for which there may be no real solution. That image is extremely useful for political leaders, for whom taking action may be the most important value. Further, as with some of the budgetary "reforms," structural reforms may give the illusion that public expenditures have been reduced when in fact they are only being made at another level of government, or by a quasi-public organization that does not show up in the budget (Hood and Schuppert 1988; Peters and Heisler 1983). We should not be too quick to condemn all reorganizational efforts as political shams, but neither should we be too willing to accept them at face value.

PROCEDURAL REFORMS. Along with changing the structures, governments have sought to alter the procedures by which they conduct their business and make their decisions. Again, unlike many of even the non-budgetary procedural reforms adopted during the 1960s and early 1970s, such as Management by Objectives (MBO), many procedural reforms emerging in the later 1970s and into the 1980s were not very concerned with substantive rationality. Rather, these "remedies" were more concerned with the simpler task of trying to produce some improvements in output per unit of input, or at a minimum making those individuals managing programs in government conceptualize their tasks in such terms. Other reforms were concerned with procedural accountability and rationality and with creating the appearance that government does, in fact, perform its role properly.

One focus for the procedural reforms has been increased accountability and enhanced scrutiny of administrative performance by the political institutions of government and by the public. With many components in this category, it is difficult to separate procedural reforms from structural ones. Procedures rarely can be introduced on their own; they require an organization to develop and implement them. So, for example, were the Rayner scrutinies (Metcalfe and Richards 1984) into program efficiency in Britain a procedural reform, or were they a structural change that led to the creation of the efficiency unit? We consider reforms of this type to be procedural, because the change in procedure, or the addition of new ones, was designed to produce the result. Reorganization or the creation of a new organization was coincidental with the procedural change. Further, some procedural reforms may come very close to being budgetary. The Financial Management Initiative in Britain, for example, had a good deal to do with the spending of money (Gray and Jenkins 1986). The primary purpose of the reform, however, appeared to be altering how government did its business rather than focusing on the saving of money through the formal budgetary process.

As in the budget and especially organizational reforms, some of the most important and effective procedural reforms have involved reducing the number of procedures. This reduction is seen externally through deregulation and governments' decisions to impose fewer rules on the conduct of economic and social life in their countries. Internally, in government itself, this type of reform has manifested itself in several ways. One has been through paperwork reduction acts and their equivalents. Another has been the abrogation of some procedures that may have protected civil servants, such as the Priestley system of pay research in the United Kingdom, or the principle of pay comparability between the public and private sectors in the United States. One meaning of "reform" has been simply to eliminate what were perceived as slow and costly procedures (for France, see Fournier

1987) in favor of quick decisions by elected political leaders or their appointees. As is so often the case (Simon 1947), however, procedural reforms designed to produce one kind of benefit (speed of decision) may do violence to other important values (accountability and due process).

RELATIONAL REFORMS. Finally, governments have sought to address their political demands for retrenchment by altering the relationships between career civil service and temporary political executives. A dominant theme of most of the "ideological" governments in the 1970s and 1980s (especially those of the political Right) was that policymaking in their governments was dominated by the career civil service. The poor management skills of the civil service, and their thinly disguised policy agendas, have been argued to be a fundamental cause of all that is wrong with government in Washington, Whitehall, or wherever. Further, the protection offered by civil service systems is argued to protect and disguise a cadre of organizational politicians who have their own views about policy and who have been successful in implementing those views (see Hoskyns 1983). Given that these ideological governments came to office with radical agendas, the civil service's status quo orientation was considered a major impediment. This obstructionist characterization of the civil service has proved popular. The public bureaucracy has become a scapegoat for the very need for retrenchment, and many political leaders have been effective in deflecting attention from their own managerial shortcomings onto perceived failures of the civil service (see Milward and Rainey 1983).

The remedies prescribed to government for its "illness" should not be surprising. In the 1980s, so many attempts were made to interject more political control, and more political appointees, into the career civil service that politicization of the civil service became a significant concern in a number of countries (Meyers 1985). Even in countries such as the United Kingdom with a long tradition of an apolitical and largely respected and influential civil service, attempts were made to impose greater political control and involvement of outsiders (Drewry and Butcher 1988, 166–86; Ridley 1985). In countries such as France and West Germany, where civil servants have been more identified with political parties, the importance of that identification appears to have intensified (Derlien 1988; Mayntz and Derlien 1989; *Pouvoirs* 1987).

Apparently many elected political leaders believe that if only they can get more politically committed people into management and leadership positions in government, then the commonly identified problems of government will have been solved, or at worst ameliorated. Yet even if the number of political appointments is not increased, the prevailing atmosphere makes it less feasible for civil servants to attempt to impose their own views on policy. Through the "law of anticipated reaction," they may bow to the wishes of their political masters. This acquiescence may, in the long run, squander a valuable resource in government that could have prevented political leaders from making the mistakes that others have made before them.

Styles of Reform

The reforms that have been adopted by European governments can also be classified according to the style of change they attempt to impose. Although some styles appear especially closely tied to specific contents— for example, automaticity with budgetary mechanisms—there is a rather wide distribution of almost all reform styles among the several content categories. Faced with the daunting problem of attempting to change the manner in which government conducts its business, political (and administrative) leaders have cast their net very widely and have tried a number of "solutions." What does appear general, however, is the denigration of "rationality" in favor of more political, ideological, and nonanalytic responses to managerial problems. This does not mean that all the tools taught to students in schools of public administration and policy around the country are being allowed to rust. Rather, the tools appear now to be used more overtly to justify and prop up preconceived notions rather than to "discover" new solutions and new information about the policy issues (Aberbach and Rockman 1989).

LOAD SHEDDING. One of the simplest strategies governments can adopt for dealing with the perceived need to retrench is to shed some of the loads they have been carrying. We have already noted that this is not feasible for many large expenditures resulting from entitlement programs, but it has proved to be very possible for a number of other programs. The greatest success in load shedding has been for large-scale public involvement in the economy (Savas 1987; Veljanovski 1987), whether through government ownership of industries or through economic regulation. Some governments have undertaken serious evaluations of the possibilities of privatization even for the big-ticket social service items.

While space constraints preclude description of all the privatization activities of all the governments in Western Europe, something of their scope is presented in Table 7.1. From that table and a reading of newspapers, we can gain some idea of the magnitude of privatization. It should also be noted that load shedding can produce (short-term) financial benefits. When public assets are sold, they bring a return. Some governments—perhaps especially the United Kingdom—have been able to bring their budgets into closer balance through the revenue from asset sales. This is true even though, perhaps for ideological reasons, the government has sold off some assets (especially council housing to sitting tenants) at below market value (Silver 1990). Such sales have made the opportunity to buy stock and houses more widely accessible. While privatization may have been opposed at the outset, it has created in Britain and to a lesser extent elsewhere property-owning democracies not thought possible previously. In so doing, privatization may have created a whole new group of conservative voters and perhaps altered the political landscape for some time to come.

Load shedding need not just be privatization, however. Deregulation is another important form that has been adopted in varying degrees in different countries.[2] Further, to some degree the policymaking load may be shed *upward* in the organization by civil servants giving greater responsibility to political appointees. This may be especially true when policy advisory functions are handed over to political appointees. Such work transfers presumably would provide civil servants with more time to master their managerial tasks. If the structures of government are somewhat flexible, this could, in principle, permit greater specialization and presumably improve the quality of both policymaking and administration.

SNAKES AND LADDERS. Load shedding redistributes the tasks of government among different types of actors in response to the managerial ills of government. Similar to this style is a reform style of tinkering with who does what within the public sector, even if all the activities do remain governmental responsibilities. Some functions may be centralized and others decentralized, but if there is a problem then shifting the level of government may be proposed as the answer. Of course, all this shifting around of responsibilities may only be a façade to hide the intractability of the problems. Or one level of government may be trying to gain some apparent fiscal responsibility at the expense of others. This strategy may be especially powerful for a goal of fiscal probity if the function can be forced onto a level of government that cannot run an operating deficit, as most states in the United States (Beam 1984; Nathan and Doolittle 1987). As with privatization, the same function performed elsewhere still costs somebody something, but the political appearance is often as important as the reality of the reform.

Interestingly, when faced with somewhat similar demands for retrenchment or at least improvement of governmental performance, different governments have approached the problem of who does what somewhat differently. To some degree this may be a function of their respective starting points; highly centralized regimes could centralize further only with great difficulty. Yet in the United States, which began as a decentralized regime, decentralized even more during the Reagan administration. Germany and Switzerland appear to have had something of the same experience. Of the two types of reforms, decentralization appears to be the more popular choice. France, Spain, and Italy have undertaken major decentralization efforts in what had been centralized regimes (Keating 1988; Putnam 1988). Local government reforms in a number of European countries appear to have made giving more power to the localities a real possibility (Gustafsson, 1981). Only the United Kingdom (Jones 1988) has seen a major effort at centralization of control over local government, although this movement is combined with a broad effort at load shedding to the private sector. This centralizing push in Britain is especially noticeable with respect to the Greater London Council and the other metropolitan governments (HMSO 1983). This metropolitan tier of government has been abolished, eliminating a major challenge to central government authority. Other countries have, however, centralized some functions formerly managed by local authorities in an attempt to enhance their control.

The game of snakes and ladders is increasingly being played at the level of the European Community. With the push toward full integration by 1992, Brussels will have to perform more economic and social functions. This does two things for national governments. First, it allows them to shed certain programs and to have more money for the functions for which they continue to be responsible. In addition, the European government in Brussels becomes a convenient scapegoat for things that go wrong. That level of government can be made to appear more remote from citizens, more bureaucratic and inefficient, and it can be argued to be absorbing too much tax money. In this comparison, the managers of national governments may appear to be efficient and responsible—whether they are or not.

AUTOMATICITY. As noted, automaticity is especially closely associated with problems in the budget. It is often difficult for political organizations, or public organizations with close links to clients, to make difficult decisions about reducing public expenditure. Therefore, if those actors can agree on automatic mechanisms for imposing reductions, then some of the political onus will be removed from those decisions. American audiences will recognize the logic of Gramm-Rudman-Hollings and others in this statement, and similar mechanisms have been imposed in other political systems. In some, such as Japan, similar automatic mechanisms have been applied to the civil service (Muramatsu 1988). The fundamental idea here is to remove as much discretion as possible from those whose careers might be damaged by making decisions to reduce expenditures or services. In addition, automatic increases in social program benefits can be considered a way of preventing a parliament from accepting even larger increases. An effective campaign strategy for an incumbent government would be to raise the benefits for government programs. It is easier to defeat such increases if there are already automatic changes based on a principle of fairness (keeping up with inflation) scheduled to go into effect.

Automaticity has also been introduced as a means of preventing government from enhancing its revenues through inflation. With a progressive income tax, as their incomes increase, taxpayers move into higher brackets and have to pay a larger proportion of their income in tax. If increases in income are due to inflation rather than real economic growth, individual taxpayers will retain a smaller real income after taxes. To correct for this, a number of European governments have introduced automatic adjustments of bracket thresholds for inflation (Rose 1985). With this arrangement, if governments want more tax revenues they have to go through the difficult political battle to change the law, rather than receiving a "fiscal dividend" of changes in price levels. Given the conservative bent that politics has taken in many European countries, this automatic indexation of tax brackets should be an enduring brake on the capacity of any future government to expand significantly the scope of its activity.

PRIORITY SETTING. One of the standard complaints about "big government" is that it has been allowed to grow without much rhyme or reason, and hence has grown in very incoherent, and therefore excessively costly, ways (Bladh 1987; Rothstein 1986). Thus if clear policy priorities could be established, then the "burdens" of government perhaps could be reduced and better government produced for all. The need for priority setting is argued to exist especially in the budget (see Natchez and Bupp 1973), but also exists across a whole range of governmental activities. Further, while some of the rational reforms of the 1960s and 1970s also sought to impose priority setting (Klein et al. 1988), largely with the goal of improving the quality of services, governments in the 1980s sought to determine those priorities by more politicized means, by terminating programs and lowering total expenditures.

Placing a greater emphasis on priority setting in government will tend to drive decision making upward, away from the career civil service and toward the political executives. This description of the effects of priority setting is similar to Colin Campbell's (1983, 24) "planning and priorities" style of executive behavior and to some extent similar to Israeli policy analyst Yehezkel Dror's (1986) concept of the "central mind of government." In moving decisions upward, the relationships between civil servants and politicians will be affected. Thus initiatives such as the Financial Management Initiative and its sequel, Next Steps, in the United Kingdom have made civil servants the managers of the policy frameworks established elsewhere, and have thereby reduced their importance in governing.

Another effect of a priority-setting style is to increase the power of central agencies (Campbell and Szablowski 1979) in governing. These agencies, located around the prime minister (or the president in France), are charged with ensuring that his or her programs are adopted by the ministries and then implemented. Central agencies use some simple but extremely powerful tools to enforce the political leaders' priorities. Among the most potent of these is the public budget. Either by simply reducing the amount of money available to everyone and pressing for greater efficiency, or by making more selective cuts, budget control is an overwhelmingly powerful tool at the disposal of ministries of finance. Control of personnel is almost as powerful an instrument. This power can extend not only to the numbers who work for government (or a particular agency) but also to the pay and conditions under which they work. Finally, central agencies have access to law, especially the right of issuing secondary legislation, and can in many instances write rules with the force of law to produce the changes they want. Thus to the extent that the central agencies rather than the ministries and service-delivery agencies are in charge of policymaking, then political leaders can get what they want from the policy process.

SQUEEZING. If it is assumed that government budgets and staffs are almost inherently too large to meet the demands of the tasks that are to be performed, one important strategy to improve efficiency would be to squeeze the "fat" out of those budgets. While the squeezing may be done through the automatic methods just discussed, it can also be done more selectively. It may be done on the grounds of efficiency—for example, selecting targets regardless of their political popularity because they appear to have a great deal of available resource slack. Reviews of defense procurement (even prior to the bribery scandals in several countries) would be an example of this approach. A more common strategy would be to select as targets programs that are politically unpopular and then scrutinize their budgets very carefully. Finally, often the most politically popular, even if logically undesirable, method of approaching this problem is across-the-board cuts, or the allocation of "equal misery."

One way to produce the squeeze on government is to bring in people who have little or nothing to protect in the current programs and administration. This is typified both by the Grace Commission (Goodsell 1984;

Kelman 1985) in the United States, and a very similar mechanism employed in Canada (Wilson 1988) in the form of the Nielsen Task Force, in which a number of private citizens examined the efficiency of government operations. Some of the commissions and inquiries in continental countries have efficiency and budgetary responsibility (Germann 1981). Those countries that do not permit outsiders to delve into the workings of their government cannot enjoy all the benefits of these exercises. However, the Rayner scrutinies in the United Kingdom serve much of the same purpose by using insiders (Metcalfe and Richards 1984). This search-and-destroy tactic provides a great deal of ammunition for those who want to reduce the size of government, although it runs the risk of cutting the good with the bad especially because, as we point out in the next section, the analogies between the public and private sectors may well be false.

MANAGERIALISM. Finally, there has been a major movement in government circles to attempt to make the public sector as a whole more like private enterprise and to make running government organizations more like private-sector management. This approach sometimes parades under the banner of "managerialism," as if there had been no management in government prior to the time that it was advocated. Managerialism tends to ignore all the warnings about the fundamental differences between government and business (Allison 1986; Rainey, Backoff, and Levine 1976), and proceeds to attempt to transplant private-sector ideas into government. As might be imagined, this approach has been championed especially by the political Right, although it has not been without its more moderate, and even Socialist, advocates. Some scholars, however, have characterized managerialism as almost hopelessly muddled and as a "reign of error" (Metcalfe 1988; see also Pollitt 1986). The question is whether any of the programmatic difficulties that beset government can be solved simply by managing them better, or whether the problems arise from the policies themselves.

The managerial approach to improving government's performance in the face of retrenchment has been widespread; some find it very comforting to think that all that is really wrong with government can be cured without addressing any fundamental value choices. Although advocated in Europe, managerialism has been more common in other industrialized countries. The Reagan administration, through such projects as the Grace Commission and "Reform 88," a detailed program to promote efficiency in government, sought to make government function more like a business (Newland 1983). Similar themes have emerged in Canadian and Australian government (Aucoin 1988; Wilenski 1986; Yeatman 1987).

In Western Europe, major efforts at understanding and improving government management are currently under way in the Scandinavian countries (Olsen 1988). The French government (under a Socialist president) has also sought to improve public program performance (Fortin 1988; Fournier 1987). The Netherlands has undertaken several initiatives in managerial reform. Nowhere, however, has managerialism been a more visible and important strategy for coping with the public sector than it has been in Mrs. Thatcher's Britain. Beginning with the MINIS, an information system for ministers (Likierman 1982), going through the Financial Management Initiative to make civil servants responsible for "cost centers" (Lee 1984; Gray and Jenkins 1986), and now pushing even farther along the managerial trail with the Next Steps program to create quasi-autonomous agencies (Jenkins, Caines, and Jackson 1988), the Conservative governments since 1979 have been attempting to produce a basic change in the culture of the British civil service. The fundamental idea is that career civil servants should serve as managers, and policy ideas should be the province of the political executives. Although this thinking pervades several of the substantive areas of reform, it is especially evident in thinking about relational issues in governance such as the relationship between elected and career officials.

Summary

Governments have not been remiss in trying to cope with the problems presented them by retrenchment politics. Rather, they have been extremely creative in producing reforms that address, if at times in no more than symbolic terms, the challenges they face. Our classification and enumeration of reforms in many ways only scratch the surface of the complexity of change. They do, however, serve as the background for understanding the ability of government executives, whether operating from a political or a career base, to supply real leadership in coping with the problems that will inevitably arise. As is always the case for government, and other organizations, the last round of solutions becomes the source of the problems the next wave of executives confronts.

Executive Leadership

Each of the types of reform just mentioned will impose some possible burdens, as well as provide some possible benefits, for subsequent executive leaders. We will discuss the implications of those reforms while answering some of the general questions posed for executive leadership by the emphasis on retrenchment in government. As intimated earlier, the current climate for executive leadership may not be as positive as that which awaited leaders who came to office in Western European governments just following the economic crises of the 1970s. To some extent those leaders had a window of opportunity in which bold action on their part was possible, even if that action was largely to reduce the role of government. That window has since been closed, and, with some of the lingering effects of the leaders of the 1970s—a negative perception of government as well as objective conditions, such as large debt interest payments—is likely to remain so for some time.

To Boldly Go

One characteristic of executive leadership has been the ability to impose a vision on a government and make the operational components of the public sector respond to it. We noted earlier that prime ministerial government appears increasingly to be the pattern in Western European governments. Those executives have been accomplishing things. These accomplishments may come about by force of personality, by good organization and management, or by mere persistence. In any case, effective leaders are usually thought to be those who produce an order of magnitude difference in what government does, or perhaps in the efficiency with which it functions.

In the era of retrenchment, strong executive leadership has been associated with doing less rather than doing more. Political leaders such as Thatcher, Reagan, Rudd Lubbers of the Netherlands, and many others have made their marks by shedding responsibilities and making government smaller and apparently less expensive.[3] This load shedding has now been accomplished, and rather thoroughly in many countries. Although some ultra-conservatives would certainly disagree, in most industrialized democracies most programs that reasonably can be eliminated from the public sector (either terminated completely or privatized) have been, and most reasonable cuts in the remaining programs have been implemented. The question now arises as to what comes next. What can subsequent executive leaders do to demonstrate their leadership and their vision of the good life for their countries?

The capacity for new executive leaders to appear to be doing something is especially constrained if we assume that many fiscal problems of government will persist, and with increased interest payments on debts some may even be exacerbated. Leaders' capacity to accomplish things will be reduced even more if the negative conceptions of government that have been popular in many industrialized countries persist. The current stock of conservative political leaders have to some extent done most of the easy things, and have appeared effective by so doing. Those who follow will face the difficult choice of being seen to do little or nothing, or being seen as violating what has become an apparent commitment of government to keep costs (and taxes) down. Either choice is unpalatable to most potential leaders. Their choices may be especially difficult because lowering taxes has produced deficits and an increased public debt that requires servicing, and cheap "profits" from asset sales have been largely exhausted.

The capacity of political leaders "to boldly go" is further inhibited by the crowding of the policy space that characterizes most industrialized countries (Heclo 1975; Hogwood and Peters 1983). That is, there are few social or economic problems that governments have not already addressed. Governments in most industrialized countries have a program, or more than one, for most clientele groups and identifiable problems in their societies; a dominant feature of "overload" that is presumed to afflict European governments may be the complexity and interconnectedness of programs in the public sector (King 1975). Policymaking in this context becomes coordinating and integrating existing organizations and programs as much as pushing forward with new initiatives. It becomes "rationalizing politics" rather than "breakthrough politics" (Brown 1983, 7). As Heclo (1975, 404) wrote more than a decade ago: "The challenge confronting social policy is not a discontinuity but a cumulation of historical developments common to Europe and the United States. . . . Frontiers of policy development no longer stretch toward a horizon of unimpeded growth amid cheap resources but are now internal frontiers of integration, coordination, and trade-offs." This type of decision making is a particularly executive form of action, focused primarily on rationalizing the internal structure of the executive branch of government and attempting to make that set of programs and institutions function better and with greater coordination. Certainly the legislative branch must be involved, because there are budgetary implications if nothing else, but legislators must function in a role secondary to that of executive officials.

Despite executive leaders' central position in the process, dealing with the coordination of existing policies presents them with some major challenges, especially for leaders with a political base. Policy coordination is a very worthy activity, but it is difficult to transform into exciting headlines for the nightly news. Therefore, the capacity of political leaders to *appear* to exercise policy leadership is diminished just when the need for such leadership is enhanced, because moving into crowded policy spaces involves bumping up against existing programs, which have existing clienteles and workers. Any intrusion into such an ongoing policy system is likely to produce greater concern and resistance than would moving into relatively virgin territory (Hogwood and Peters 1983). The capacity of career civil servants to lead is perhaps particularly constrained in these circumstances, given that most who would be concerned with the issue area are members of one of the existing organizations. They therefore would be expected to fight to defend that organization's turf (budget and policy latitude) rather than cooperate with other organizations in the name of sweet reason or "rationalization." Political executives are forced into the central position for policy leadership, but it is not very comfortable for them.

In Western Europe the capacity to exercise any bold leadership in policy will be further constrained by the increasing role of the European Community in most policy areas. That role has been present in some economic policy areas for some time, but has become more intrusive in all areas as full integration in 1992 approaches. In addition, European agricultural, regional, and social policies are all now encountering more frequent conflicts with existing domestic policies. In short, to exercise national leadership will require a capacity to integrate and harmonize with the rest of Europe—an activity that will create headlines only when it goes badly wrong. Further, to the extent that nationalist sentiments remain, as they certainly do in some countries, success in dealing with the rest of Europe may actually be a political negative for leaders.

Still the Century of Corporatism?

The constraints on executive leadership are not just those arising within the executive branch of government; they also arise from the relationship between the public and private sectors in most industrialized countries. This is true on both the input and output sides of government, to use Eastonian language. First, on the input side, a dominant characteristic of politics in most industrialized societies during the 1960s and 1970s was some form of neocorporatism (Schmitter and Lehmbruch 1982). As noted in Chapter 5, there has been a linking of private-sector interest groups to government, with a consequent loss of autonomy for both actors. This arrangement appeared to work well in these countries as long as there was growing affluence, with interest-group quiescence on some decisions being repaid with their participation in all.

This agreed-upon system for sharing the fiscal dividend of growth enabled corporatist countries to undergo large-scale economic and social change with a minimum of disruption. The system does not appear to have worked so well on the economic downside, and many states have appeared to become virtual hostages to the participatory commitments they had made earlier (Bekke 1985; Nobelen 1983). These commitments to participation accumulated much as did European governments' commitments to provide social policy benefits and have severely limited the capacity of many countries to respond to a rapidly changing international marketplace and to make the tough, internal redistributive decisions that were required; some groups held virtual vetoes over policy changes. In some cases, such as with Mrs. Thatcher in Britain, any existing corporatist arrangements were broken, but this has been harder to do in West Germany, the Netherlands, and the Scandinavian countries. If distributive politics worked so well during times of affluence, times of retrenchment appear to require redistributive politics that corporatism may not be able to supply readily (Nedelman and Meier 1982; Wassenberg 1982).[4] Some political leaders in states with some tendencies toward corporatism have been able to break or modify the system, but many nations lack such decisive leadership. This is especially true for Labor and Social Democratic political leaders who have direct ties to unions and who have championed the role of organized labor in public policymaking.

The Loosening of Linkages

Some of the same loss of leadership capacity that resulted from linkages to the private sector on the input side appears to occur on the output side as well. According to the literature on guidance and control in the public sector (Kaufmann, Majone, and Ostrom 1986), there is clearly some reduction in the steering capacity in most modern governments, when compared to governments during the 1950s and 1960s. This has been in part a function of popular attitudes but has been more a consequence of the structural changes in the provision of public services just described, especially the tendency to use lower levels of government or nongovernmental organizations to provide these services. Thus even if a central government organization still determines the ostensible direction in policy areas, program implementation may not be determined—and that implementation may be crucial in defining the true nature of the policy (O'Toole 1986; Sabatier 1986; Toonen 1985). Changes in service delivery that made sense to reduce the apparent costs of government may, in the long run, make government appear less effective and further diminish popular support for the public sector.

Likewise, old democratic values such as accountability may be threatened when a significant portion of the real policymaking action in the public sector is located outside organizations over which elective or appointed officials have any direct control. The development of "third-party govern-ment" (Hood and Schuppert 1988; Salamon 1981a) has produced some real financial and administrative benefits for government, but those benefits may have been purchased at some real cost as well. Further, given the changes in popular attitudes toward government that have occurred, it may be difficult for future executives to return some of these functions to government administration. The increased apparent costs that a return of programs to the public sector would imply would be unacceptable to many voters in the early 1990s, and it is unclear just how long this rejection will persist.

The tightness or looseness of the linkages in government need not, however, depend totally on the utilization of third-party actors to imple-ment public programs. Some political systems may be more closely linked within their own executive establishments than are others. For example, the decentralized nature of the executive branch (Seidman and Gilmour 1986) in the United States makes executive leadership a more difficult commodity to supply, even when more appointed political executives are available to manage government (Heclo 1988). Much the same would be true for Sweden, and to some degree Finland, with their board structure for imple-mentation. This internal decentralization may be contrasted with the greater domination of the ministry structure in Britain, which, combined with a rather tightly organized career civil service, puts government more directly in the command of the prime minister and the cabinet.

Other industrialized countries vary along this control dimension as well, with factors such as the overall structure of the political system, the struc-ture of ministries, the personnel system, and the system of advice and analysis all influencing the relative degree of linkage within government. As we have argued elsewhere, a key point in any analysis of government is the ability of those at the top of the system to manage it and to govern (see Peters 1988). Some substantial variations in effectiveness of executive lead-ers can be discerned based on the closeness of the linkages within the political system. While certainly related to the political system's capacity to reduce its involvement in the economy and society, this closeness of linkage also seems related to the system's ability to increase that involvement, as in the case of France under the first few years of Socialist governments.

Where Politicians Fear to Tread

Another barrier to executive leadership arising in the era of retrenchment to some degree seems to contradict the first. This barrier is the fact that the problems that appear to face society are perhaps too massive and/or too inadequately understood to be ripe candidates for effective government intervention. Government is involved in everything but yet does not address some fundamental structural social problems. This fact is perhaps particularly evident in the United States, where social dislocation, the widespread demand for drugs, poor school performance, a rapidly aging population and equally a rapidly aging industrial structure, and a host of other major problems await some effective solution. At present, government does not appear to offer answers and seeks to run away from them as much as address them directly. This avoidance was most pronounced in the Reagan administration, but to some degree it is found in the states and even in the cities where these problems are most manifest.

The problem of massive need for social and environmental programs is not, however, confined to the United States. Much the same would be true for many Western European democracies that currently face more or less severe versions of most of the same difficulties. The combination of conservative politicians who have been willing to permit the free market, or voluntary organizations, or the family, or whatever to take care of the problems and a slowing of the fiscal dividend of economic growth to government has made attacking these social problems difficult. They are, however, very apparent as fish die by the thousands in the Rhine and people die by the dozens on city streets in winter.

The accumulation of large-scale problems for society poses at least two difficulties for executive leaders.[5] The first problem is directly related to the usual, fiscal, interpretation of retrenchment. Any attempt to address most of these significant problems is likely to be very expensive. Previous attempts to address major public problems—whether they were social (the War on Poverty) or merely engineering (man on the moon)—involved a commitment to spend, and to spend almost without limit. Such a deep-pockets strategy does not appear possible in the 1990s, with the real problems of public deficits and the perceived popular resistance to government taxation and expenditure.

The second difficulty with the accumulation of problems is more political and perceptual, although it is linked with the cultural changes associated with retrenchment. Few politicians want to be associated with failures, and especially with expensive failures; blame avoidance may be a preferable option to the possibility of credit claiming (Weaver 1986). In this retrenchment period politicians are presented with opportunities that are primarily very risky, with a real possibility or even probability of failure. Government does not have a ready methodology for attacking most of these problems, or even a very well-accepted definition of what the problem really is. The problems being faced are definitely ghetto-type ones, to use Nelson's "moon and the ghetto" analogy (1977), for which there are no ready engineering solutions. Nelson argued that getting to the moon was easier than solving social problems in the ghetto because there was an accepted technology for space travel but not for social policy. Thus if leadership is to be built on success, the current possibilities of success are limited. So too is the likelihood of democratic political systems to push forward people with bold visions about the future who are willing to stake their careers and their futures on attacking "wicked" problems.

Conclusion: All Dressed Up and Nowhere to Go

This analysis leads to a somewhat paradoxical, but even more a depressing, conclusion about the prospects for executive leadership in an age of retrenchment in Western democracies. If we are conceptualizing leadership as a significant addition to what might have been accomplished without a leader's intervention, this is especially true. On the one hand it appears that executive leaders (meaning here primarily political leaders) have been blessed with a range of new leadership tools and possibilities. Some of the institutional politics of the 1980s was about reducing the role of the career civil service and giving political executives greater capacity. While most of the roadblocks to political leaders' power that have been cataloged in the past remain, they are somewhat diminished. Further, when necessary, political leaders have developed new mechanisms for circumventing or surmounting the barriers to policy change that the institutions they manage may have presented. In fairness, of course, another reaction to retrenchment has been to push so much of government out to third-party institutions and quasi-governmental organizations that some control over programs is lost, although at the gain of lower costs and less apparent public responsibility. Even with that caveat, however, one consequence of the age of retrenchment is that executive leaders have a diminished capacity to lead.

In what direction is leadership to go? The direction of government is less certain at the end of this age of retrenchment. One might argue that political ideas have been exhausted, except for ideas about what tasks need *not* be done in government. While some ideas about minimizing the role of government are creative, and may require some leadership to bring to fruition, at a broader level politics does seem to lack new policy directions. This lack appears to be in direct proportion to the number of times that the need for new policy ideas is mentioned in political campaigns—usually by someone who claims to have them.

The prevalence of the theme of new ideas and new policies in political campaigns highlights some of the paradox mentioned earlier. Citizens appear to want government to do something positive for them, but they are very wary (and weary?) of the costs and the possible failures that this could involve. How can the political system cope with these seemingly contradictory demands? A simple answer is to argue for greater leadership, but a leadership that shapes ideas rather than merely reacts to them. As Theodore Lowi has argued for years, policies shape politics, and perhaps a new style of politics to cope with the new policy demands must be developed (1972). Jimmy Carter, rather than Ronald Reagan, may be the wave of the future. That is, executive leadership may have to be more technocratic (and bureaucratic) and less photogenic if it is to be successful.

Another answer, somewhat more complex, might be that those in government need to recapture a bit of the hubris of old. This would not mean relying on the rational, analytic methods of the 1960s to provide solutions, but at least relying on analytic methods to understand their own actions. Any such analysis should focus as much on the instruments of intervention as on a simple question of whether to intervene or not. Such analyses can be performed in many ways, some of which may provoke reactions against government and others of which may not. This has been well demonstrated for tax policies and will probably be true in other policy areas as well. Returning to William Gormley's ideas about institutional policy analysis, the need may be for less coercive and more catalytic controls, and toward very subtle manipulations of instruments already in place. This may not be the stuff of great political drama, but it may be the stuff of successful executive leadership in an era of ongoing retrenchment and political skepticism.

Again, in Western Europe the technocratic and incremental elements may be especially important for coping with the changes brought about by the European Community. Much of the progress of the EC, in terms of its gaining power in policy, has been the result of just those sorts of strategies and forces. Thus if national political leaders are to be successful either in maintaining their own powers or in getting the best deal they can for their own countries, they may have to play a different political game than they might when dealing only with domestic interest groups and parties. Although it is easy to make sweeping statements that the nature of politics may have changed, there is some evidence that the upcoming decades will place changing demands on leaders. The period of the effective, personalized political executive with ideology and conviction may have been a very short-lived and transitional era.

Notes

1. As indicated by Table 1.3, economic growth has returned to most of the industrialized world. It is not so great as in the pre-1973 days, but it is real and rather steady. What may be different is how the economy is perceived and what confidence there is in government to manage the economy and use its resources wisely.

2. Privatization may limit the possibilities of deregulation. For example, privatizing such firms as British Telecom has required the development of the Office of Telecommunications to regulate the rates and operation of the new private firms.

3. The ability to shed responsibility is, as ever, especially valuable if the politician can shed responsibility for failures. Blame avoidance is as much, or more, valuable than credit claiming in the politics of most contemporary political systems (Weaver 1986).

4. Although the argument could not be forced too far, there does appear to be some relationship between corporate structures for participation and the rate of economic growth in industrialized countries. Before the oil crisis, that relationship appears to have been positive; but in the years after the oil crisis, it appears to have become negative. Such an appearance is much too preliminary to make much over, but it is suggestive.

5. We are using "large-scale" to describe problems very much as Schulman (1980) did: a large-scale problem is one with relatively indivisible outcomes that must be addressed with comprehensive solutions. The NASA program to get a man to the moon is a classic example. It was no good to get the astronaut halfway, or even 99 percent of the way to the moon; it was all or nothing. Therefore, a government undertaking of sufficient magnitude was required to ensure that the goal could be attained.

Chapter

8

WHAT FUTURE FOR THE WELFARE STATE?

The development of the welfare state has been one of the great triumphs of government in Western Europe. In the eyes of many observers, however, the welfare state has now become the victim of its own successes. While the welfare programs were once a major source of comfort and security for citizens, and a mechanism for legitimating the state in the face of many potentially destabilizing forces, the viability of this form of state structure is now questioned, and it faces numerous challenges. This chapter will describe the political and economic sources of the European welfare state, what services it currently produces, and what emerging challenges may fundamentally alter its character during the late twentieth century.

The last portion of the analysis is largely speculative, as many of the changes to be described have yet to occur. The analysis is, however, also realistic because many of the socioeconomic forces that will motivate political and policy changes are already in operation and are very real. Some of those impending forces, such as the changing demographic structure of most European countries, will be almost impossible for governments to avert. This discussion will not be apocalyptic, and no one should expect modern European government to return to the nightwatchman state of the nineteenth century. On the other hand, however, "If things are to stay the same, something has to change."[1]

Before we embark on our analysis of the contemporary welfare state, we should be clear about what the term means. We will be referring primarily to the system of social benefits provided by governments in Western Europe. Unlike "welfare" in the United States, however, the programs of the European welfare state are largely universal benefits available to all citizens, or at least to all citizens (and their families) who have contributed to social insurance programs. These universalistic programs have supplanted means-tested benefits that require an individual to prove need before becoming eligible. Most welfare-state programs are entitlements for citizens and are received (or potentially received) by all citizens. Hence, there is not the degree of stigma attached to receiving these social benefits that there has been to receiving "welfare" (Aid to Families with Dependent Children) in the United States. Means-tested benefits have not been eliminated entirely, however, and continuing unemployment for many former industrial workers in rapidly changing economies has forced more people onto programs more like American "welfare."

Most of the programs of the welfare state are insurance programs. Like Social Security in the United States, to be eligible for any benefits the citizen, and/or his or her employer, must have contributed to the insurance funds that finance the largest portion of the benefits. If an individual is unemployed, unemployment compensation (itself a form of social insurance in most countries) will continue payments to other (especially health) social insurance programs. This permits the unemployed worker and his or her family to remain eligible for other important programs. Since citizens pay insurance premiums (actually obligatory taxes) to finance the programs, they become thought of as a right to an even greater extent than other public programs might be. The insurance basis, along with their universality, makes the programs less stigmatizing than means-tested programs.

Although the exact nature of the social program packages available to citizens varies across countries, they do have a number of common elements. The most widely available and expensive single programs are pensions, designed to provide the insured individual with an income in retirement, or support for the survivors of a worker who dies prior to retirement. While the amount received from a public pension is rarely if ever sufficient for the life-style of a *bon vivant,* a public pension usually does provide a *basic* living for a retiree. Further, in addition to their basic pension schemes, a number of European countries have developed supplementary, earnings-related pensions. These programs enable participants with a higher income during their working lifetime to accumulate sufficient resources for a more comfortable life in retirement.

In addition to being protected against poverty in old age, workers in most countries are also protected against loss of earnings during the normal working years. These protections include industrial accidents insurance, sickness insurance, disability insurance, unemployment insurance, and paid maternity leaves (in some countries for the mother or father). Thus if the worker is not able for almost any reason to earn a living, there will be an income for him or her and the family. Family allowances are available if there are children in a family, whether the parents are working or not, usually based on the number of children below a certain age. These benefits, which go to all families with children, regardless of their earned incomes, are intended to enable the family to cope better with the costs of raising those children. Again, this will not pay for all costs but it does make family life easier. Also, public health insurance or, in the United Kingdom, the National Health Service provides full medical care for families. Most health insurance programs do, however, charge a fee (sometimes as little as the equivalent of a dollar or less) for each visit to the doctor. This is in part to deter needless visits and in part to pay for the costs of care. With all these benefits, plus other minor ones such as death benefits, the average Western European citizen is well protected against the vicissitudes of life and the capitalist market. To these benefits should be added government-financed education, enabling children to receive as much education as they require and can absorb without having to worry about the expense. As with health care, there may be some modest fees at the university level, but rarely enough to deter any student who wants an education.

Although generally referred to as the "welfare state," it may be more appropriate to refer to the political economy of contemporary Western Europe as the "mixed-economy welfare state." Along with providing social insurance and other social benefits, a significant portion of government activity has been devoted to making the free market function more predictably and more humanely (Shonfield 1965). Some of this government activity has been directed toward smoothing the business cycle that has at times shattered the economic prospects of individuals and nations alike, a goal largely achieved from the 1950s onward. Governments have had less success in managing the economy since the mid-1970s, but compared to many historical periods of recession and depression, even the post-1973 economic world has been very benign. By maintaining effective demand in the market with payments to the unemployed and retired, the social insurance programs have made a major contribution to smoothing the business cycle (Albeda 1986) and should be considered as automatic economic stabilizers. Another focus of government activity in the mixed economy has been on economic regulation and consumer protection—concerning prices, quality, and safety—so that individuals could enter the marketplace with some assurance about the quality and safety of what they were buying. Although certainly public ownership is more widespread in Europe than in the United States, most of the economic goals of a mixed economy—low unemployment, relatively stable prices, economic growth—have been attainable without large-scale nationalization of industry. While most West European countries may have social economies, they do not have socialist economies.

The Origins and Development of the Welfare State

Selecting the starting point for the welfare state is difficult, as it actually has several roots and several intellectual points of departure. Usually Germany in the 1880s (Kohler and Zacher 1982) is cited. Before then, however, some form of relief for the poor was found in almost all countries. Such relief was, however, a last resort for most people, no matter how poor they may have been. It required proof of indigence, usually loss of civil rights, and perhaps even virtual imprisonment in a workhouse. The first major programs of social insurance, in contrast to poor relief, were sickness insurance, followed closely by industrial accidents insurance (see Table 8.1). Both programs compensated the worker if he or she could not work because of illness or work-related accidents. These insurance programs were begun in Germany in 1883 and 1884 respectively, under the leadership of Otto von Bismarck. While that conservative regime may seem unlikely to have initiated major social reforms, the reforms were not undertaken simply to improve the lot of the working man; social control and the foreclosure of potential socialist political mobilization were much more important factors.

For whatever reasons, however, these two social insurance programs were adopted in Germany, and they became models for similar programs that were to spread around Western Europe (see Table 8.1; Flora and Alber 1981; Heclo 1974). Although at times implemented for reasons of social justice, other countries often adopted industrial accidents insurance (and other forms of social insurance) with an eye to some of the same political pressures that were facing Bismarck. The revolution in the Soviet Union in 1916–17, for example, spurred several northern European countries to adopt social insurance programs. These programs were frequently conceptualized as mechanisms for co-opting the working classes and legitimating the existing regimes. Groups interested in social justice and social reform supported the programs, but more pragmatic considerations frequently dominated government decisions.

Although the history of each country varied, the most common pattern was for sickness and industrial accidents insurance to be adopted first.

TABLE 8.1

Timing of Welfare-State Program Initiations

	Industrial Accidents	Sickness Insurance	Pensions	Health Insurance	Unemployment Insurance
Austria	1887	1888	1906	1888	1920
Belgium	1903	1894	1900	1894	1907
Denmark	1898	1892	1900	1892	1907
Finland	1895	1963	1937	1963	1917
France	1898	1930	1910	1898	1914
W. Germany	1884	1883	1889	1883	1927
Italy	1898	1886	1898	1928	1919
Netherlands	1901	1913	1913	1929	1916
Norway	1894	1909	1936	1909	1906
Sweden	1901	1891	1913	1891	1934
Switzerland	1911	1911	1946	1911	1924
United Kingdom	1906	1911	1908	1911	1920

SOURCE: Based on data from P. Flora and J. Alber, "Modernization, Democratization and the Development of Welfare States in Western Europe," in *The Development of Welfare States in Europe and North America*, ed. P. Flora and A. Heidenheimer (New Brunswick, NJ: Transaction, 1981), and P. Flora et al., *State, Economy, and Society in Western Europe, 1815–1975: A Data Handbook* (Frankfurt: Campus, 1983).

These programs provided benefits if a employee could not work because of illness or an accident at the workplace. These forms of insurance were followed by old-age pensions, beginning again in Germany, in 1889.[2] Although major innovations at the time, these forms of social insurance did not produce a large conservative reaction, in part because they were not perceived as tampering excessively with the need of workers actually to work. Industrial accidents insurance in particular was acceptable to most conservatives because it merely provided a public means of compensation for employers' long-standing potential liability for accidents at work (Flora and Alber 1981, 53). Likewise, eligibility for sickness and accident insurance required certification by a physician,[3] so that malingering was not expected to be a problem. As for public pensions, if someone lived to age sixty-five at around the end of the nineteenth century, it was unlikely that he or she could be a very productive worker anyway (life expectancy in Germany at the time the old-age pensions were adopted was substantially less than sixty-five for males). Unemployment insurance, which was seen as potentially damaging to the incentive to work, was not introduced until much later; the first compulsory program not introduced until 1911 in the

United Kingdom. Many countries did not adopt unemployment insurance until the time of the Great Depression.

To this point we have been discussing the introduction of *compulsory* social insurance, designed primarily for the working classes. Voluntary programs had begun earlier, in some cases as early as the guilds during the Middle Ages. The existence of voluntary programs was at once an alternative source of initiation for government programs and a barrier to those programs. Sometimes a public program grew out of the private, voluntary one, but more often the private program blocked a public one. Not only could any conservative opponents claim that the problem was being addressed, but also those who ran the private funds did not want their program to be superseded by a government program. The Friendly Societies in the United Kingdom (Furniss and Tilton 1977, 103), organizations of workers founded originally for burial insurance but that later branched out to provide other forms of social insurance, were especially reluctant to give up their functions to the public sector. Government programs never fully supplanted private programs, which have again become a major element of social protection as uncertainty about the solvency and generosity of government programs increases (O'Higgins 1986b; Rein and Rainwater 1986). Further, to some extent the public sector continues to depend on the private sector to fill in any gaps that may be left in public programs.

Health insurance and other health services provided through the public sector have had a varied history in the West European countries, in part because of the differential power and prestige of the medical profession. Some countries, such as Sweden, began some form of public medical services as early as the mid-eighteenth century, although health insurance as we now know it did not develop there until later. In other countries, public health insurance, or in the case of the United Kingdom direct provision of health services,[4] was not initiated until after World War II. In almost all nations, however, some form of indigent health care developed very early. This medical care was frequently of extremely poor quality and also was associated with all the deprivations and stigmatization of receiving poor relief. Public provision of treatment was often also available for certain dread infectious diseases, such as tuberculosis.

Although health insurance is the primary mode of public intervention in health care, some programs besides Britain's National Health Service, which is the only comprehensive public system for health service delivery in Western Europe, directly provide medical care. In most countries, private physicians who treat their own patients and then bill the public health insurance system for most of the costs serve as the general practitioner component of medical care. In a number of countries, however, the government directly provides hospitals and other more specialized care. So, for example, in Sweden the major activity of the twenty-four county *(lansting)* governments is hospital management (Carder and Kongeberg 1980). The hospital sector is organized on a similar basis in Denmark, while in most other countries it is partly public and partly private. Thus the health care sector is one area of the welfare state—along with education—that involves large numbers of public employees as well as significant public expenditures (Rose et al. 1985), although those employees may be technically the employees of quasi-governmental authorities.

Finally, although it is sometimes excluded from a discussion of the welfare state, some mention should be made of government housing programs for low- and middle-income families. These programs were initiated somewhat later than most of the social insurance programs, and many housing programs did not expand significantly until the end of World War I, or even World War II. Yet housing programs are a major component of the welfare state. Either by providing better living accommodations than could be obtained through the private market, or by providing a decent house at a lower price and thereby freeing family resources to be used for other purposes, they do improve the living conditions of poor families. Governments have utilized a number of policy instruments to intervene in the housing market, although over time most programs have gravitated away from direct construction of public housing (with the United Kingdom until the Thatcher government the exception). Instead, a variety of rent or mortgage supplements, low-interest loans to builders of low-rent housing, and assistance to housing cooperatives have been used (Headey 1978; Roistacher 1987). In addition to direct government subsidization of housing, subsidies through the tax system have been more important here than in other social policy areas, although the subsidies have benefited the middle class substantially more than less affluent citizens. As well as supplying housing, these programs also provide a great deal of private employment in the construction industry, and therefore receive support from directions that might not have been anticipated.

After the pioneering social insurance programs just described were adopted, the welfare state as we have come to know it developed during the late nineteenth and the twentieth centuries. These developments have taken place in several ways, and for a variety of reasons. One of the principal forces involved in the expansion of the welfare state was diffusion (Collier and Messick 1975). After a program is adopted and works successfully in one country, other countries may want to imitate it. The idea may spread through experts in the public bureaucracy who are interested in the policy area (Heclo 1974), or through labor unions and socialist parties with international contacts, or through more specialized social reform organizations. Once in operation, a successful social program has a powerful appeal for other countries. This was especially true among countries with some geographical proximity and cultural affinity, as in the countries of northern Europe.

Wars, depressions, and other crises also have been a source of social program expansion. The most obvious case was the British government's formation of the Beveridge Commission during World War II. A bargain was made, almost explicitly, between the government and the public that if they endured the hardships of the war, they would be rewarded with a better Britain. That better Britain was to include a fully developed welfare state. It has also been argued that the end of a major war creates slack tax resources that, no longer needed for defense, can then be put to use for social purposes (Peacock and Wiseman 1967). In addition to wars, the hardships of the Great Depression and mass unemployment provoked a social policy response of some sort in almost all European countries, as well as a lessened resistance to paying taxes to fund those programs.

Another factor in the expansion of the welfare state has been the extension and elaboration of existing programs. Within a single country, there has been a tendency to expand programs beyond their original target populations—usually the working classes or the poor—to make them universal. Again, this expansion may occur for a variety of reasons. One is that once a program has demonstrated that it can work for one segment of the population, other segments will demand it. As usually the more politically influential middle classes were excluded initially, their subsequent demands are likely to be effective. In addition, programs may be extended to remove any remaining stigma from receiving the benefits. Finally, the programs may be extended by bureaucratic organizations that want to expand their own power base in budgetary politics, or by other social policy organizations that want to expand the tax base that pays for the programs. For whatever reasons, once begun, social programs have a tendency to become universal rapidly.

To this all-too-brief introduction to the formation and early history of the welfare state in Western Europe we must add several important background features of the complex array of programs. The first is that this development was not a coherent and integrated set of planned events, but rather a sequence of incremental additions of programs across decades. The complexity and the multiplicity of welfare-state programs have been a source of concern to program critics and also to advocates seeking to provide comprehensive services to citizens. Despite some commonalities, every country has a different welfare state and a different welfare-state history (Flora 1986a, 1986b). One important commonality in the development of the programs has been the movement away from means-tested benefits to universal programs based on insurance principles. The welfare state has become a right of all citizens, as long as they (or someone in their family) have made the requisite contributions.

Finally, although less obvious than the first points, social insurance programs are not really radical redistributive programs. They tend to extract tax money from all economic classes and return benefits to all classes.[5] What most programs do is to smooth the flow of income across a person's lifetime. If age, accidents, or infirmity diminish an insured person's ability to earn an income, the social insurance system minimizes the economic impact of that change in the person's life. Insurance does not guarantee the same income as when working but tries to provide something approaching a living income based on family needs. In addition to social insurance, all countries have retained some means-tested benefits for people who might otherwise not be eligible for any assistance, and in those cases the impact clearly is redistributive. Some changes in the distribution of income do occur when governments operate (see Table 8.1; OECD, annual), but the welfare state tends to build floors below which people cannot fall, rather than to build ceilings above which they cannot rise.

The Recent History of the Welfare State

Most major programs of the European welfare state developed during the period from about 1885 to 1950, with the major spurts of activity occurring during the periods following both world wars. During these decades in almost all European countries, the major forms of social insurance just described were adopted and extended to cover virtually the entire population. Western European countries entered the period of postwar affluence and rapid economic growth with a social safety net protecting their citizens already in place. Although this safety net included a substantial basic system of benefits, there were still political pressures for improving it, and hence there were changes in the welfare state at a time when low unemployment and high economic growth made it appear less relevant to many citizens. Jobs were plentiful and income was rising rapidly, but some people—mainly in the civil service—continued to press ahead with new social policy ideas and plans for new programs. This was in many ways the best time to press for such an expansion. Economic growth appeared limitless, and the costs of new programs could be paid easily—it was then thought—by new resources produced through economic growth. If the same program expansion had been attempted after the mid-1970s, it is extremely unlikely that it could have been successful.

Earnings-Related Benefits

One very important social policy question was what to do about different earnings during a person's lifetime and whether there should be differential pensions when workers retired. After the welfare state was made comprehensive, its programs provided benefits for everyone from the very bottom of the income ladder to the very top. This variation produced political pressures for making retirement pension earnings related. This was less of an issue for other programs because most already paid a percentage of income, while many public pensions paid a flat rate or had very modest differences based on levels of contribution.

There were good arguments on both sides of earnings-related benefits issue. On the one hand, it could be argued that government should be in the business only of providing basic social benefits for all citizens; if someone wanted more he or she could provide for that privately. As it was primarily the middle-class members of the insurance systems who wanted differential benefits, they would be in a good position to supplement the basic retirement benefits provided by government. On the other hand, however, fairness could also argue that those who pay more into the system, since contributions were earnings related even if benefits were not,[6] should receive more benefits back when they retired. Further, if the idea of the public pension was to provide for retirement, those who have earned more during their working lifetime would have different expectations about their life in retirement than would lower-paid employees. Few argued that the differences among pensions should be directly related to contributions, but there was a rather widespread feeling that some differentials could be justified. Finally, as societies became more affluent, the supplemental pensions issue affected more people, so that some earnings-related system may have been necessary to maintain political support for the welfare-state system.

The question of earnings-related benefits became a heated political issue in many countries during the 1960s and 1970s (Kuhnle and Solheim 1981; Molin 1965; Schneider and Peters 1989). Not only were there issues of justice and political power involved, but there were very real fiscal issues as well. If public pensions suddenly were made earnings related, a short-term drain on the insurance funds might result. Although European social insurance programs did receive revenues from sources other than earmarked payroll taxes (unlike the United States), there was a sense of separate fund accounting and also that the system could be "bankrupted" by a decision to increase pension benefits overnight for higher-income earners. The solution that most countries hit on was a separate state-sponsored system of earnings-related pensions on top of the state basic pension. Membership in the earnings-related system was voluntary in some countries and compulsory in others. In most instances these systems were closer to being actuarially sound (benefits would equal payments into the system plus interest) than the basic pension programs and would not "mature" until participants had been contributing for a number of years. Hence there would be no immediate drain on the public purse.

Indexing

Another issue about the welfare state that also had justice as well as fiscal questions attached to it was relating benefits to changes in the economy. If there is no economic change (particularly inflation), then the level of benefits that an individual receives upon retirement should be adequate for the remainder of the retirement. Economic change is, however, almost certain, and therefore governments had to develop some means of relating social benefits to those changes. One way would be for government to decide periodically to adjust benefits, when and if it believes an adjustment is necessary. While such changes would certainly satisfy any demands for a democratic solution, they would have several possible negative side effects. One is that an incumbent government could use social benefits as a campaign weapon by providing generous benefit increases just before an election. Or, conversely, a government might find it expedient to cope with its own financial problems by keeping social benefits lower than they should otherwise be for recipients' well-being. In either case, the welfare state would become a political pawn, rather than the more objective system of well-being that its advocates believed it to be.

An alternative mechanism for coping with economic change is to adjust the levels of benefits automatically (Weaver 1988), a process called *indexation*. The adjustment of benefits is usually related to the level of prices in the economy, so that beneficiaries do not lose any purchasing power during inflation; most countries do not have provisions for reducing benefits if there is deflation. Some countries also have decided to index benefits to reflect changes in the level of wages, so that if there is economic growth pensioners and other social beneficiaries are able to share in that as well. With this automatic system of adjustment, beneficiaries of social programs are guaranteed that their purchasing power will not be reduced through inflation and that it may even increase with economic growth. Further, the temptation for politicians to raid the treasury to attempt to win reelection is largely eliminated. For those reasons, indexation has become a common feature of public social programs, and one that has been protected vigorously if an incumbent government attempts to save money by tampering with it. During the early 1980s, a West German government attempted to delay indexing pensions by six months, but rescinded the order within a few days after a huge political furor arose.

The only real problem with indexation is that it can be expensive, especially if it must take both price and wage increases into account ("double indexing") and they are both increasing. Although potentially expensive in real terms, when most countries adopted indexation its relative costs were not perceived as being very great, because tax revenues went up as rapidly or even more rapidly (due to the progressive rate structure) as did the cost of benefits. Many conservative governments that came to power in the 1980s changed policy to index taxes as well as benefits, so that tax rates and the threshold of rate changes are adjusted annually for inflation. As governments no longer receive more real revenues from inflation, they may have to strain to maintain their social payment commitments, especially if benefits are double-indexed.

New and Expanded Benefits

One of the age-old questions of politics is "What have you done for me *recently?*" This question appeared to arise in reference to the welfare state during the 1960s and into the 1970s. The basic structure of the major welfare-state programs was laid years, or even decades, previously. Thus those programs appeared stable and not particularly interesting, especially during a period of affluence when unemployment or other hardships appeared unlikely threats to most workers. It was difficult for politicians to gain any advantage simply by continuing programs that had become so much a part of the social and economic life of West European countries. These programs had become entitlements, as much a part of citizenship in a country as the right to vote or the right to be treated equally in a court of law.

Politicians who wanted to use the welfare-state programs as the focus of their activities and as the basis for a career faced at least two problems. The first is, again, the simple problem of the costs. As the postwar period of affluence began to wane following successive oil crises in the 1970s, programs that cost more money became suspect. Many in government came to feel that in order to do something new, something old would have to be terminated, and little or nothing in the domain of social programs was a ready candidate for termination. As the "scrap and build" ethic became institutionalized in government, and as the prevailing ideology came to question government action generally, promoting new programs became a difficult if not impossible political exercise.

The second problem was what to do. The major targets of government activity had already been attacked, and the easy changes had already been made. The tasks remaining required government to become involved in very difficult social problems for which there was no ready solution. As in Nelson's analogy of the "moon and the ghetto" (1977) cited earlier, putting a man on the moon was a simple engineering problem, while solving the problems of the ghetto required a technology that did not exist. Much the same could be said of the differences between the old and the new social policy problems. At one level, caring for the elderly was relatively simple: give them pensions and cheap housing. Trying to make the lives of the elderly meaningful and enjoyable, however, involved extremely difficult social, cultural, and economic changes. The disintegrating family structure, the perpetuation of poverty in the midst of affluence, substance abuse, homelessness, and many of the other problems of modern society could not be solved so easily as were the original problems of the welfare state. To involve government in those types of policy problems was almost certainly to condemn it to failure, and failure was something with which few politicians wanted to be involved (Weaver 1986).

One sure thing that a politician could do was to expand the real value of the benefits being offered. This strategy, of course, could encounter opposition on financial grounds. Further, it appears to violate the principle of indexing as a means of automatic adjustment of benefits. Yet in many countries—especially the Scandinavian ones (Johansen and Kolberg 1985), but also elsewhere—the real (adjusted for inflation) value of basic social benefits has tended to increase. Table 8.2 provides some idea of the increases that have been occurring. While program enhancement is not as exciting politically as developing whole new programs, it is a strategy that allows politicians to say that they are indeed producing some social benefits for their constituents.

In summary, in the postwar period the European welfare state has been faced with new political and financial questions. Most of these questions were concerned with the extension of the basic set of programs, either by adding new programs or making the existing ones more generous. Until the economic downturns in the 1970s, such expansion was perfectly possible and appeared the only right thing to do. Economic growth in the 1960s and early 1970s still appeared assured, and any program enhancements could be paid for out of the fiscal dividend of economic growth (Rose and Peters 1978). As was pointed out in Chapter 4, questions of justice and equality came to be considered more important than economic restraints in the "postmaterialist" era. These extensions and enhancements of benefit programs, as well as changes in the underlying nature of welfare-state programs themselves, created some real financial difficulties for governments in the 1980s. As important as the financial problems are, however, they may be more soluble than the other challenges to the welfare state.

The Welfare State in Crisis

In the late 1970s and into the 1980s it became fashionable to discuss the "crisis" that was confronting government (Abel-Smith 1985; Douglas 1989; OECD 1981). That crisis was conceptualized in a number of ways, but the discussion revolved around some very fundamental changes that had been occurring in industrialized societies and the need of government to adjust to those changes. Such words as "governability" (Crozier, Hunt-

TABLE 8.2

Changing Real Value of Social Benefits (1970 = 100)

| | United Kingdom | |
	Pension	Unemployment
1970	100	100
1974	103	105
1976	105	108
1978	107	104
1980	110	100
1982	117	99
1984	116	103
1986	116	104

| | Scandinavia | | | | | |
| | Denmark | | Norway | | Sweden | |
	Old Age	Disability	Old Age	Disability	Old Age	Disability
1970	100	100	100	100	100	100
1975	107	106	101	105	134	147
1980	111	103	130	118	167	185
1985	116	106	141	129	170	196

SOURCE: Central Statistical Office, *Social Trends* (London: HMSO, annual); L. N. Johansen and J. E. Kolberg, *Welfare State and Its Aftermath*, ed. S. N. Eisenstadt and O. Ahimein (Totowa, NJ: Barnes and Noble, 1985).

ington, and Watanuki 1975; Rose 1974), "unmanageability" (Scharpf 1977), and "overload" (King 1975) became very common in the discussion of the welfare state and the governments of advanced industrial societies more generally. While the word crisis implies a sharp and decisive point of decision, the reality for most welfare states has been a long, grinding series of adjustments. Nothing really has been solved in any final sense about the nature of the public sector since the first oil crisis in 1973. There have been more or less stable resolutions about government in different countries, but those are still subject to change and reinterpretation. The United Kingdom, for example, has probably made the sharpest break with its immediate past (Gamble 1988), but even Sweden has been forced to reconsider its welfare-state programs. On the other hand, countries such as West Germany, Denmark, and Belgium appear to have adjusted very little to the new realities (Marsh 1987) and have maintained all or most of their social and economic policy structures. All these governments and their citizens have been facing a long series of decisions and adjustments rather than a sharp, definitive crisis.

The resolution of welfare-state issues has been delayed to some extent because of the continuing large-scale structural changes in the economies of European countries and the need to relate social programs to the social problems generated by those changes. The welfare state was originally developed to provide a safety net for workers in the capitalist economy, and that protection is still necessary. But the economic system has become very different from the one upon which the welfare state was premised, if for no other reason than that the internationalization of markets has placed effective economic management beyond the certain reach of most governments. For many individuals, economic change has meant that the nature of their employment is now very different. For blue-collar workers employment is not as certain as it was, as likely to be in manufacturing industries, or likely to be as lucrative as it once was. Likewise, the welfare state was designed to protect families, but family structure has changed so much that the protections that were successful in the past must be reexamined. Government attempts to adjust social programs to the changing economy and the changing society have involved trying to hit a moving target, and further to hit a target that is moving increasingly beyond its control. These have not been the happiest times for politicians called upon to govern their societies.

Financial Problems

The most obvious problems facing the welfare state are financial. Newspapers and journals of opinion have been filled with discussions of the costs of welfare-state programs, the possibilities of "bankruptcy," and feasible and infeasible solutions to government's financial problems. The fiscal problems of the welfare state are also in many ways the easiest to solve—all they require for solution is more money. That sounds simple, but it disguises a somewhat more complex reality. Therefore it is important to understand the nature and extent of public expenditures for social programs, and the dynamics that result in their steady, and seemingly inevitable, increases in all European countries.

Tables 8.3 and 8.4 display data about the development of social welfare expenditures in the European countries from 1960 to 1985, with projections through 1990. These data demonstrate very clearly several pertinent facts about social expenditures. The first is that social expenditures have been increasing rapidly, both in absolute terms and as a percentage of total public expenditure. Although governments in the 1980s, for ideological and financial reasons, attempted to contain their level of social spending, social expenditures continued to increase almost as rapidly (or in some cases even more rapidly) as they did during the 1960s and early 1970s. The welfare state is simply a very big "business," and it is one that any government will find very difficult to control effectively. Governments adopted insurance principles very early and created enduring entitlements to citizens who have made their contributions. Subsequently they have found it difficult to reduce, or even slow, the growth of expenditures.

The other major fact that these tables point out is that, although almost all European countries (Britain is something of an exception) spend a great deal of money for social welfare purposes, significant differences do exist among them. At one end of the scale, the Low Countries, the Scandinavian countries, and several continental powers have extremely large social expenditures, accounting for over 70 percent of all public expenditures in some. At the other end of the spectrum are Greece and the United Kingdom. These countries have rather low levels of social expenditures—lower than even the United States, which is usually cited as a "welfare-state laggard" (Wilensky 1975). The southern European countries such as Greece have not been as wealthy as the other European countries and have had fewer available resources to devote to social expenditures. Their rapid economic development, combined with their entry into the European Community and pressures to conform to Community standards, is producing very rapid expansions in their social services, and equally rapid increases in their costs.

The financial problems of the welfare state have been related to some extent to slowed economic growth, but some critics attribute that slowed growth to increased government expenditure. Conservatives, and some

TABLE 8.3
Social Welfare Expenditures, 1960–85
(as percentage of total government expenditure)

	Including Education			
	1960	1970	1980	1985
Austria	NA	56.5	57.4	61.7
Belgium	57.2	68.2	72.8	73.0
Denmark	NA	63.3	61.9	64.0
Finland	58.2	63.9	66.4	67.9
France	NA	NA	60.5	62.5
Germany	65.3	63.2	66.0	68.1
Greece	36.2	38.8	40.0	51.1
Ireland	36.4	45.0	52.3	56.7
Italy	56.4	64.2	64.2	60.4
Netherlands	54.2	71.7	62.4	64.4
Norway	44.3	55.0	55.8	57.3
Sweden	49.3	52.9	53.2	56.7
Switzerland	NA	59.3	65.7[a]	66.2
United Kingdom	41.9	48.9	49.8	48.6

	Without Education			
	1960	1970	1980	1985
Austria	NA	49.5	49.4	52.7
Belgium	42.7	56.0	57.6	58.1
Denmark	NA	46.2	47.7	55.2
Finland	33.4	43.6	50.3	49.5
France	39.7	43.2	48.1	55.6
Germany	57.7	52.4	55.0	57.1
Greece	29.3	32.1	32.9	41.5
Ireland	27.1	31.4	39.1	42.3
Italy	43.9	50.8	50.9	47.3
Netherlands	39.1	46.3	49.7	49.6
Norway	29.7	39.4	43.0	42.7
Sweden	34.6	38.6	43.0	44.8
Switzerland	NA	39.8	46.6[a]	48.4
United Kingdom	30.9	34.9	37.2	35.4

SOURCE: Based on data from the Organization for Economic Cooperation and Development, *National Accounts of OECD Member Countries* (Paris: OECD, annual); OECD, *Social Expenditure 1960–1990: Problems of Growth and Control* (Paris: OECD: 1985); plus national sources.

[a] 1978.

analysts who are not so conservative, argue that by high levels of taxing and spending governments remove incentives for hard work for individuals and remove incentives for investments from businesses (Saunders and Klau 1985). They argue that government programs are a "leaky bucket" to carry money to the poor and that more positive change could be achieved by more rapid economic growth (see Korpi 1985; Okun 1975). The evidence on the impact of public expenditures on economic growth is extremely contradictory, but it cannot be linked conclusively with slow growth (Gilsdorf 1989). That absence of conclusive evidence does not, however, stop political argument or even political actions to reduce public expenditure.

DEMOGRAPHY. Several factors are driving the increases in social expenditures. Among the most important of these is demography. An aging population is expensive for the welfare states of Western Europe. In the first place, those over sixty-five are eligible for public pensions, which is the largest single program in terms of expense. In addition, the elderly consume proportionately more health care than do other segments of the population, so the costs of public health insurance programs also will increase. A few programs—unemployment and maternity benefits, for example—may experience declining costs, but those will be more than offset by costs in the two large programs of health and pensions. Further, on the revenue side of the equation, an aging population implies a smaller proportion of the population paying into social insurance funds—or perhaps

TABLE 8.4

Projected Increase of Social Expenditures
(as percentage of Gross Domestic Product), 1981–90[a]

Finland	4.8
France	27.7
W. Germany	0.0
Ireland	42.7
Italy	63.5
Netherlands	16.5
Norway	11.1
Sweden	6.6
United Kingdom	−8.5

SOURCE: Based on data from the Organization for Economic Cooperation and Development, *Social Expenditure 1960–1990: Problems of Growth and Control* (Paris: OECD, 1985).

[a] Based on same average real benefit increase as 1975 to 1981.

paying any taxes at all—and hence more problems in balancing the public budget.

We have already pointed out that the population of Western Europe has been aging and that a significant share of the population in all the countries is at or over retirement age. In some countries fully one person in five is over sixty-five and is therefore likely to be drawing a public pension. The demographic future for European countries will be even more expensive, as the proportion of the population of retirement age is projected to continue to increase for at least the next several decades (OECD 1988). Projections indicate that demographic changes will account for 50 percent of the increase in social program expenditures for the largest OECD countries and a larger share than that in most of the smaller ones (OECD, 1985). Further, not only is the proportion of the population over sixty-five increasing rapidly, but the proportion over eighty-five is increasing even more rapidly. This segment of the population is an extremely heavy consumer of medical services, and the increase in this age bracket will place even greater financial pressure on already rising medical costs.

In addition to the increased cost of benefits associated with demographic changes in Western Europe, there is also the revenue side to be considered. Benefits for retirees are paid largely out of the taxes paid by people who are still working. This is certainly true for the portion of social insurance expenditures financed directly from payroll taxes or contributions. This averages 85.5 percent in all European social security programs, although five countries finance social insurance entirely from payroll taxes. It is also largely true for general revenues such as the income tax that are used to top up the social insurance funds. At present, there are on average 4.6 people of working age in Western Europe for each person of retirement age. That figure varies from a low of 3.9 in Sweden to a high of 6.2 in Portugal. In all these countries, the number of workers supporting each retiree will continue to decrease; projections are that by 2000 there will be 4.2 workers, and by 2020 only 3.5 workers, per retiree. These demographics imply that—unless significant expenditure reductions can be made in other programs—taxes will have to increase. But the conservative regimes that have taken office in many Western European countries appear reluctant to increase taxes. This places their welfare state in something of an impasse.

RELATIVE PRICES. Although we will not become too technical in our discussion of the financial problems facing the welfare state, we should point out that just to stay even—in terms of services delivered—the costs of social service programs probably will have to increase. This phenomenon is called the "relative price effect," and it also affects other public programs

(Beck 1976). The problem is that most public programs are relatively labor intensive. As yet, there are no good mechanized means of providing social services, or of delivering the mail, or of policing. Certainly equipment such as computers do help to make these services more efficient, but most do not provide the return to capital investment that is found in most manufacturing industries. Even capital investments, such as CAT-scan equipment in hospitals, that have improved services may have *increased* prices rather than reduced them. Therefore, when wages are increasing—as they continue to do, although slowly in real (deflated) terms in Western Europe—the price of labor-intensive services such as those in government will increase relative to other prices. This, in turn, means that the costs of providing the same volume of government services will increase relative to other costs, and to stay even (in services provided) government will have to become bigger. The increasing power of public-sector unions relative to those in the private sector exacerbates this effect.

Although it is a technical problem, the relative price effect produces some very real consequences for governments. The Organization for Economic Cooperation and Development (OECD), an economics and social research organization for Western Europe, estimates that social expenditures in the largest European countries grew by an average of 0.7 percent of *Gross National Product* during the period from 1975 to 1981 just because of the relative price effect. OECD projects that this factor will continue to boost the costs of government social services by a similar percentage (OECD 1985). Providing government services is expensive and will continue to be increasingly so. Unfortunately for those managing national treasuries, many social services cannot be delivered any more cheaply. Furthermore, to attempt to do so would eliminate some of the value of those services; citizens value the personal touch in medicine and social welfare services even if those are the factors that may be driving up the costs, and the taxes. Further, the new social services that appear necessary for dealing with family problems, drug abuse, and the like may be even more labor intensive than existing programs.

PROGRAM CHANGES. Finally, welfare-state costs may increase because the programs are changed, or because the characteristics of the people eligible for them change (in addition to the demographic changes already mentioned). Even though the 1980s saw a number of conservative governments come to power, there were still some program enhancements. They occurred in part because social change and economic change have been taking place even under conservative governments. Whether through the actions of the public bureaucracy, or through the need of incumbent governments to ensure their electoral support, governments have responded to those changes. Many of the socioeconomic changes have affected family structure. Assisting families in coping with the increasingly common pattern of both adults in the family working at least part time has been a major impetus in social policy (Adams 1980; Moen 1989). Thus programs for maternal (and paternal) leaves, child care benefits, and the like have all been expanding. These family changes are likely to make residential care for the elderly even more in demand, as fewer families are able to care for their aging parents. These types of public intervention are very different from the social insurance programs that began the welfare state, but then family life and economic life are very different than they were a century ago as well.

Besides the quantitative enhancements in social programs, there have also been qualitative improvements in programs. Many have come in health care, as government programs have attempted to keep abreast of the advances in medical science and technology, all of which are expensive. Further, government programs increasingly have had to keep up with the competition arising from the private sector and the real or threatened privatization of medical services. Although less positive than the changes occurring in health care, unemployment insurance, job retraining, related benefits have had to be extended for longer periods as long-term unemployment has followed the economic slowing in many industries and the increasing international nature of economic life. Finally, citizens have become increasingly resentful of poor-quality services delivered by government and paradoxically have been demanding better public services at the same time that they have been demanding to pay lower taxes (Sears and Citrin 1982; Taylor-Gooby 1985).

SUMMARY. Despite widespread public concerns about the costs of government, and despite the widespread success of conservative politicians, the costs of the welfare state have continued to increase. Once the dynamic of insurance programs and other entitlement programs were placed in motion, controlling costs became very difficult without major (and probably unacceptable) political actions. Again, the reaction of much of the public to the welfare state is a paradox. On the one hand, most citizens consider its programs to be excessively expensive and the benefits to be perfectly acceptable for someone else but not for them or their families (Hadenius 1987; Taylor-Gooby 1985, 1986). On the other hand, any attempt to tamper with those programs would be, from both survey evidence and the limited evidence of governments that attempted even modest modifications, potentially very dangerous for a politician. As they are not in responsible offices, citizens do not have to reconcile these apparently contradictory stances; governments, however, do.

Management

In addition to the "mere" financial problems facing the mixed-economy, welfare state, there are substantial questions about its governance and its management. The social insurance systems of the larger industrialized countries handle volumes of money greater than the Gross National Product of some poorer countries. These huge economic institutions are not as easy to manage as organizations of similar size in the private sector might be. The goals of social policy organizations are not nearly as clear as those for a business; there is no criterion, such as profit, to determine effectiveness. In addition, the legal rules—both for the distribution of benefits and the management of personnel—that surround a public organization tend to slow its operations. Further, demands for participation, from employees and clients alike, have rendered decision making in social policy organizations very difficult and ponderous. Many citizens look to such organizations to provide crucial benefits, but when they look they often see apparent waste, inefficiency, and bureaucracy.

Not only conservatives complain about the bureaucratization of the welfare state. For many citizens and analysts on the political Left the bureaucratization of the system is as maddening as it is to those on the Right, although for different reasons. While those on the Right may see waste and inefficiency in public organizations and think the market could deliver the services more efficiently, those on the Left tend to see the dehumanization of clients (and perhaps also workers) by large, impersonal organizations (Weale 1985). Political campaigns by Green parties have targeted the excessive bureaucratization of government. Further, especially when means-tested benefits are being administered, the welfare state is conceptualized as intrusive and as unnecessarily controlling over citizens' lives. Systems established for commendable humane purposes appear to have become rigid and more concerned with their own definitions of clients' needs than with what the clients think they themselves really require. Further, social service providers have offered substantial resistance to less bureaucratized programs—for example, the negative income tax—that might both simplify administration and reduce total costs. Some of these objections have been for humane reasons—many program beneficiaries need counseling and comfort as well as a check—but some resistance may simply be to protect jobs and the status quo.

Finally, the problems of internal management of public organizations appear to be matched by problems of relationships with their environment. As we have discussed previously with respect to corporatism and the management of the economy, making decisions in government can become complicated by ties to interest groups. In addition, the environment of one public organization contains other public organizations, and there have been difficulties in making one program work effectively with others. These problems of coordination have been especially evident between social and tax programs (Piachaud 1980), but they arise in other areas as well. For example, expanding programs of day care for children of working mothers typically involves education, social welfare, and labor-market organizations.

The coordination problems that arise inside and outside of government make doing anything to change the status quo and its programs difficult if not impossible (King 1975; Scharpf 1977). Again, programs established to produce benefits for citizens run the risk of becoming unresponsive and ossified to the point that critics question their ability to respond effectively to changing socioeconomic conditions. Further, they may be managed more for the benefit of the service providers than for the clients. The survival of existing means-tested benefits in the face of the possibility of a negative income tax, which would greatly simplify social policy administration (Lenkowsky 1987), appears to confirm the power of social service providers. In short, problems in the welfare state involve much more than just money—they also involve the style in which services are delivered and the efficient management of the programs.

The Potential Irrelevance of the Welfare State

It is almost certainly hyperbolic to say that the welfare state is in the process of becoming irrelevant in Western Europe. Too many people depend on its programs for health care, retirement pensions, child benefits, and a panoply of other benefits. Further, if the publicly provided educational system is included as a part of the welfare state, this system of benefits is also responsible for fostering and enculturating the next generation of Europeans. The public welfare system does not exist in a vacuum, and supplementary private programs for retirement and health care are premised upon the existence of the public systems. Almost every citizen in Western Europe receives at least one benefit from welfare-state programs, and most receive multiple benefits (Rose et al. 1985). Therefore it does not appear likely that this complex and well-developed system will be going out of business in the foreseeable future. However, for many people in Western Europe, the welfare state may be of declining relevance and utility. This fact may require some rethinking of the entire system, and perhaps some adjustment of the mechanisms for financing the benefits. The adjustment, however, has the potential of undermining the egalitarian principles that have been a major component of the system's success.

Irrelevance I: Work and Social Insurance

As we have noted several times earlier, social insurance is the principal instrument of intervention utilized by the welfare state. The concept of social insurance is that while people are working, they should make contributions that "buy" them protection. If for any reason—disability, illness, or retirement—an insured worker can no longer participate in the labor force, the insurance will provide him or her with benefits sufficient for survival, if not an elegant life-style. Social insurance also protects survivors in the event of the wage-earner(s)' untimely death. Although these social programs are often discussed as the rights of citizens, they are rights that are largely conditional upon work or upon having some member of the immediate family working.

The difficulty that many Europeans are now facing is that the pattern of employment in their economies is changing. No longer can an individual expect to go to work after leaving formal education and then work at a reasonable wage, perhaps in the same job, with few interruptions until it is time for retirement. The emerging pattern of work is one of more interruptions in a work history, with an individual having to be retrained at least once and perhaps several times during a working lifetime. Further, part-time workers (especially women) apparently will become a more significant component of the labor force, whether through choice or through the functioning of the economic marketplace. Finally, apparently there will be more lower-wage jobs, especially in the service industries, where the bulk of the new jobs are being created in most industrialized countries. There are certainly a number of very well-paid jobs in service industries—stockbrokers, computer engineers, and the like—but many of the new jobs will be at the bottom of the economic ladder and offer little chance for advancement. These jobs are replacing very well-paid jobs in manufacturing industries, so that even if employment remains high, earnings may not. The average industrial workers' expectation of being able to work in a job that earns a middle-class income after a rather basic education, and doing this year after year until retirement, appears to have become a thing of the past.

In addition to the possible irregularity of work for many employees, some face an even more foreboding future. Many middle-aged employees who lose their jobs and who do not have high levels of formal education may never again have a good job. It had been widely thought that long-term unemployment was a problem of the past, and that with proper government management of the economy there would be jobs for everyone who wanted them. This was true during the 1950s, 1960s, and into the early 1970s, but in many declining industrial areas long-term unemployment is very real. In the Ruhr and especially Essen—once the heart of the steel industry for Germany and perhaps Europe as a whole—a number of former coal and steel workers cannot expect to work again at anything like their former wages. Lacking formal education, and having a relatively short working lifetime remaining, they are not good candidates for retraining for the skilled jobs that are becoming available. Although there are economic costs in this unemployment, the human costs may be even greater. And this has happened, not just in the Ruhr, but in Lille and the Pas de Calais in France, Namur and Liège in Belgium, the Basque region of Spain, Glasgow and Sheffield in the United Kingdom, and a large number of other former industrially powerful cities and towns.

These changes in the employment patterns of Western Europeans (not to mention North Americans) arise from several factors. One is the replacement of manufacturing industries with service industries. For many of the same reasons discussed for social services, service industries do not have the return to investment that manufacturing industries do, and to keep prices down wages must also be low. Associated with this is the internationalization of the economy. Not only have many manufacturing jobs already gone to Japan, and then on to Korea, Taiwan, and other newly industrializing economies, but the product cycle of moving those manufacturing jobs around has been accelerating. This means that training and retraining are increasingly important, along with necessary interruptions in the individual's working life. Finally, service industries and high-technology firms need fewer nonprofessional employees and may hire them on a part-time basis. Unskilled and semiskilled workers will not have the opportunities that have been available even in the recent past.

These economic changes present obvious difficulties for workers, and they also present difficulties for governments attempting to provide welfare-state services. In the first place, the average worker/citizen is now more likely to be a recipient of social benefits during his or her working lifetime than would have been true previously. These benefits will be expensive not only because the workers will be receiving those benefits, but also because they will not be making contributions and paying taxes. The declining number of workers, and hence the greater importance of each (and his or her contributions to social insurance funds) exacerbates the problem. More workers be receiving benefits and, because of long-term unemployment, they will be in need of them for a longer period of time.

In many countries, long-term unemployment may mean that the beneficiaries move off unemployment insurance and on to means-tested benefits, such as the Supplementary Benefit program in the United Kingdom. Even if still eligible for unemployment benefits, the long-term unemployed may need additional assistance from means-tested programs. These expensive social programs also involve many of the stigmatizing and socially divisive characteristics that the more thoughtful architects of the welfare state, such as Richard Titmuss, William Henry Beveridge, André Fouillee, and Per Albin Hansson, had sought to eliminate when conceiving and designing the programs (Ashford 1986). The workhouses have been eliminated, but many of the psychological deprivations of the preinsurance system may still exist for workers whose insurance benefits are exhausted.

In addition to the problems encountered during their normal working lifetime, employees in the contemporary European economy may also face difficulties when they are ready to retire. Although the schemes differ in each country, and are complicated in each, eligibility for a pension depends on a certain number of contributions of at least a certain amount to the pension funds. Further, any earnings-related pensions on top of the basic pensions are directly related to the amount of money contributed during the working lifetime. Thus not only may employees be denied the style of living during their normal working years that they had expected, but this deprivation may be compounded by reduced eligibility for pensions after retirement. For these workers, the welfare-state system will be if not wholly irrelevant, certainly a less than adequate source of protection.

This discussion has focused on the industrial worker who has been put out of work, or who may have to undergo a more disorderly pattern of work than would have been true prior to the 1970s. We have not said anything yet about those individuals who, for whatever reasons, have not had and/or do not want a conventional relationship with the industrial economy. Although not of the same magnitude as that in the United States, there is a homeless population in Western Europe. Whether because of little or no preparation for the labor market, addictive diseases, mental illness, or whatever, an increasing number of people apparently simply do not fit into the niches provided by the economy and society and therefore really do not fit into the welfare state. The countries of Western Europe do not seem to have made any more progress in coping with this problem than has the United States. Other former workers in the industrial economy have dropped out but not to live on the streets. They have entered the "black economy" and often live very well on untaxed income. This may serve them well while they are young and fit enough to work, but it does not provide the safety net (other than means-tested benefits) that exists for regular employees in the welfare state.

In addition to the homeless population, poverty still persists in Western Europe. One report from the European Community (Commission of the European Communities 1981) found that an average of over 12 percent of the population of the Community, including almost one-fourth of the Irish population, lived in relative poverty; that figure would almost certainly be higher after the admission of the southern European countries. The benefits provided through the welfare state—especially means-tested ones—may not provide more than a minimal existence, and some people may still be reluctant to apply. Especially for larger families, the existence provided by the welfare state may still be a very meager one indeed, and nothing has been able to replace full employment as a social program.

In summary, the changing world economy has played major havoc with the welfare state in Western Europe. To a system premised on work, and actually on regular work at a good wage, the changes that have occurred to make work less stable and less predictable have been major blows. As a result, the welfare state faces very real problems. Some involve the "mere" question of how to pay for it all, but more fundamental ethical and social problems also have arisen. The most important of these is the possible return to a social service system that depends more on means-tested benefits and, through those programs, produces stigmatization and alienation. Associated with a possible return to means-tested benefits for a portion of the population is the development of a two-class system even within the social services, with those individuals who have jobs being on one track and those out of work or who have had less stable employment histories being on a separate and much less comfortable track. Beneath both of those tracks, however, will be those who fall through the cracks of the system entirely.

Irrelevance II: The Private Welfare State

If economic change has made some programs of the welfare state irrelevant or unattainable for one segment of the population, other social and economic changes have been making the system increasingly irrelevant, and even undesirable, for another portion. While one segment of the population has been faced with long-term unemployment and its consequences for their economic fortunes and personal lives, another part has been doing extremely well economically. The economic successes of that portion of the population, and a loss of the spirit of community and altruism (Silver 1980) that had characterized earlier periods of welfare-state development, have led some politicians and analysts to advocate that the size of social programs be reduced or that they be terminated or privatized. Social insurance programs, it has been argued, are bad investments, and citizens should be allowed to use the money they would have used to pay social security taxes to purchase private schemes to care for them in retirement or in ill health (Boskin 1977; Donnison 1984). This argument is made even though it is extremely difficult to purchase indexed pensions in the private market. Such investment logic is, quite naturally, closely related to the success of conservative political ideologies and of critics of the welfare state and of government more generally.

Conservative attacks on the welfare state have taken two forms. One is the direct frontal assault, arguing that the system is an inappropriate activity for government and that the market can provide the same services better and cheaper. This attack would lead to privatization of any services that reasonably could be marketed or provided by employers rather than through the public sector. Certainly health care, retirement pensions, disability insurance, and perhaps even personal social services (counseling and so on) would fit into that category. Most advocates of privatization do recognize that not all citizens are capable of providing for their own social protection, and vestigial schemes might be maintained to care for those who could not otherwise provide for themselves. Also, the bolder attempts at privatization, such as Mrs. Thatcher's selling off of council housing to sitting tenants, have taken differences of circumstances into account and have sold the assets at very low costs.[7] That differentiation among clients may not be possible, however, in other types of social services unless there is a public subsidy.

The other assault on the welfare state is more incremental, but probably no less serious. Rather than attacking the existing system, this attack involves an undermining and evasion of the existing programs by aiming to supplement existing services for those who can afford them. This supplementing of government programs certainly has existed for retirement pensions for some time, as, for example, people in better-paying jobs receive private retirement benefits from their companies. The same has been true of education, when the more affluent send their children to private schools and in some instances negotiate to have the school fees paid by their employers. Under the label of employee benefits, companies can provide services that, if they were provided by government, would be called social welfare. Even in countries with well-developed social programs, there has been an increased demand for access to private services. For example, in the United Kingdom there has been a rapidly increasing demand for private medical insurance as a means of avoiding the long lines now common in the National Health Service. As private services become more widespread, the need for the welfare state diminishes, as does its base of political support.

PRIVATIZATION. In the frontal attack on the welfare state, it is argued that some public services should be sold to the private sector, while others may be contracted out to private-sector providers. Privatization has occurred primarily in state-owned enterprises, but some aspects of the welfare state could also, at least in principle, be privatized. Many of the services provided by government through welfare-state programs are similar to those already provided privately. Health care certainly can be provided through the market, although some would argue that it is not a service that is ideally suited to being marketed (Culyer 1983). Retirement pensions and disability insurance are also marketed privately, and can be provided through insurance companies or not-for-profit associations. A major difference between private schemes and public social insurance is that almost no private plans are indexed to keep up with inflation. Education is marketed to some extent in almost all countries, and private social workers and counselors can provide personal social services. In principle, there is very little that government does in the welfare state that is intrinsically public and that could not also be done through the private sector.

Some countries have made attempts at privatizing at least a part of their social services. In many instances this has gone no further than contracting out laundry, cleaning, and other ancillary services in public facilities such as hospitals. A next level has been to contract out some of the actual medical services provided in public hospitals, such as laboratory testing. Other countries have made some limited efforts at privatizing social insurance, through means such as requiring employers to pay the equivalent of sickness insurance benefits (income while an employee is too ill to work), with the employers then being able to deduct these payments against their taxable profits. Other countries have contracted out at least a portion of the management of their social insurance funds, while retaining them as public or quasi-public entities. Governments have been much slower to look into this more extreme form of privatization, perhaps because it affects so many people and is potentially politically charged, than they have into the privatization of industries. Nonetheless, more extensive privatization of social services continues to be considered by governments.

The attempts to privatize welfare-state services point to the very real conflicts existing between efficiency and equity goals in most contemporary political systems. It may well be that private-sector suppliers and contractors can supply social services more cheaply than does the public sector

(Smith and Stone 1988). Management in the public sector is more difficult than in the private sector (Allison 1986), and government must attend to more goals than simple economic efficiency. The question becomes whether, in the pursuit of efficiency and lower costs, we are willing to sacrifice other goals and other values embodied in welfare-state programs (Starr 1990)? Most important of those may be the concept that all citizens should be equal in their dealings with the state and receive approximately equal benefits. Privatization implies (although does not necessarily require) differential benefits based on the criteria that would prevail in the marketplace.

PRIVATE SUPPLEMENTS. The second form of erosion of the public nature of the welfare state is through the addition of private benefit schemes on top of public ones, whether or not the same individual is eligible for both. Although schemes of this sort have been proposed (and even implemented) in several policy areas, apparently the greatest amount of supplementation of public benefits has been occurring in health care. Having private medical insurance allows the more affluent to go to private doctors and to go to private hospitals with better facilities. Also, some services may be available privately that are considered frivolous (plastic surgery), experimental (liver transplants), or too expensive by public insurance schemes. While in some cases private insurance may buy better quality care, it almost always purchases more convenient, comfortable, and personalized care.

The supplementation of health benefits is somewhat important in countries that have relied on public health insurance, but it is extremely important in the United Kingdom with the National Health Service (NHS) (West 1984). Over time the NHS has gradually become less well funded, relative to what might be needed to run a fully modern, state-of-the-art health care system. Britain now spends a smaller proportion of its Gross National Product on health care than do most industrialized countries—a triumph of financial control or the starving of the health care system, depending on the observer's perspective. This incremental reduction of funding (in relative if not absolute terms) for health has been especially evident in the Thatcher government, whether for ideological or merely financial reasons. Waiting times for any elective surgery have increased, and the quality of services in the NHS appears to have declined. These problems, in turn, have led to a very rapid increase in the number of people buying private health insurance—one estimate is that the number doubles every year. Holders of private insurance can avoid the lines in NHS hospitals and for NHS doctors and get the kind of care they want. Ironically, some labor unions have begun to negotiate for private health insurance as a benefit of employment,

TABLE 8.5

Social Protection Benefits from the Public and Private Sectors, 1977
(as percentage of Gross Domestic Product)

	Private	Public	Total	Private as Percentage of Total Benefits
Austria	1.9	22.8	24.5	7.7
Belgium	1.6	22.5	24.1	6.6
France	1.1	22.0	23.1	4.8
W. Germany	1.1	22.3	23.4	4.7
Netherlands	2.7	25.3	28.0	9.6
Italy	2.1	19.6	21.7	9.7
Sweden	1.2	29.8	31.0	3.9
Switzerland	2.0	15.1	17.1	11.7
United Kingdom	2.6	15.5	18.1	14.4
United States	3.8	12.8	16.8	22.9

SOURCE: Reprinted with permission from M. Rein and L. Rainwater, "The Public/Private Mix," in *Public-Private Interplay in Social Protection,* ed. M. Rein and L. Rainwater (Armonk, NY: M. E. Sharpe, 1986), 17.

an action that must make some of their predecessors in the Labour party who fought for so long to defend the NHS cringe.

Although health care is the most visible policy area with private supplementation of public social benefits, the private sector is becoming involved in other policy areas as well. Further, it is becoming involved even in countries such as the Netherlands and Sweden, with well-developed social service systems. Table 8.5 shows the magnitude of public and private expenditure for social benefits in a number of OECD countries. Clearly the United States and the United Kingdom have the largest share of such benefits, but some continental countries also supply a significant private welfare state. Other studies (Eriksen 1981; O'Higgins 1986) demonstrate a growing private role in retirement pensions, with some preliminary moves toward making private pensions adjust their benefits for inflation.

We must remember that government has been a witting or unwitting accomplice to some of these attacks on the welfare state. This is certainly true of privatization, which could not have occurred without overt government activity, but it is also true of the supplementation of the welfare state by private programs. Much less private supplementation would occur, in all likelihood, if it were not for the benefits provided to private social services through the tax system and the unwillingness of most national tax systems to tax social benefits from employers in the same way that they tax other forms of income. So, for example, if a worker does not like the health care provided through public health insurance, he or she may be free to purchase private health insurance, but with after-tax income. A health insurance policy that costs £100 per month, for example, requires £200 of earned income if the total tax rate imposed by government is 50 percent. On the other hand, if the worker's employer provides the benefit, in most countries it is not taxed (OECD 1988). Therefore, employers can increase the well-being of their employees relatively efficiently by providing supplementary insurance protection, thanks in large part to the subsidy provided through the tax system.

It is not only employers, however, who can use the tax system to subsidize a private welfare state. Individuals have been doing this for years. The most commonly used subsidy is for housing, with mortgage interest and possibly some taxes on houses being deductible against tax in most industrialized countries (MacDaniel and Surrey 1985; OECD 1986). This, in effect, means that the public pays a significant share of the cost of an individual's purchasing a home, just as it would pay a subsidy if a builder were to build low-income housing units. Governments may also provide favorable tax treatment for private life insurance and retirement annuities, so that an individual can provide for retirement and for any survivors. In some cases, even the costs of the private health insurance just mentioned might be subsidized through taxes. In short, the public sector helps to subsidize, however indirectly, programs that may be in competition with its own programs and that may be undermining public support for the government-provided services. These tax-subsidy programs have, however, become so widespread throughout the society (especially for housing) that any attempt to eliminate them would likely be political suicide.

Irrelevance III: Does It Really Matter?

A final question that could be asked about the welfare state in its current manifestations is whether it is really producing anything for citizens. At one level it has become a massive machine that takes in huge volumes of money, spends equally huge volumes, but does not really change economic circumstances very much for most citizens. One of the basic emerging characteristics of the welfare state is its fragmentation (Dente 1985). Spending programs are isolated from taxing programs (Piachaud 1980), and from one another, and the several sides of the public ledger usually are not put together. It is a system in which everyone pays and everyone benefits, but at the end of the day, most people receive back about what they pay into the system. It is a system that may have originally been thought to be re-

TABLE 8.6

Income Taxes and Cash Benefits for Average Production Worker, 1986
(as percentage of gross earnings)

	Income Tax	Cash Benefits
Austria	8.3	14.7
Belgium	17.0	12.1
Denmark	36.0	3.8
Finland	24.5	6.1
France	0.0	7.4
W. Germany	8.3	4.6
Greece	3.4	20.0
Ireland	16.9	3.7
Italy	13.7	8.1
Luxembourg	2.1	10.1
Netherlands	8.5	7.7
Norway	15.1	8.1
Portugal	2.5	5.4
Spain	9.6	0.5
Sweden	34.5	8.7
Switzerland	6.9	7.0
United Kingdom	17.4	8.0
AVERAGE	13.3	8.0

SOURCE: Based on data from the Organization for Economic Cooperation and Development, *Tax/Benefit Position of Production Workers, 1983–86* (Paris: OECD, 1987).

distributive but that has become largely distributive, even in the more developed welfare states of Scandinavia (see Heckscher 1984). This distributive character is in part a function of the insurance nature of most programs, but also in part a function of the numerous programs—tax benefits as well as public expenditures—providing benefits to virtually all segments of the population.

The distributive nature of the welfare state in Western Europe can be seen in Table 8.6. This shows the average payment for income taxes (including local, where applicable) for the average industrial worker with two children, along with the average cash benefits from government to his or her family. This demonstrates that everyone pays (except in France) and especially in Sweden and Denmark and everyone receives some cash benefits, even if working. If the family did not have someone working, the taxes would be lower and the benefits higher. However, even if the total family income were from social transfer payments, they would still be paying taxes because of the significant rate of value-added tax on goods and services in Europe. Likewise, the average industrial worker in the table is paying more tax (insurance contributions and indirect taxes such as value-added tax) but is also receiving more benefits (schools, health services, roads, and so on).

Some greater understanding of the impact of the welfare state on citizens can be gained from the information in Table 8.7. This table contains data on the net impact of taxes and expenditures on different income groups in two European countries. Although these data involve some significant assumptions about the incidence of taxes and benefits, they do point out that although there is some improvement in the status of the poor because of government programs, the poor remain poor. Likewise, although the most affluent have less money after public-sector programs operate, they remain relatively wealthy. The principal determinant of economic well-being in European countries remains the free market. What the welfare state has done, however, is to remove some of the uncertainty about income over time, in case of disability, unemployment, or when the workers in the family retire. That is an important benefit, but many may not perceive it to be sufficient for all the taxing and spending that now takes place.

Although social insurance programs may distribute income across time rather than across economic classes, the direct provision of services may be thought to have a better chance of being redistributive across classes. That, however, does not appear to be the case. First, in health care, the evidence is that Britain's National Health Service has not markedly changed the distribution of health status by class in its over fifty-year history. All social classes are healthier than they were when the NHS was introduced, but the differentials among the classes remain relatively unchanged. For example, as shown in Table 8.8, infant mortality and adult mortality in males have retained much of the inequality by class that was found in the 1930s, and in some measures that inequality actually has increased.[8] Second, public programs such as education (especially higher education) are utilized differentially by the more affluent, and these programs tend to perpetuate class differences rather than erase them. In short, while the welfare state may have removed the worry of personal expense from some services, it has yet to make access to public services equal. Many citizens seem to question the extent to which the insurance benefits received justify the large-scale taxation, and the large-scale bureaucracy, that the welfare state has produced in European countries.

TABLE 8.7

Redistributional Effects of Government Taxes and Expenditures

Switzerland, 1980
(percentage of total income pre- and postgovernment, by deciles)

Decile	Pregovernment	Postgovernment
1	0.1	1.9
2	1.6	4.1
3	3.8	6.2
4	6.0	8.0
5	7.8	8.3
6	9.2	9.1
7	10.7	10.2
8	12.7	11.7
9	15.8	14.2
10	32.3	26.3

United Kingdom, 1986
(average income per household, in £)

Average	Bottom	2nd	Quintiles 3rd	4th	Top
Original Income	130	2,800	8,030	13,180	24,790
plus cash benefits	3,370	2,730	1,250	870	680
less direct taxes	−10[a]	330	1,490	2,710	5,650
less indirect taxes	880	1,540	2,280	2,900	4,250
Income After Cash Benefits and Taxes	2,620	3,650	5,520	8,450	15,560
plus benefits in kind[b]	1,510	1,500	1,500	1,670	1,700
Final Income	4,130	5,150	7,020	10,120	17,260

SOURCE: For Switzerland, based on data from R. E. Leu, R. L. Frey, and B. Buhmann, "Taxes, Expenditures, and Income Distribution in Switzerland," *Journal of Social Policy* 14 (1985): 341–60; for the United Kingdom, "The Effects of Taxes and Benefits on Household Income, 1986," *Economic Trends* 422: 89–99.

[a] Rebates through tax system greater than amount of tax paid.
[b] Not all services created by the public sector can be attributed directly to households.

Summary

We began by noting the importance of the welfare state for Western European politics in the postwar period. The development of these social programs, and the extension of existing programs, was important in making the state appear a benign and positive force in social life after almost a decade of conflict and mass destruction in the name of governments. The welfare state helped legitimize some potentially shaky regimes and to make

TABLE 8.8

Inequalities in Health Outcomes, United Kingdom

| | Infant Mortality[a] | | | |
	1930–32	1949–53	1970–72	1984
Occupational Class[b]				
I	32	19	12	6
II	46	22	14	7
III	59	28	16	8
IV	63	35	20	11
V	80	42	31	13
I as a % of V	40.0	45.2	38.7	46.2

| | Male Mortality | | | |
	1930–32	1949–53	1959–63	1970–72
I	90	86	76	77
II	94	92	81	81
III	97	101	100	104
IV	102	104	103	114
V	111	118	143	137
I as a % of V	81.1	72.9	53.1	56.2

SOURCE: Reprinted from D. Black, N. J. Morris, C. Smith, and P. Townsend, *Inequalities in Health* (London: Penguin, 1988), 59, 63.

[a] Deaths in the first year of life per 1,000 live births
[b] I Professional
II Intermediate (manager, schoolteacher)
III Skilled
IV Semiskilled
V Unskilled

fundamentally legitimate regimes even more confident and secure. More than what it did for governments, however, the welfare state (along with the mixed economy) improved the daily lives and expectations of most ordinary citizens. It provided them with some sense of economic security, both during their working lifetimes and during retirement. It also enabled them to regain some optimism about the future prospects of Western European society after a war that had exposed the fragility of that society. Finally, it gave them a sense of citizenship and equality, even in the context of free-market economies that tended to produce economic inequalities.

Yet now the welfare state faces a number of major challenges. Some involve only the need to firm up the financial foundations of the programs, which have deteriorated as a part of the general fiscal crisis that has affected all aspects of government. The other challenges are more fundamental, and involve questions about the real utility of the system for citizens. These challenges come, in part, from the ideological Right, which wants to privatize the social service system and to allow a marketplace in social benefits and health care to develop. The challenges also come from ordinary citizens, who perceive that the programs associated with the welfare state no longer meet their needs as well as they once did. The changing political economies of Western Europe have produced a pattern of employment and a labor market that is substantially different from the one on which most welfare-state programs are premised. The probable continuation of the economic circumstances that developed during the 1980s will require some reconceptualization of how the welfare state should be structured.

We cannot expect the apocalyptic vision of some politicians and ideologues to come true. The existing system of welfare-state benefits is likely to remain in place for the foreseeable future. What may change, however, is the manner in which citizens relate to the welfare state. There may be mechanisms for the more affluent to opt out of taxes and benefits. There may be schemes that supplement the publicly provided programs with private insurance and employer-provided benefits. Many displaced industrial workers may have to depend on means-tested benefits or on assistance from voluntary agencies. That may mean that an already not very redistributive social service system may become even less likely to take from the affluent and give to the poor. Following from those changes, social programs may become more community based than national. Most of the welfare-state program structure will remain intact; what may be different is the meaning of the programs and the sense of equality of citizenship that they once created.

Notes

1. Taken from *The Leopard* by G. di Lampedusa (New York: Pantheon, 1960).

2. There were publicly subsidized voluntary programs of social insurance in Italy prior to the introduction of Germany's *compulsory* program.

3. There may or may not be separate programs for disability. This protection may be simply a part of sickness and accident insurance. See Stone (1984). Further, disability has now become in some cases a disguised form of social assistance because the long-term unemployed soon exhaust their unemployment benefits. See Emanuel (1980).

4. A small program of health insurance was begun in Britain in 1911 as a part of Lloyd George's social programs. Access was limited and any comprehensive medical program had to wait until the Beveridge programs after World War II.

5. It is difficult, however, to assign the benefits of many public programs. Who wins and who loses by the provision of such programs as defense, police protection, and even highways?

6. In many programs social insurance contributions cease after a certain annual maximum has been paid, in part to preserve the "insurance" concept for these programs. Even so, however, workers with higher incomes will pay more than lower-paid workers and might expect higher benefits also.

7. In this case, the opportunity to create a "property-owning democracy," which would be more in tune with the Conservative party than a democracy of public tenants, was deemed worth the loss of potential revenue by selling houses at below-market values.

8. This is in part because of a number of factors contribute to health besides access to medical care, such as diet, housing, and knowledge. Further, middle-class employees have the freedom to take time off work for medical care without loss of income that many working-class individuals do not have, and middle-class patients have their own transportation to get to medical facilities.

POSTSCRIPT

Writing a book about European politics in the early 1990s is a difficult task. Reading the newspapers each morning may mean that some assumption or another, or some fact or another, is out of date, and changes must then be made. The daily events reported in the papers range from simple changes in governments and their officials to very fundamental changes in the manner in which politics, and indeed Western Europe, must be conceptualized. Therefore, the discussion above is very much *in medias res,* and the world is changing faster than we can document, or perhaps even notice, the changes that are taking place. Western Europe appears to be racing ahead toward a new and promising future which, however, is not without its problems and dangers.

Europe East and West

The most fundamental change in the politics of Western Europe has been headline news more often than not in 1989 and 1990—that is, the radical changes taking place in what had been referred to since the 1950s as Eastern Europe. It now appears that it is better to think of Europe more as a whole, extending from County Kerry in Ireland to the borders of the Soviet Union. Historically, countries such as Hungary and Poland have been an important part of general European social, cultural, and political history, and there is now every indication that their relative isolation of four decades will be reversed. The reintegration may be slow, but it does appear both possible and inevitable.

Almost certainly the most dramatic change of all has occurred in Germany. As of July 1990 it makes relatively little sense to speak of East and West Germany as separate countries. The reunification of the two parts of Germany began when the Berlin Wall was first breached and then destroyed, and has continued rapidly thereafter. It continued even after Chancellor Kohl of West Germany suffered some political defeats based, in part, on his advocating the swift rejoining of the two countries. On July 1, 1990, the two halves of a divided Germany became one country economically, with the West German Deutschmark as the common currency. Goods that had never been available appeared on East German shelves, and goods and services could move freely between East and West. An agreement with the Soviet Union permitting a unified Germany to join NATO, and an agreement with Poland to respect the postwar boundary, has opened the way to full political unification.

These changes, while generally welcomed by observers, are not without their immediate and potential problems. The immediate problems involve such tasks as dismantling the repressive state apparatus in eastern Germany and meeting increased consumer demands for goods and services. And while there is no longer a Communist government in the East, it is still not clear what will happen to the army and the bureaucracy that had served the old regime. They now have few tasks to perform, and many citizens and politicians in the western part of the country consider these military or government officials tainted for future service in a democratic regime.

In addition to internal political concerns, there are also concerns about what the merger of the two countries implies for their combined economy. On the one hand, East Germany brings with it a large, relatively skilled, and vigorous work force, which is a valuable asset for a rapidly aging West Germany. Further, it brings with it a huge market for consumer goods, with demand for products that are now very commonplace in the West. Along with these benefits, however, come a number of costs. For one thing, East Germany is an underdeveloped economy compared to the West, which is in need of massive investment, even in the basic economic infrastructure, in order to bring it up to the standards found in the remainder of the country. There are also huge environmental problems caused by the outdated machinery, and outdated values, of the former East German regime. The Deutschmark weathered reunification without losing its strength on world currency markets, but fears of inflation still remain. Finally, there are potentially very large obligations for social services and pensions for which the East Germans, as citizens of the Federal Republic, are eligible. There is a complex and worrisome balance of costs and benefits to consider after the euphoria of reunification passes.

There are also some very significant concerns about German reunification outside of Germany. Again, some of these are political and some are economic. The political concerns revolve around the seeming superpower status that the new unified Germany has achieved, with a population of almost 80 million people and a level of industrial production far in excess of other European countries. Some of these concerns are residual fears left from the events of two world wars, but others simply result from the economic imbalance between a unified Germany and other European countries. Some British politicians have expressed their concerns about Germany very openly. One lost his seat in the cabinet, but he appeared to have been supported by many citizens. Associated with those fears is a concern that Germany will become more preoccupied with its internal affairs and therefore less interested in European affairs more broadly. This is of particular concern as the European Community moves toward more complete economic integration in 1992.

The futures of the other countries of (the former) Eastern Europe, and their integration with Western Europe, are also dependent upon a number of other factors. One of these factors is simply economics. As with East Germany, there is a tremendous need for capital investment to provide not only consumer goods but also the basic social and economic infrastructure needed for a modern society. Economically, East Germany was perhaps the most advanced of the countries of Eastern Europe, so the demands are even more pressing in the other countries. Integrating the eastern countries into the European economy will require large-scale investment from the West, although some of this may be paid by the peace dividend from the apparent end of the Cold War. In addition, there is the economic problem of retraining a work force that is unaccustomed to working at the pace and with the technology required in Western industry.

Politically there are concerns about the future of the newly freed countries in Eastern Europe. One is that disappointments arising when all the economic goods found in the West are not immediately available will provoke disillusionment and political change away from the liberal regimes established in most countries. Another is that the ethnic tensions that have been submerged in the communist-dominated regimes will emerge and provoke internal conflicts and political instability. Finally, there is the question of what the future course of Soviet policy will be, and if the Soviet Union might at some time want to reverse the political changes in its former satellites. Most of these questions are unanswerable at present, but they do pose serious questions and insecurities for the countries of Western Europe.

At least as potential adversaries, the countries of Eastern and Western Europe have had their fates intertwined since the end of World War II. That interconnection now takes on a very different character, but is no less important. The two sets of countries now become, in many ways, one Europe but a Europe with several internal differences. One portion of Europe is affluent and has (even in the case of Spain, Greece, and Portugal) a democratic experience spanning a number of years. The other portion of Europe is relatively underdeveloped economically, and has only very recently begun to experiment with democratic governance. Although different, these two portions of Europe cannot ignore each other and must both accommodate to the needs and demands of the other.

The European Community

Looking only at the countries usually identified as Western Europe, one of the most significant ongoing changes is the continuing movement toward economic and even political integration. From the announcement of 1992 as the target date, the European Community has appeared capable of overcoming the previous diagnosis of "Eurosclerosis" and moving toward a more fully integrated economy, society, and political system. The less committed Europeans, such as Margaret Thatcher, continue to express their doubts about that integration, but even they appear reluctant to express those doubts too strongly lest they miss the dynamic train of European history as it pulls away. Being a part of those events, and therefore having some ability to shape them, may be even more important than winning on particular points of policy or national pride.

The pace of Western European integration has accelerated, and the discussions have even come to the point of considering full monetary union, as has now occurred with German unification. This is a significantly greater level of economic integration than might have been expected even one year ago. Monetary unification will mean that each member country of the European Community would surrender a good deal of its independence in making economic policy. A member country will find it difficult to use changes in exchange rates or even domestic inflation as a policy instrument. One further factor that must be considered is that monetary unification will give Germany an even more dominant position in Europe. The Deutschmark is the strongest currency among the EC members, and would serve as the standard for all the other currencies. The movement toward greater monetary unity is being resisted by the United Kingdom, and there are doubters in other countries as well, but such monetary unification may be an inevitable extension of the movement toward full European economic union.

The movement toward economic unification is also playing a significant role in national politics. This is true first within the member countries. The domestic effects of EC politics has been most evident in the United Kingdom since Mrs. Thatcher's reluctance to become more European has at times produced a political backlash, as it did in the 1990 European elections. The Conservatives did rather poorly while parties more committed to Europe (including the Greens) did much better. Although Britain has been the most obvious case of caution in movement toward greater European unity, a number of other countries have found that costs as well as benefits are associated with membership in the European Community.

Within the European Community there also appears to be a substantial need for political and institutional change. The institutions of the Community are perceived by some citizens, and by many national politicians, as being remote and bureaucratic. The phrase "democratic deficit" has been coined to describe the apparent absence of a direct political connection between the EC and the mass public. This perceived deficit exists despite the existence of a European Parliament directly elected by the people. Therefore, if the EC is to become an effective supranational government, it will apparently require a stronger set of legitimating institutions, especially if the costs associated with membership become more visible.

For countries outside the Community, the increasing pace of unification within the European Community is causing a great deal of political pressure. Some countries such as Austria have begun to apply actively for membership, and Sweden and Finland have been moving closer to the market economically. Other countries, however, continue to debate the advisability of closer ties. For Switzerland in particular this appears to be a difficult political choice. The requirement for a national referendum, their historical policy of neutrality, and the need to protect a highly regulated internal market all appear to make Swiss entry problematic. However, remaining outside the Community (especially if Austria should enter) may be even more problematic. Even if Austria, Switzerland, or Sweden wants to join the Community, it is less clear now that the EC wants or needs new members. The Community may have enough to do to produce greater unity among the current members, and new members would only be a further impediment to achieving the goals current members have set for themselves.

The Public Sector

A final challenge for European politics as it enters the 1990s is what to do about government itself. The 1980s were a period in which the virtues of government institutions were thought to be few, and the vices of those institutions to be numerous. All over Europe, even in countries with socialist or labor governments, there was a tendency to reduce the size of the public sector, privatize services, and see what the private sector could do to achieve the social and economic goals previously pursued by the public sector. That approach to providing for the public needs of societies may now have gone as far as it can go, and there appears to be a need to revitalize some aspects of the public sector. This is especially true for the economic infrastructure of some countries, and will become more of a necessity in dealing with the needs of a rapidly increasing elderly population in almost all countries.

It is also almost certain that Europe, and the rest of the world, will have to cope with a range of complex environmental and distributional issues. The probable warming of the earth's atmosphere from burning fossil fuels, the probable depletion of ozone and decrease of the protection it provides from ultraviolet rays, and the exhaustion of natural resources will require global solutions in a manner not usually conceivable. Further, the restraints imposed by these policies will make the developmental aims of the less developed countries difficult or impossible to achieve. It is easy for wealthy Europeans and North Americans to discuss curtailing growth when they begin from a very high plateau, but that is a much more difficult task for the underdeveloped countries. This is not a strictly European political problem, but it will impinge on the political and economic future of the continent.

Significant changes are also taking place in the social structures of the European countries. The rapid aging of the populations, and the concomitant need for social and health services, has already been mentioned. In addition, the ethnic composition of many countries continues to change. Countries such as those in Scandanavia, which historically have been very homogeneous, find themselves with significant non-native populations. Switzerland, which is itself divided by language and religion, now must accommodate to an increasing non-Swiss population. The list could go on, but the basic point is that new modes of accommodation must be developed within many European countries to cope with their changing populations.

Reform and change in the public sector were a consistent theme in the 1980s, and may continue to be so in the 1990s. In the 1980s, this theme almost always implied "less"—less cost, certainly, and perhaps less service. In the 1990s a simple pursuit of "less" will be almost impossible. Most public-service managers believe that all the fat has already been taken out of their programs, and along with that some of the muscle. The reductions in the 1980s also have made the task of political leaders in the 1990s that much more difficult. They will have to try to repair some of the real damage done to public services while at the same time trying to keep taxes down. Further, they will have to do this with public servants who often have been demoralized by the cutbacks and general denigration of the public sector during the previous decade. The 1990s will be a decade of real challenge for politicians and for civil servants.

The shape of the public sector for the 1990s may cause difficulty for the average citizen as well. The privatization of government services and the mixed models of provision make public service provision even more of a jungle than it had been. The (allegedly) imperious bureaucracy may have been replaced by a system of service delivery in which no one really is in charge. Certainly there are problems with traditional service delivery through bureaucratic agencies, but privatized services also have their problems with responsibility and accountability. The 1990s will require some rethinking of the nature of the public sector, the types of services that it must provide, and the most appropriate manner in which to provide those services.

The Future of European Politics

The future for Europe as it enters the 1990s appears brighter than perhaps at any time since World War II. If the Cold War is not over entirely, it has certainly thawed greatly, and there is a justifiable belief that most of Eastern Europe can never return to being what it was. This not only makes the lives of citizens of those countries more bearable, but it should free a great deal of energy and resources in Western Europe to address other social and economic problems, rather than worrying about building more tanks and missiles. In addition, there is a sense that Western Europe itself is entering an era of greater unity and economic progress through the European Community. The full ramifications of the program for integration by 1992 have not been made manifest, but it appears clear that there will be a new Europe.

All of these positive aspects of the European future bring their own dangers and their own impediments. Many of the positive developments require a reduction of nationalist sentiments, and that may not be as easy to sustain as it has appeared to date in the European Community. Moreover, many of the changes depend upon continued economic growth, and the willingness to share that growth with countries in Eastern Europe, and perhaps even the world more broadly. The positive future also depends upon political leadership and perhaps on a more positive conception of the possibilities of public action. The future for Europe appears bright, but it must be considered in the light of hard economic and political realities if any meaningful and sustainable change is to be achieved.

REFERENCES

Abel-Smith, B. 1985. Major Problems of the Welfare State: Defining the Issues. In *The Welfare State and Its Aftermath*, ed. S. N. Eisenstadt and O. Ahimeir, pp. 31–43. Totowa, NJ: Barnes and Noble.

Aberbach, J. D., and B. A. Rockman. 1989. On the Rise, Transformation and Decline of Analysis in the U.S. Government. *Governance* 2: 293–314.

Aberbach, J. D., R. D. Putnam, and B. A. Rockman. 1981. *Bureaucrats and Politicians in Western Democracies*. Cambridge, MA: Harvard Univ. Press.

Adams, C. T. 1980. *Mothers at Work*. New York: Longman.

Adams, W. J., and C. Stoffäes. 1986. *French Industrial Policy*. Washington, DC: Brookings Institution.

Albeda, W. 1986. *The Future of the Welfare State*. Maastricht: Presses Interuniversitaires Européenes.

Allardt, E. 1964. Social Sources of Finnish Communism: Traditional and Emerging Radicalism. *International Journal of Comparative Sociology* 5:49–72.

Allardt, E. 1979. *Implications of Ethnic Revival in Modern Industrialized Societies*. Helsinki: Societas Scientiarum Fennica.

Allardt, E. 1984. Representative Government in a Bureaucratic Age. *Daedalus* 113:172–87.

Allison, G. T. 1986. Public and Private Management: Are They Fundamentally Alike in All Unimportant Respects. In *Current Issues in Public Administration*, ed. F. S. Lane, pp. 16–33. New York: St. Martin's

All Souls-Justice. 1988. *Administrative Justice: Some Necessary Reforms*. Oxford: Oxford Univ. Press.

Almond, G. A., and G. B. Powell. 1966. *Comparative Politics: A Developmental Approach.* Boston: Little, Brown.

Almond, G. A., and S. Verba. 1963. *The Civic Culture.* Boston: Little, Brown.

Anastassopoulos, J.-P. 1985. State-owned Enterprises Between Autonomy and Dependency. *Journal of Public Policy* 5:521–39.

Andersen, J. G. 1984. Decline of Class Voting or Change in Class Voting? Social Classes and Party Choice in Denmark in the 1970s. *European Journal of Political Research* 12:243–59.

Anderson, C. W. 1970. *The Political Economy of Modern Spain.* Madison, WI: Univ. of Wisconsin Press.

Antoni, P., and D. Antoni. 1976. *Les Ministres de la 5e Republique.* Paris: Presses Universitaires de France.

Ardant, G. 1965. *Théorie sociologique de l'impôt.* Paris: SEVPEN.

Armstrong, J. A. 1973. *The European Administrative Elite.* Princeton, NJ: Princeton Univ. Press.

Ascher, K. 1987. *The Politics of Privatization* London: Macmillan.

Ashford, D. E. 1986. *The Emergence of the Welfare State.* Oxford: Basil Blackwell.

Aucoin, P. 1988. Contraction, Managerialism and Decentralization in Canadian Government. *Governance* 1:144–61.

Bahema, W. E., and I. P. Secher. 1988. Ministerial Expertise and the Dutch Case. *European Journal of Political Research* 16:153–70.

Baker, K., R. Dalton, and K. Hildebrandt. 1981. *Germany Transformed.* Cambridge, MA: Harvard Univ. Press.

Barker, A. 1982. *Quangos in Britain.* London: Macmillan.

Barnes, S., and M. Kaase. 1979. *Political Action.* Beverly Hills, CA: Sage.

Bay, C. 1965. *The Structure of Freedom.* New York: Atheneum.

Beam, D. 1984. New Federalism, Old Realities: The Reagan Administration and Intergovernmental Reform. In *The Reagan Presidency and the Governing of America,* ed. L. Salamon and M. Lund, pp. 415–42. Washington, DC: Urban Institute.

Beck, M. 1967. The Expanding Public Sector: Some Contrary Evidence. *National Tax Journal* 29:1–21.

Bekke, A. J. G. M. 1985. Private Organizations and the State: Mutual Prisoners Blocking De-bureaucratization. In *Limits to Government: Dutch Experiences,* ed. I. T. M. Snellen, pp. 53–70. Amsterdam: Kobra.

Bell, D. 1960. *The End of Ideology.* New York: Free Press.

Bell, D. 1973. *The Coming of Post-Industrial Society.* New York: Basic Books.

Benjamin, R., and R. Duvall. 1985. The Capitalist State in Context. In *The Democratic State,* ed. R. Benjamin and S. L. Elkin, pp. 19–57. Lawrence, KS: Univ. Press of Kansas.

Benjamin, R., and R. T. Kudrle. 1984. *The Industrial Future of the Pacific Basin.* Boulder, CO: Westview.

Beyme, K. von. 1981. Der liberale Körporatismus als Mittel gegen die Unregierbarkeit? In *Neokörporatismus,* ed. U. von Alemann, pp. 117–44. Frankfurt: Campus.

Beyme, K. von. 1985. *Political Parties in Western Democracies*. New York: St. Martin's.

Birnbaum, P. 1985. The Socialist Elite, "les Gros," and the State. In *Socialism, the State and Public Policy in France*, ed. P. G. Cerny and M. A. Schain, pp. 129–42. London: Frances Pinter.

Bjorkman, J. W. 1982. Professionals in the Welfare State: Sociological Saviours or Political Pariahs. *European Journal of Political Research* 10:407–28.

Black, D., J. N. Morris, C. Smith, and P. Townsend. 1988. *Inequalities in Health*. London: Penguin.

Blackmer, D. L. M., and S. Tarrow. 1975. *Communism in Italy and France*. Princeton, NJ: Princeton Univ. Press.

Bladh, A. 1987. *Decenteraliserad Forvaltning: Tre Ämbetsverk i Nya Roller*. Lund: Studentlitteratur.

Blake, D., A. Blais, and S. Dion. (In press). The Public-Private Sector Cleavage in North America: The Political Behavior and Attitudes of Public Sector Employees. *Comparative Political Studies*.

Blanco, J. J. et al. 1977. *La Consciencia Regional en España*. Madrid: Centro de Investigaciones Sociológicas.

Blondel, J. 1985. *Government Ministers in the Contemporary World*. London: Sage.

Blondel, J. 1988. Ministerial Careers and the Nature of Parliamentary Government: The Cases of Austria and Belgium. *European Journal of Political Research* 16:51–71.

Body, R. 1982. *Agriculture: The Triumph and the Shame*. London: Macmillan.

Bonnett, K. 1985. Corporatism and Thatcherism: Is There Life after Death? In *Organized Interests and the State*, ed. A. Cawson, pp. 85–105. London: Sage.

Bortolotto, G. 1934. *Diritto Corporativo*. Milan: U. Hoepli.

Boskin, M. J. 1977. *The Crisis in Social Security*. San Francisco: Institute of Contemporary Studies.

Bracher, K. D. 1974. Die Kanzlerdemokratie. In *Die Zweite Republik*, ed. R. Lowenthal and H.-P. Schwartz, pp. 179–202. Stuttgart: Seewald.

Brass, P. 1985. *Ethnic Groups and the State*. Totowa, NJ: Barnes and Noble.

Brown, L. D. 1983. *New Policies, New Politics: Government's Response to Government's Growth*. Washington, DC: Brookings Institution.

Buchan, B. 1989. Millan Aims to Iron Out Community Inequalities. *Financial Times*, 5 January.

Budge, I. 1982. Electoral Volatility: Issue Effects and Basic Change in 23 Post-War Democracies. *Electoral Studies* 1: 31–61.

Buerklin, W. 1981. Die Grünen und die "Neue Politik." *Politische Vierteiljahrschrift* 22:359–82.

Buerklin, W. 1985. The Greens: Ecology and the New Left. In *West-German Politics in the Mid-Eighties*, ed. H. G. Wallach and G. Romoser, pp. 187–218. New York: Praeger.

Cagan, P. 1958. The Demand for Currency Relative to Money Supply. London: NBER Occasional Paper 62.

Campbell, C. 1983. *Governments Under Stress: Political Executives and Key Bureaucrats in Washington, London and Ottawa.* Toronto: Univ. of Toronto Press.

Campbell, C., and B. G. Peters. 1988. *Organizing Governance: Governing Organizations.* Pittsburgh: Univ. of Pittsburgh Press.

Campbell, C., and G. Szablowski. 1979. *The Superbureaucrats: Structure and Behaviour in Central Agencies.* Toronto: Macmillan of Canada.

Carder, M., and B. Kongeberg. 1980. Towards a Salaried Medical Profession: How "Swedish" Was the Seven Crowns Reform. In *The Shaping of the Swedish Health System,* pp. 143–72. New York: St. Martin's.

Cassese, S. 1980. Is There a Government in Italy? Politics and Administration at the Top. In *Presidents and Prime Ministers,* ed. R. Rose and E. Suleiman, pp. 171–202. Washington, DC: American Enterprise Institute.

Castles, F. G. 1987. Neocorporatism and the "Happiness Index," or What Did the Trade Unions Get for Their Cooperation? *European Journal of Political Research* 15:381–94.

Cawson, A. 1982. *Corporatism and Welfare.* London: Heinemann.

Cawson, A. 1985. *Organized Interests and the State: Studies in Meso-Corporatism.* London: Sage.

Central Statistical Office. Monthly. *Economic Trends.* London: Central Statistical Office.

Chubb, B. 1963. Going Around Persecuting Civil Servants: The Role of the Irish Parliamentary Representative. *Political Studies* 11:272–86.

Collier, D., and R. E. Messick. 1975. Prerequisites versus Diffusion: Testing Alternative Explanations of Social Security Adoption. *American Political Science Review* 69:1299–1315.

Commission of the European Communities. 1981. *Final Report on the First Programme of Pilot Schemes and Studies to Combat Poverty.* Brussels: Commission of the EC, Com (81) 769.

Cook, C., and J. Paxton. 1986. *European Political Facts* London: Macmillan.

Coombes, D. 1976. *The Power of the Purse.* London: Allen and Unwin.

Coughlin, R. M. 1979. Social Policy and Ideology: Public Opinion in Eight Rich Countries. In *Comparative Social Research,* ed. R. F. Tomasson, vol. 2, pp. 1–40. Greenwich, CT: JAI.

Coughlin, R. M. 1980. *Ideology, Public Opinion and Welfare Policy.* Berkeley, CA: Institute of International Studies, Univ. of California.

Crewe, I. 1986. On the Death and Resurrection of Class Voting: Some Comments on How Britain Votes. *Political Studies* 34:620–38.

Crozier, M., S. P. Huntington, and J. Watanuki. 1975. *The Crisis of Democracy.* New York: New York Univ. Press.

Culyer, A. J. 1983. Public or Private Health Services? A Skeptic's View. *Journal of Policy Analysis and Management* 2:386–402.

Daalder, H. 1984. In Search of the Center of European Party Systems. *American Political Science Review* 78:92–109.

Dalton, R. J. 1988. *Citizen Politics in Western Democracies*. Chatham, NJ: Chatham House.

Dalton, R. J., S. Flanagan, and P. Beck, eds. 1984. *Electoral Change in Advanced Industrial Democracies*. Princeton, NJ: Princeton Univ. Press.

Daltrop, A. 1982. *Politics and the European Community*. London: Longman.

Darbel, A., and D. Schnapper. 1969. *Les Agents du Système Administratif*. Paris: Mouton.

Darbel, A., and D. Schnapper. 1972. *Le Système Administratif*. Paris: Mouton.

Davis, P. K., and B. G. Peters. 1986. Migration to the United Kingdom and the Emergence of a New Politics. *The Annals* 485:129–38.

de la Mahotiere, S. 1970. *Towards One Europe*. Harmondsworth: Penguin.

Delruelle-Vosswinkel, N., and A. P. Frognier. 1980. L'Opinion Publique et les Problemes Communautaires. *Courrier Hebdomadaire du CRISP* 10:1–22.

Denison, E. F. 1967. *Why Growth Rates Differ: Postwar Experience in Nine Western Countries*. Washington, DC: Brookings Institution.

Dente, B. 1985. *Governare la Frammentazione*. Bologna: Il Mulino.

Derlien, H.-U. 1988. Repercussions of Government Change on the Career Civil Service in West Germany: The Case of 1969 and 1982. *Governance* 1:50–78.

DeSwann, A. 1973. *Coalition Theories and Cabinet Formation*. Amsterdam: Elsevier.

Deutsch, K. W. 1952. *Nationalism and Social Communications*. New York: Free Press.

Deutsch, K. W., L. J. Edinger, R. C. Macridis, and R. L. Merritt. 1967. *France, Germany and the Western Alliance*. New York: Scribners.

Diamant, A. 1968. Tradition and Innovation in French Administration. *Comparative Political Studies* 1:251–74.

Dogan, M. 1975. *The Mandarins of Western Europe*. New York: John Wiley.

Dogan, M., and D. Pelassy. 1987. *Le Moloch en Europe*. Paris: Economica.

Doig, A. 1984. *Corruption and Misconduct in Contemporary British Politics*. Harmondsworth: Penguin.

Donnison, D. 1984. The Progressive Potential of Privatisation. In *Privatisation and the Welfare State*, ed. J. LeGrand and R. Robinson, pp. 45–57. London: George Allen and Unwin.

Douglas, J. D. 1989. *The Myth of the Welfare State*. New Brunswick, NJ: Transaction.

Downs, A. 1957. *An Economic Theory of Democracy*. New York: Harper & Row.

Downs, A. 1967. *Inside Bureaucracy*. Boston: Little, Brown.

Downs, A. 1972. Up and Down with Ecology—The Issue-Attention Cycle. *The Public Interest* 28:38–50.

Downs, G. W., and P. D. Larkey. 1986. *The Search for Government Efficiency: From Hubris to Helplessness*. New York: Random House.

Drewry, G. 1981. Legislation. In *The Commons Today*, ed. S. A. Walkland and M. Ryle, pp. 87–117. London: Fontana.

Drewry, G., ed. 1985. *The New Select Committees*. Oxford: Clarendon Press.

Drewry, G., and T. Butcher. 1988. *The Civil Service Today*. Oxford: Blackwells.

Dror, Y. 1986. *Policymaking Under Adversity*. New Brunswick, NJ: Transaction.

Dunleavy, P. 1979. The Urban Basis of Political Alignment. *British Journal of Political Science* 9:409–44.

Duverger, M. 1964. *Political Parties*. New York: John Wiley.

Duverger, M. 1987. *La Cohabitation des Français*. Paris: Presses Universitaires Françaises.

Eatwell, R., and N. O'Sullivan. 1989. *The Nature of the Right*. London: Pinter.

Egeberg, M. 1981. *Stat og Organisasjoner*. Bergen: Universitetsforlaget.

Elder N., A. H. Thomas, and D. Arter. 1983. *The Consensual Democracies?* Oxford: Martin Robertson.

Eliasson, G., and B.-C. Ysander. 1981. Picking Winners or Bailing Out Losers? *Working Paper*, no. 37. Stockholm: Industriens Utredningsinstitut.

Elvander, N. 1972. The Politics of Taxation in Sweden, 1945–70: A Study of the Function of Parties and Organizations. *Scandinavian Political Studies* 7:63–82.

Emanuel, H. 1980. Factors in the Growth in the Number of Disability Beneficiaries in the Netherlands. *International Social Security Review* 33:41–60.

Ericksson, B. 1983. Sweden's Budget System in a Changing World. *Public Budgeting and Finance* 3:64–80.

Eriksen, T. E. 1981. Some Reflections on the Role of National Supplementary Pensions Scheme in the Swedish Pensions System. *International Social Security Review* 34:36–44.

Featherstone, K., and D. K. Katsoudas. 1987. *Political Change in Greece: Before and After the Colonels*. London: Croom Helm.

Feige, E. L. 1979. How Big Is the Irregular Economy? *Challenge* 22:5–13.

Feigenbaum, H. B. 1985. *The Politics of Public Enterprise: French Oil and the State*. Princeton, NJ: Princeton Univ. Press.

Financial Times. 1988. Law Report, June 20, p. 36.

Flora, P. 1986a. *Growth to Limits: The Western European Welfare States since World War II*, vol. 1. Berlin: DeGruyter.

Flora, P. 1986b. *Growth to Limits: The Western European Welfare States since World War II*, vol. 2. Berlin: DeGruyter.

Flora, P., and J. Alber. 1981. Modernization, Democratization and the Development of Welfare States in Western Europe. In *The Development of Welfare States in Europe and North America*, ed. P. Flora and A. Heidenheimer, pp. 37–80. New Brunswick, NJ: Transaction.

Flora, P., et al. 1983. *State, Economy, and Society in Western Europe, 1815–1975: A Data Handbook*. Frankfurt: Campus.

Fortin, Y. 1988. Reflection on Public Administration in France, 1986–87. *Governance* 1:101–110.

Fournier, J. 1987. *Le Travail Gouvernmental*. Paris: Dalloz.

Franklin, M. N. 1985. *The Decline of Class Voting in Britain*. Oxford: Clarendon Press.

Franklin, M. N., and T. T. Mackie. 1984. Reassessing the Importance of Size and Ideology in the Formation of Governing Coalitions in Parliamentary Democracies. *American Journal of Political Science* 28:671–92.

Frears, J. R. 1981. Parliament in the Fifth Republic. In *The Fifth Republic at Twenty*, ed. W. G. Andrews and S. Hoffman, pp. 57–78. Albany: State Univ. of New York Press.

Frey, B. S., and H. Weck. 1983. Estimating the Shadow Economy: A Naive Approach. *Oxford Economic Papers* 35:23–44.

Frey, L. 1979. Del Lavoro Nero alla Misurazione del Reddito "Sommerso." *Notizario Ceres di Economia del Lavoro* 6:1–4.

Furniss, N. 1984. Devolution and Identity in Scotland and Wales. In *Dilemmas of Change in British Politics*, ed. D. T. Studlar and J. L. Waltman, pp. 126–54. London: Macmillan.

Furniss, N., and T. Tilton. 1977. *The Case for the Welfare State*. Bloomington, IN: Indiana Univ. Press.

Gamble, A. 1988. *The Free Economy and the Strong State*. Durham, NC: Duke Univ. Press.

Gaudin, J., and M. Schiray. 1984. L'Economie Cachée en France: Etat du Debat et Bilan des Travaux. *Revue Economique* 4:691–733.

Germann, R. E. 1981. *Ausserparlamentarische Kommissionen: Die Milizerverwaltung des Bundes*. Berne: Haupt.

Germann, R. E. 1985. *Experts et commissions de la Confederation*. Lausanne: Presses Polytechniques Romandes.

Gilbert, M. 1989. *World War II*. London: Weidenfeld and Nicolson.

Gilsdorf, R. R. 1989. Government, Equality and Economic Growth in Western Europe: A Cross-National Empirical Study. *Governance* 2:422–56.

Goodsell, C. T. 1984. The Grace Commission: Seeking Efficiency for the Whole People? *Public Administration Review* 44:196–204.

Goodsell, C. T. 1985. *The Case for Bureaucracy*, 2d ed. Chatham, NJ: Chatham House.

Gormley, W. T. 1982. Alternative Models of the Regulatory Process: Public Utility Regulation in the States. *Western Political Quarterly* 35:297–317.

Gormley, W. T. 1987. Institutional Policy Analysis: A Critical Review. *Journal of Policy Analysis and Management* 6:153–69.

Gourevitch, P. A. 1986. *Politics in Hard Times: Comparative Responses to International Economic Crises*. Ithaca, NY: Cornell Univ. Press.

Gray, A., and W. I. Jenkins. 1986. Accountable Management in British Central Government: Some Reflections on the Financial Management Initiative. *Financial Accountability and Management* 2:171–85.

Grosser, A. 1975. Quoted in M. Dogan, *The Mandarins of Western Europe*. New York: John Wiley.

Gunlicks, A. B. 1981. *Local Government Reform and Reorganizations*. Port Washington, NY: Kennikat.

Gunther, R., G. Sani, and G. Shabad. 1988. *Spain after Franco: The Making of a Competitive Party System*. Berkeley, CA: Univ. of California Press.

Gustafsson, G. 1981. Local Government Reform in Sweden. In *Local Government Reform and Reorganization*, ed. A. B. Gunlicks, pp. 76–92. Port Washington, NY: Kennikat.

Haas, E. B. 1964. *Beyond the Nation State*. Stanford, CA: Stanford Univ. Press.

Hadenius, A. 1978. Ämbetsverkens Styrelsen. *Statsvetenskapliga Tidskrift* 81:19–32.

Hadenius, A. 1986. *A Crisis of the Welfare State.* Stockholm: Almqvist and Wiksell.

Hall, P. A. 1986. *Governing the Economy: The Politics of State Intervention in Britain and France.* New York: Oxford Univ. Press.

Hartley, T. C. 1988. *The Foundations of European Community Law: An Introduction to the Constitutional and Administrative Law of the European Community.* New York: Oxford Univ. Press.

Hatfield, M. 1978. *The House the Left Built: Inside Labour Policy-making, 1970–75.* London: Gollancz.

Hay, P. R., and M. G. Haward. 1988. Comparative Green Politics: Beyond the European Context. *Political Studies* 36:433–48.

Haycraft, J. 1985. *Italian Labyrinth.* London: Secker and Warburg.

Hayward, J. 1966. *Private Interests and Public Policy: The Experience of the French Economic and Social Council.* London: Longman.

Hayward, J. 1983. *France: The One and Indivisible Republic,* 2d ed. New York: Norton.

Hayward, J. 1986. *The State and the Market Economy: Industrial Patriotism and Economic Intervention in France.* New York: New York Univ. Press.

Headey, B. 1974. *British Cabinet Ministers.* London: Macmillan.

Headey, B. 1978. *Housing Policy in the Developed Economy.* London: Croom Helm.

Heath, A., R. Jowell, and J. Curtice. 1985. *How Britain Votes.* Oxford: Pergamon.

Heckscher, G. 1984. *The Welfare State and Beyond: Success and Problems in Scandinavia.* Minneapolis, MN: Univ. of Minnesota Press.

Heclo, H. 1974. *Modern Social Politics in Britain and Sweden.* New Haven, CT: Yale Univ. Press.

Heclo, H. 1975. The Frontiers of Social Policy. *Policy Sciences* 6:403–21.

Heclo, H. 1988. The In and Outer System: A Critical Assessment. *Political Science Quarterly* 103:37–56.

Heisler, B. S., and M. O. Heisler. 1986. Transnational Migration and the Modern Democratic State: Familiar Problems in New Form or a New Problem? *The Annals* 485:12–22.

Heisler, M. O. 1979. Corporate Pluralism Revisited: Where Is the Theory? *Scandinavian Political Studies* 2 (n.s.), 3: 277–98.

Heisler, M. O., with R. B. Kvavik. 1974. The European Polity Model. In *Politics in Europe,* ed. M. O. Heisler, pp. 27–89. New York: David McKay.

Henig, J. R., C. Hamnett, and H. B. Feigenbaum. 1988. The Politics of Privatization: A Comparative Perspective. *Governance* 1:442–68.

Hennessy, P. 1986. *Cabinet.* Oxford: Basil Blackwell.

Her Majesty's Stationery Office. 1983. *Streamlining the Cities.* Cmnd. 9063. London: HMSO.

Hessing, D. J., H. Elffers, and R. H. Weigel. 1986. Self-Report versus Behavior: An Examination of the Correlates of Tax Evasion. Report I-15, Research Project on

Tax Evasion and Social Security Fraud, Faculty of Law, Erasmus University, Rotterdam.

Hewstone, M. 1986. *Understanding Attitudes to the European Community*. Cambridge: Cambridge Univ. Press.

Hirsch, F. 1976. *The Social Limits to Growth*. Cambridge, MA: Harvard Univ. Press.

Hirschman, A. O. 1970. *Exit, Voice and Loyalty*. Cambridge, MA: Harvard Univ. Press.

Hogwood, B. W. 1988. *From Crisis to Complacency: Policymaking in Britain*. Oxford: Oxford Univ. Press.

Hogwood, B. W., and B. G. Peters. 1983. *Policy Dynamics*. Brighton: Wheatsheaf.

Hollingsworth, J. R., and L. N. Lindberg. 1985. The Governance of the American Economy: The Role of Markets, Clans, Hierarchies and Associative Behavior. In *Private Interest Government*, ed. W. Streeck and P. C. Schmitter, pp. 221–54. London: Sage.

Hood, C., and G. F. Schuppert. 1988. *Delivering Public Services in Western Europe*. London: Sage.

Hoskyns, J. 1983. Whitehall and Westminster: An Outsider's View. *Parliamentary Affairs* 36:137–47.

Huntington, S. P. 1974. Postindustrial Politics: How Benign Will It Be? *Comparative Politics* 6:164–92.

Inglehart, R. 1977. *The Silent Revolution: Changing Values and Political Styles Among Western Publics*. Princeton, NJ: Princeton Univ. Press.

Inglehart, R. 1979. Value Priorities and Socio-economic Change. In *Political Action*, ed. S. Barnes and M. Kaase, pp. 305–42. Beverly Hills, CA: Sage.

Inglehart, R. 1981. Post-Materialism in an Age of Insecurity. *American Political Science Review* 75:880–900.

Inglehart, R. 1984. The Changing Structure of Political Cleavages in Western Society. In *Electoral Change in Advanced Industrial Societies*, ed. R. J. Dalton, S. C. Flanagan, and P. A. Beck, pp. 25–69. Princeton, NJ: Princeton Univ. Press.

Inglehart, R., and J.-J. Rabier. 1978. Economic Uncertainty and European Solidarity: Public Opinion Trends. *The Annals* 440:66–87.

Ingraham, P. W., and B. G. Peters. 1988. The Conundrum of Reform. *Review of Public Personnel Administration* 8:3–16.

International Labour Office. 1987. *Annotated Bibliography on Clandestine Employment*. Geneva: ILO.

Jenkins, K., K. Caines, and A. Jackson. 1988. *Improving Management in Government: The Next Steps* (Ibbs Report). London: HMSO.

Jenkins, P. 1988. *Mrs. Thatcher's Revolution: The End of the Socialist Era*. Cambridge, MA: Harvard Univ. Press.

Jessop, B. 1978. Capitalism and Democracy: The Best Possible Shell? In *Power and the State*, ed. G. Littlejohn, pp. 132–64. London: Croom Helm.

Johansen, L. N., and J. E. Kolberg. 1985. Welfare State Regression in Scandinavia?: The Development of the Scandinavian Welfare States from 1970 to 1980. In *The*

Welfare State and Its Aftermath, ed. S. N. Eisenstadt and O. Ahimeir, pp. 143–76. Totowa, NJ: Barnes and Noble.

Johansen, L. N., and O. P. Kristensen. 1982. Corporatist Traits in Denmark, 1946–1976. In *Patterns of Corporatist Policy-Making*, ed. G. Lehmbruch and P. C. Schmitter, pp. 189–218. London: Sage.

Johnson, C. 1982. *MITI and the Japanese Miracle*. Berkeley, CA: Univ. of California Press.

Johnson, N. 1979. Committees in the West German Bundestag. In *Committees in Legislatures*, ed. J. D. Lees and M. Shaw, pp. 102–47. Durham, NC: Duke Univ. Press.

Johnston, M., and D. Wood. 1986. Right and Wrong in Public and Private Life. In *British Social Attitudes, 1986*, ed. R. Jowell et al., pp. 121–47. Aldershot: Gower.

Jones, G. W. 1988. The Crisis in Central-Local Government Relations in Britain. *Governance* 1:162–83.

Jordan, A. G. 1981. Iron Triangles, Woolly Corporatism and Elastic Nets: Images of the Policy Process. *Journal of Public Policy* 1:95–124.

Jordan, A. G., and J. J. Richardson. 1982. The British Policy Style or the Logic of Negotiation. In *Policy Styles in Western Europe*, ed. J. J. Richardson, pp. 80–110. London: George Allen and Unwin,

Kaase, M. 1988. Political Alienation and Protest. In *Comparing Pluralist Democracies: Strains on Legitimacy*, ed. M. Dogan, pp. 114–42. Boulder, CO: Westview.

Katz, R. S. 1985. Measuring Party Identification with Eurobarometer Data: A Warning Note. *West European Politics* 8:104–108.

Katz, R. S. 1987. *The Future of Party Government: European and American Experiences*. Berlin: DeGruyter.

Katzenstein, P. J. 1985. *Small States in World Markets*. Ithaca, NY: Cornell Univ. Press.

Kaufmann, F. X., G. Majone, and V. Ostrom. 1986. *Guidance, Control and Evaluation in the Public Sector*. Berlin: DeGruyter.

Kavanagh, D. 1987. *Thatcherism and British Politics: The End of Consensus?* Oxford: Oxford Univ. Press.

Keating, M. 1988. Does Regional Government Work?: The Experience of Italy, France and Spain. *Governance* 1:184–209.

Keating, M., and B. Jones. 1985. *Regions in the European Community*. Oxford: Oxford Univ. Press.

Keegan, W. 1984. *Mrs. Thatcher's Economic Experiment*. London: A. Lane.

Keeler, J. T. S. 1981. Corporatism and Official Union Hegemony: The Case of French Agricultural Syndicalism. In *Organizing Interests in Western Europe*, ed. S. Berger, pp. 185–208. Cambridge: Cambridge Univ. Press.

Kelman, S. 1985. The Grace Commission: How Much Waste in Government? *The Public Interest* 78:62–882.

Kemp, P. 1990. The Next Steps Initiative in British Government. *Governance* 3:86–96.

Kerr, H. K. 1974. *Switzerland: Social Cleavages and Partisan Conflict.* London: Sage.

Kessler, D., and A. Masson. 1985. What Are the Distributional Consequences of Socialist Government Policy in France? *Journal of Social Policy* 14:403–18.

Kettl, D. 1987. *Government by Proxy.* Washington, DC: Congressional Quarterly Press.

King, A. 1975. Overload: Problems of Governing in the 1970s. *Political Studies* 23:284–96.

Kitschelt, H. 1989. *The Logics of Party Formation: Ecological Parties in Belgium and West Germany.* Ithaca, NY: Cornell Univ. Press.

Kitzinger, U. 1973. *Diplomacy and Persuasion: How Britain Joined the Common Market.* Oxford: Basil Blackwell.

Klein, R. 1983. *The Politics of the National Health Service.* London: Longman.

Klein, R., et al. 1988. *Joint Approaches to Social Policy.* Cambridge: Cambridge Univ. Press.

Kohler, P. A., and H. F. Zacher. 1982. *The Evolution of Social Insurance, 1881–1981.* London: Frances Pinter.

Kommers, D. P. 1976. *Judicial Politics in West Germany.* Beverly Hills, CA: Sage.

Korpi, W. 1985. Economic Growth and the Welfare State: Leaky Bucket or Irrigation System. *European Sociological Review* 1:97–118.

Kraemer, P. E. 1955. *The Societal State.* Meppel: Boom en Zoon.

Krasner, S. 1978. *Defending the National Interest.* Princeton, NJ: Princeton Univ. Press.

Krejci, J., and Velimsky, V. 1981. *The Ethnic and Political Nations of Europe.* London: Croom Helm.

Kuhnle, S. 1975. *Patterns of Social and Political Mobilization: A Historical Comparative Analysis.* London: Sage.

Kuhnle, S., and L. Solheim. 1981. Party Programs and the Welfare State: Consensus and Conflict in Norway 1945–1977. *Skrifter,* no. 3. Sosiologisk Institutt, Bergen, Norway.

Laegreid, P., and P. G. Roness. 1983. *Sentraladministrasjon.* Bergen: Tiden Norsk.

Lafferty, W. M. 1971. *Economic Development and the Response of Labor in Scandinavia: A Multilevel Analysis.* Oslo: Universitetsforlaget.

Lafferty, W. M., and O. Knutsen. 1985. Postmaterialism in a Social Democratic State: An Analysis of the Distinctness and Congruity of the Inglehart Value Syndrome in Norway. *Comparative Political Studies* 17:411–31.

Lane, J.-E., and S. Ersson. 1987. *Politics and Society in Western Europe.* London: Sage.

LaPalombara, J. D. 1966. The Decline of Ideology: A Dissent and an Interpretation. *American Political Science Review* 60:5–16.

LaPalombara, J. D. 1987. *Democracy Italian Style.* New Haven, CT: Yale Univ. Press.

Laurin, U. 1986. *På Heder och Samvete.* Stockholm: P. A. Norstedts.

Lawson, K., and P. H. Merkl. 1988. *When Parties Fail: Emerging Alternative Organizations.* Princeton, NJ: Princeton Univ. Press.

Layton-Henry, Z. 1988. The Political Challenge of Migration in Western European States. *European Journal of Political Research* 16:587–96.

Lee, J. M. 1984. Financial Management and the Career Service. *Public Administration* 62:2.

Leemans, A. 1976. *Managing Change in Government*. The Hague: Martinus Nijhoff.

Lehmbruch, G. 1979. Liberal Corporatism and Party Government. In *Trends Toward Corporatist Intermediation*, ed. P. C. Schmitter and G. Lehmbruch, pp. 147–83. Beverly Hills, CA: Sage.

Lenkowsky, L. 1987. *Politics, Economics and Welfare Reform*. Lanham, MD: Univ. Press of America.

Lepper, M. 1983. Internal Structure of Public Offices. In *Public Administration in the Federal Republic of Germany*, ed. K. König, H. J. von Oertzen, and F. Wagener, pp. 83–93. Boston: Kluwer.

Leu, R. E., R. L. Frey, and B. Buhmann. 1985. Taxes, Expenditures, and Income Distribution in Switzerland. *Journal of Social Policy* 14:341–60.

Levine, C. H. 1978. Organizational Decline and Cutback Management. *Public Administration Review* 38:316–25.

Levine, C. H. 1980. *Managing Fiscal Stress: The Crisis in the Public Sector*. Chatham, NJ: Chatham House.

Lewis, A. 1982. *The Psychology of Taxation*. Oxford: Martin Robertson.

Lijphart, A. 1968. *The Politics of Accommodation*. Berkeley, CA: Univ. of California Press.

Lijphart, A. 1977. *Democracy in Pluralist Societies*. New Haven, CT: Yale Univ. Press.

Lijphart, A. et al. 1987. *Las Democracias Contemporaneas; Un Analisis Comparativo*. Barcelona: Ariel.

Likierman, A. 1982. Management Information for Ministers: The MINIS System in the Department of the Environment. *Public Administration* 60:127–42.

Lindbeck, A. 1974. *Swedish Economic Policy*. Berkeley: Univ. of California Press.

Lindberg, L. N., and S. A. Scheingold. 1970. *Europe's Would-Be Polity*. Englewood Cliffs, NJ: Prentice-Hall.

Listhaug, O., and A. H. Miller. 1985. Public Support for Tax Evasion: Self-Interest or Symbolic Politics. *European Journal of Political Research* 13:265–82.

Lodge, J. 1986. *Direct Elections to the European Parliament*. London: Macmillan.

Lorwin, V. R. 1966. Belgium: Religion, Class and Language in National Politics. In *Political Oppositions in Western Democracies*, ed. R. A. Dahl, pp. 147–87. New Haven, CT: Yale Univ. Press.

Lowi, T. 1972. Four Systems of Politics, Policy and Choice. *Public Administration Review* 32:298–310.

Luethy, H. 1955. *France Against Herself*. New York: Praeger.

Lundqvist, L., and K. Ståhlberg. 1983. *Byråkrater i Norden*. Åbo, Finland: Åbo Akademi.

MacDaniel, P., and S. Surrey. 1985. *International Aspects of Tax Expenditures*. Deventer, The Netherlands: Kluwer.

Macgill, S. M. 1987. *The Politics of Anxiety*. London: Pion.

Machin, H. 1977. *The Prefect in French Public Administration*. New York: St. Martin's.

Mackie, T. T. Annual. General Elections in Western Nations. *European Journal for Political Research*.

Mackie, T. T., and B. W. Hogwood. 1985. *Unlocking the Cabinet: Cabinet Committees*. London: Sage.

Mackie, T. T., and R. Rose. 1982. *International Almanac of Electoral History*. New York: Facts on File.

MacRae, D. 1967. *Parliament, Parties and Society in France, 1946–58*. New York: St. Martin's.

Mair, P. 1984. Party Politics in Contemporary Europe: A Challenge to Party? *West European Politics* 7:170–84.

Manoïlesco, M. 1934. *Le Siècle du Corporatisme*. Paris: F. Alcan.

Marples, E. 1969. A Dog's Life in a Ministry. In *Policymaking in Britain*, ed. R. Rose, pp. 128–31. London: Macmillan.

Marsh, A. 1975. The "Silent Revolution," Value Priorities, and the Quality of Life in Britain. *American Political Science Review* 69:21–30.

Marsh, D. 1987. In the Clutch of Corporatism. *Financial Times*, November 5.

Mauco, G. 1984. *Les Étrangers en France et le Probleme du Racisme*. Paris: Pensee Universelle.

Mayntz, R., and H.-U. Derlien. 1989. Party Patronage and Politicization of the West German Administrative Elite 1970–1987—Toward Hybridization? *Governance* 2:381–401.

Meijer, H. 1969. Bureaucracy and Policy Formation in Sweden. *Scandinavian Political Studies* 4:103–16.

Metcalfe, L. 1988. The Logic of Public Management. Paper presented at IPSA World Congress, Washington, DC, August 29–September 1.

Metcalfe, L. and S. Richards. 1984. Raynerism and Efficiency in Government. In *Issues in Public Sector Accounting*, ed. Hopwood and C. Tompkins, pp. 188–211. Oxford: Philip Allan.

Meyers, F. 1985. *La Politisation de l'Administration*. Brussels: Institut International des Sciences Administratives.

Michiletti, M. Forthcoming. Interest Groups in Post-Industrial Sweden. In *Interest Groups in Post-Industrial Democracies*. ed. C. S. Thomas.

Mielke, S. 1983. *Internationales Gewerkschaftshandbuch*. Opladen: Leske & Budrich.

Mierlo, H. J. G. A. van. 1986. Depillarisation and the Decline of Consociationalism in the Netherlands, 1970–85. *West European Politics* 9:97–119.

Migdal, J. S. 1988. *Strong Societies and Weak States*. Princeton, NJ: Princeton Univ. Press.

Milward, H. B., and H. G. Rainey. 1983. Don't Blame the Bureaucracy. *Journal of Public Policy* 3:149–68.

Mitrany, D. 1946. *A Working Peace System*. London: Royal Institute of International Affairs.

Moe, T. M. 1980. *The Organization of Interests.* Chicago: Univ. of Chicago Press.

Moen, P. 1989. *Working Parents.* Madison, WI: Univ. of Wisconsin Press.

Molin, B. 1965. *Tjänstepensionsfragen.* Göteborg: Akademiforlaget.

Mondari, A. 1965. *Basi statistiche e leggi assimatiche della dinamica delli evasione fiscale.* Milan: Bocconi.

Mueller, D. C. 1983. *The Political Economy of Growth.* New Haven, CT: Yale Univ. Press.

Muramatsu, M. 1988. Recent Administrative Developments in Japan. *Governance* 1:468–78.

Natchez, P. B., and I. C. Bupp. 1973. Policy and Priority in the Budgetary Process. *American Political Science Review* 67:951–63.

Nathan, R. P., and F. C. Doolittle. 1987. *Reagan and the States.* Princeton, NJ: Princeton Univ. Press.

Nedelman, B., and K. G. Meier. 1982. Theories of Contemporary Corporatism: Static or Dynamic. In *Trends Toward Corporatist Intermediation,* ed. P. Schmitter and G. Lehmbruch, pp. 95–118. Beverly Hills, CA: Sage.

Nedjati, Z. M., and E. N. Trice. 1978. *English and Continental Systems of Administrative Law.* Amsterdam: North Holland.

Nelson, R. R. 1977. *The Moon and the Ghetto.* New York: Norton.

Netherlands Scientific Council for Government Policy. 1983. *A Reappraisal of Welfare Policy.* The Hague: Netherlands Council.

Neustadt, R. 1966. White House and Whitehall. *The Public Interest* 2:55–69.

Newland, C. A. 1983. A Mid-term Appraisal—The Reagan Presidency: Limited Government and Political Administration. *Public Administration Review* 43:1–21.

Newton, K. 1977. Is Small Really so Beautiful? Is Big Really so Ugly? *Studies in Public Policy,* no. 18. Glasgow: University of Strathclyde Centre for the Study of Public Policy.

Nobelen, P. 1983. Kwijend Corporatisme en Stagnerende Verzorgingsstaat. In *Corporatisme en Verzorgingsstaat,* ed. T. Akkermans and P. Nobelen, pp. 86–108. Leiden: Univ. of Leiden.

O'Higgins, M. 1986a. Inequality, Redistribution and Recession: The British Experience, 1976–1982. *Journal of Social Policy* 14:279–307.

O'Higgins, M. 1986b. Public/Private Interaction and Pension Provision. In *Public/Private Interplay in Social Protection,* ed. M. Rein and L. Rainwater, pp. 99–148. Armonk, NY: M. E. Sharpe.

Okun, A. M. 1975. *Equality and Efficiency: The Big Tradeoff.* Washington, DC: Brookings Institution.

Olsen, J. P. 1988. The Modernization of Public Administration in the Nordic Countries: Some Research Questions. *Hallinnon Tutkimus* 8:2–17.

Olson, M. 1965. *The Logic of Collective Action.* Cambridge, MA: Harvard Univ. Press.

Olson, M. 1982. *The Rise and Decline of Nations.* New Haven, CT: Yale Univ. Press.

Organization for Economic Cooperation and Development. 1981. *The Crisis of the Welfare State*. Paris: OECD.

Organization for Economic Cooperation and Development. 1984. *Tax Expenditures: A Review of the Issues and Country Practices*. Paris: OECD.

Organization for Economic Cooperation and Development. 1985. *Social Expenditure 1960–1990: Problems of Growth and Control*. Paris: OECD.

Organization for Economic Cooperation and Development. 1986. *Living Conditions in OECD Countries*. Paris: OECD.

Organization for Economic Cooperation and Development. 1988. *Aging Populations*. Paris: OECD.

Organization for Economic Cooperation and Development. Annual a. *The Tax/Benefit Position of Selected Income Groups in OECD Member Countries*. Paris: OECD.

Organization for Economic Cooperation and Development. Annual b. *National Accounts of OECD Member Countries*. Paris: OECD.

Organization for Economic Cooperation and Development. Annual c. *Revenue Statistics for OECD Countries*. Paris: OECD.

O'Riagain, S. 1988. Cited in *Pittsburgh Press,* July 24, p. B1.

Orvik, N. 1975. *Norway's No to Europe*. Pittsburgh, PA: International Studies Association.

O'Toole, L. J. 1986. Policy Recommendations for Multi-Actor Implementation: An Assessment of the Field. *Journal of Public Policy* 6:181–210.

Oystese, O. 1980. *Staten en Skjenetime*. Oslo: Lunde.

Page, E. C. 1985. *Political Authority and Bureaucratic Power*. Knoxville, TN: Univ. of Tennessee Press.

Panitch, L. 1979. The Development of Corporatism in Liberal Democracies. In *Trends Toward Corporatist Intermediation*, ed. P. C. Schmitter and G. Lehmbruch, pp. 119–46. London: Sage.

Panitch, L. 1980. Recent Theorizations on Corporatism: Reflections on a Growth Industry. *British Journal of Sociology* 31:159–87.

Pasquino, G. 1980. *Crisi dei Partiti e Governabilità*. Bologna: Il Mulino.

Peacock, A. T., and J. Wiseman. 1967. *The Growth of Public Expenditure in the United Kingdom*. London: George Allen and Unwin.

Pedersen, M. N. 1983. Changing Patterns of Electoral Volatility in European Party Systems, 1948–77. In *Western European Party Systems*, ed. H. Daalder and P. Mair, pp. 29–66. London: Sage.

Perez-Diaz. 1984. Mesogobiernos Territoriales y Económicos: Autonomias Regionales y Corporatismo en España. *Papeles de Económica Española* 16:1–24.

Perez-Diaz, V. 1987. Economic Policies and Social Pacts in Spain during the Transition. In *Political Stability and Neo-Corporatism*, ed. I. Scholten, pp. 216–46. London: Sage.

Peters, B. G. 1981. The Problem of Bureaucratic Government. *Journal of Politics* 43:56–82.

Peters, B. G. 1987. Politicians and Bureaucrats in the Politics of Policymaking. In *Bureaucracy and Public Choice*, ed. J.-E. Lane, pp. 256–82. London: Sage.

Peters, B. G. 1988. The Machinery of Government: Concepts and Issues. In *Organizing Governance: Governing Organizations,* ed. C. Campbell and B. G. Peters, pp. 19–53. Pittsburgh, PA: Univ. of Pittsburgh Press.

Peters, B. G. 1989a. *The Politics of Bureaucracy,* 3d ed. New York: Longman.

Peters, B. G. 1989b. Changing Government in an Era of Retrenchment and Commitment. Mimeo, LOS Centre, Bergen, Norway.

Peters, B. G., and M. O. Heisler. 1983. Thinking about Public Sector Growth. In *Why Governments Grow: Measuring Public Sector Size,* ed. C. L. Taylor, pp. 177–97. Beverly Hills, CA: Sage.

Peters, B. G., and B. W. Hogwood. Forthcoming. The Application of Population Ecology Models to the Public Sector. *Research in Public Administration* 1.

Pettenati, P. 1979. *Illegal and Unrecorded Employment in Italy.* Paris: OECD Working Party on Employment and Unemployment Statistics.

Phillips, A. W. 1958. The Relation Between Unemployment and the Rate of Change of Money Wage Rates. *Economica* 25:283–99.

Piachaud, D. 1980. Taxation and Social Security. In *Taxation and Social Policy,* ed. C. Sandford, C. Pond, and R. Walker, pp. 68–83. London: Heinemann.

Poguntke, T. 1987. New Politics and Party Systems: The Emergence of a New Type of Party? *West European Politics* 10:76–88.

Pollitt, C. 1984. *Manipulating the Machine.* London: George Allen and Unwin.

Pollitt, C. 1986. Beyond the Managerial Model: The Case for Broadening Performance Assessment in Government and the Public Services. *Financial Accountability and Management* 2:155–70.

Pouvoirs. 1987. Special Issue: "Des Fonctionnaires Politises?"

Pridham, G. 1983. Not so Much a Programme—More a Way of Life: European Perspectives on the British SDP/Liberal Alliance. *Parliamentary Affairs* 36:183–201.

Pridham, G. 1986. *The New Mediterranean Democracies: Regime Transition in Spain, Greece and Portugal.* London: Frank Cass.

Pridham, G., and P. Pridham. 1979. *Towards Transnational Parties in the European Community.* London: Policy Studies Institute.

Pridham, G., and P. Pridham. 1981. *Transnational Party Cooperation and European Integration.* London: George Allen and Unwin.

Putnam, R. D. 1988. Institutional Performance and Political Culture: Some Puzzles about the Power of the Past. *Governance* 1:221–42.

Rainey, H. G., R. W. Backoff, and C. H. Levine. 1976. Comparing Public and Private Organizations. *Public Administration Review* 36:223–44.

Ravenal, E. C. 1985. *NATO: The Tides of Discontent.* Berkeley, CA: Institute of International Studies, Univ. of California.

Redwood, J. 1984. *Going for Broke: Gambling with Taxpayers' Money.* Oxford: Basil Blackwell.

Regini, M. 1982. Changing Relationships Between Labour and State in Italy: Towards a New Corporatist System. In *Patterns of Corporatist Policymaking,* ed. G. Lehmbruch and P. C. Schmitter, pp. 109–32. Beverly Hills, CA: Sage.

Reich, R. B. 1988. *The Power of Public Issues.* Cambridge, MA: Ballinger.

Rein, M., and L. Rainwater. 1986. The Public/Private Mix. In *Public-Private Interplay in Social Protection*, ed. M. Rein and L. Rainwater, pp. 3–24. Armonk, NY: M. E. Sharpe.

Remond, R., A. Coutrot, and I. Boussard. 1982. *Quarante ans de cabinets ministerials*. Paris: PUF.

Rhodes, R. A. W. 1988. *Beyond Westminster and Whitehall*. London: Unwin Hyman.

Riddell, P. 1988. Thatcher Robustly Attacks Delors' European Vision. *Financial Times*, July 28.

Ridley, F. F. 1985. Politics and the Selection of Higher Civil Servants in Britain. In *La Politisation de l'Administration*, ed. F. Meyers, pp. 151–77. Brussels: Institut International des Sciences Administratives.

Rigaud, J., and X. Delcros. 1984. *Les institutions administratives françaises, les structures*. Paris: Presses de la Fondation nationale de sciences politiques.

Riker, W. H. 1962. *A Theory of Political Coalitions*. New Haven, CT: Yale Univ. Press.

Riker, W. H., and P. C. Ordeshook. 1973. *Positive Political Theory*. Englewood Cliffs, NJ: Prentice-Hall.

Roca, J. 1987. Neo-corporatism in Post-Franco Spain. In *Political Stability and Neo-Corporatism*, ed. Ilja Scholten, pp. 247–68. London: Sage.

Rogaly, J. 1988. The Active Citizen for All Parties. *Financial Times*, October 5.

Roistacher, E. A. 1987. Housing and the Welfare State in the United States and Western Europe. *Netherlands Journal of Housing and Environmental Research* 2:143–75.

Rokkan, S. 1966. Norway: Numerical Democracy and Corporate Pluralism. In *Political Oppositions in Western Democracies*, ed. Robert A. Dahl, pp. 70–115. New Haven, CT: Yale Univ. Press.

Rokkan, S. 1967. Geography, Religion and Social Class. In *Party Systems and Voter Alignments*, ed. S. M. Lipset and S. Rokkan, pp. 367–444. New York: Free Press.

Rokkan, S. 1970. *Citizens, Elections, Parties*. Oslo: Universitetsforlaget.

Rokkan, S., and D. Urwin. 1982. *The Politics of Territorial Identity*. London: Sage.

Rose, R. 1971. *Governing Without Consensus: An Irish Perspective*. Boston: Beacon.

Rose, R. 1974. *The Problem of Party Government*. London: Macmillan.

Rose, R. 1976. On the Priorities of Government. *European Journal of Political Research* 4:247–89.

Rose, R. 1978. Ungovernability: Is There Fire Behind the Smoke? *Studies in Public Policy*, no. 16. Glasgow, University of Strathclyde, Centre for the Study of Public Policy.

Rose, R. 1985. Maximizing Tax Revenue While Minimizing Political Costs. *Journal of Public Policy* 5:289–320.

Rose, R., and B. G. Peters. 1978. *Can Government Go Bankrupt?* New York: Basic Books.

Rose, R., and I. McAllister. 1986. *The Voters Begin to Choose*. Beverly Hills, CA: Sage.

Rose, R., et al. 1985. *Public Employment in Western Nations.* Cambridge: Cambridge Univ. Press.

Rose-Ackerman, S. 1978. *Corruption: A Study of Political Economy.* New York: Academic Press.

Rothstein, B. 1986. *Den Socialdemokratiska Staten.* Lund: Studentlitteratur.

Rowat, D. C. 1985. *The Ombudsman Plan.* Lanham, MD: Univ. Press of America.

Rudig, W. 1988. Peace and Ecology Movements in Western Europe. *West European Politics* 11:26–39.

Rush, K. 1979. *NATO at 30.* Washington, DC: Atlantic Council.

Rydén, B., and V. Bergstrom. 1982. *Sweden: Choices for Economic and Social Policy in the 1980s.* London: George Allen and Unwin.

Sabatier, P. 1986. Top-Down and Bottom-Up Approaches to Implementation Research. *Journal of Public Policy* 6:21–48.

Salamon, L. 1981a. Rethinking Public Management: Third-Party Government and the Changing Forms of Government Action. *Public Policy* 29:255–75.

Salamon, L. 1981b. Reorganization—The Question of Goals. In *Federal Reorganization: What Have We Learned?* ed. P. Szanton, pp. 58–84. Chatham, NJ: Chatham House.

Samuelsson, K. 1968. *From Great Power to Welfare State.* London: George Allen and Unwin.

Särlvik, B., and I. Crewe. 1983. *Decade of Dealignment.* Cambridge: Cambridge Univ. Press.

Sartori, G. 1966. European Political Parties: The Case of Polarized Pluralism. In *Political Parties and Political Development,* ed. J. LaPalombara and M. Weiner, pp. 137–76. Princeton, NJ: Princeton Univ. Press.

Sartori, G. 1976. *Parties and Party Systems.* Cambridge: Cambridge Univ. Press.

Sartori, G. 1987. *Theory of Democracy Revisited,* vols. 1, 2. Chatham, NJ: Chatham House.

Saunders, P., and F. Klau. 1985. *The Role of the Public Sector: Causes and Consequences of Government Growth.* Paris: OECD.

Savas, E. S. 1982. *Privatizing the Public Sector.* Chatham, NJ: Chatham House.

Savas, E. S. 1987. *Privatization: The Key to Better Government.* Chatham, NJ: Chatham House.

Scharpf, F. 1977. Public Organization and the Waning of the Welfare State. *European Journal of Political Research* 5:339–62.

Schick, A. 1988. Micro-budgetary Adaptations to Fiscal Stress in Industrialized Countries. *Public Administration Review* 48: 523–33.

Schmitter, P. C. 1974. Still the Century of Corporatism? *Review of Politics* 36:85–131.

Schmitter, P. C. 1981. Interest Intermediation and Regime Governability in Contemporary Western Europe and North America. In *Organized Interests in Western Europe,* ed. S. Berger, pp. 285–327. Cambridge: Cambridge Univ. Press.

Schmitter, P. C., and G. Lehmbruch. 1982. *Trends Toward Corporatist Intermediation.* Beverly Hills, CA: Sage.

Schneider, J. 1985. Social Problems Theory: The Constructivist View. *Annual Review of Sociology* 11:209–29.

Schneider, S., and B. G. Peters. 1989. The British Welfare State. In *International Public Policy Sourcebook*, ed. J. DeSario and F. Bolotin, pp. 293–314. Westport, CT: Greenwood.

Schulman, P. R. 1980. *Large-Scale Policymaking*. New York: Elsevier.

Schulman, P. R. 1988. The Politics of "Ideational Policy." *Journal of Politics* 50:263–91.

Sears, D. O., and J. Citrin. 1982. *Tax Revolt—Something for Nothing in California*. Berkeley, CA: Univ. of California Press.

Seidman, H., and R. Gilmour. 1986. *Politics, Position and Power*, 4th ed. New York: Oxford Univ. Press.

Sharpe, L. J. 1987. The West European State: The Territorial Dimension. *West European Politics* 10:148–67.

Shils, E. 1968. The Concept and Function of Ideology. In *International Encyclopedia of the Social Sciences* 7:66–76. New York: Macmillan.

Shonfield, A. 1965. *Modern Capitalism*. New York: Oxford Univ. Press.

Silver, H. 1990. Privatizing Housing in Britain. In *Privatization and Its Alternatives*, ed. W. T. Gormley. Madison, WI: Univ. of Wisconsin Press.

Silver, M. 1980. *Affluence, Altruism and Atrophy*. New York: New York Univ. Press.

Simon, H. A. 1947. *Administrative Behavior*. New York: Free Press.

Sinnott, R. 1984. Interpretations of the Irish Party System. *European Journal of Political Research* 12:289–307.

Slayton, P., and M. J. Trebilcock. 1978. *The Professions and Public Policy*. Toronto: Univ. of Toronto Press.

Smith, S. R., and D. S. Stone. 1988. The Unexpected Consequences of Privatization. In *Remaking the Welfare State*, ed. M. K. Brown, pp. 232–52. Philadelphia: Temple Univ. Press.

Spicer, M. W., and S. B. Lundstedt. 1976. Understanding Tax Evasion. *Public Finance* 31:295–305.

Spicer, M. W., and J. E. Thomas. 1982. Audit Probabilities and the Tax Evasion Decision. *Journal of Economic Psychology* 2:241–45.

Spinelli, A. 1957. The Growth of the European Movement Since World War II. In *European Integration*, ed. C. G. Haines, pp. 37–63. Baltimore, MD: Johns Hopkins Univ. Press.

Spretnak, C., and F. Capra. 1986. *Green Politics: The Global Promise*. Boulder, CO: Bear and Co.

Ståhlberg, K., and S. Sjöblom. 1989. Styrningsstrategier i Utvecklandet av Finlandsk Förvaltning. In *Den Mangtydiga Styrningen*, ed. S. Sjöblom and K. Ståhlberg, pp. 37–90. Åbo: Academy Press.

Starr, P. 1990. The Case for Privatization. In *Privatization and Its Alternatives*, ed. W. T. Gormley. Madison, WI: Univ. of Wisconsin Press.

Steiner, J. 1981. The Consociational Theory and Beyond. *Comparative Politics* 13:339–54.

Steiner, J., and R. H. Dorff. 1980. *A Theory of Political Decision Modes*. Chapel Hill, NC: Univ. of North Carolina Press.

Steinkemper, B. 1974. *Klassische und politische Bürokratie in der Ministerialverwaltung der Bundesrepublik Deutschland*. Cologne: Carl Heymans.

Stephens, M. 1976. *Linguistic Minorities in Western Europe*. Llandyssul: Gomer Press.

Stewart, M. 1971. *Keynes and After*. Harmondsworth: Penguin.

Stone, D. A. 1980. *The Limits of Professional Power: National Health Care in the Federal Republic of Germany*. Chicago: Univ. of Chicago Press.

Stone, D. A. 1984. *The Disabled State*. Philadelphia: Temple Univ. Press.

Streeck, W., and P. C. Schmitter. 1985. *Private Interest Government: Beyond Market and State*. London: Sage.

Strömberg, L., and J. Westerståhl. 1984. *The New Swedish Communes*. Stockholm: Lerum.

Strümpel, B. 1969. The Contribution of Survey Research to Public Finance. In *Quantitative Analysis in Public Finance*, ed. A. T. Peacock, pp. 13–32. New York: Praeger.

Sundberg, J. 1986. Old Parties—New Challenges: Partisan and Social Changes in Scandinavian Welfare States. University of Helsinki, Department of Political Science, Discussion Paper #2.

Surrey, S. S., and P. R. McDaniel. 1985. *Tax Expenditures*. Cambridge, MA: Harvard Univ. Press.

Swaan, D. 1988. *The Retreat of the State*. Ann Arbor, MI: Univ. of Michigan Press.

Taagepera, R., and B. Grofman. 1985. Rethinking Duverger's Law: Predicting the Number of Parties in Plurality and PR Systems. *European Journal of Political Research* 13:341–52.

Tarschys, D. 1981. Rational Decremental Budgeting. *Policy Sciences* 14:49–58.

Tarschys, D. 1985. Curbing Public Expenditure: Current Trends. *Journal of Public Policy* 5:23–67.

Taylor, C. L., and M. Hudson. 1972. *World Handbook of Political and Social Indicators*, 2d ed. New Haven, CT: Yale Univ. Press.

Taylor, S. 1982. *The National Front in English Politics*. London: Macmillan.

Taylor-Gooby, P. 1982. Two Cheers for the Welfare State: Public Opinion and Private Welfare. *Journal of Public Policy* 2:319–46.

Taylor-Gooby, P. 1985. *Public Opinion, Ideology and State Welfare*. London: Routledge and Kegan Paul.

Taylor-Gooby, P. 1986. Consumption Cleavages and Welfare Politics. *Political Studies* 34:592–606.

Thurow, L. 1980. *The Zero-Sum Society*. New York: Basic Books.

Timsit, G. 1987. *Administrations et états: Étude comparée*. Paris: Presses Universitaires de France.

Toonen, T. A. J. 1985. Implementation Research and Institutional Design. In *Policy*

Implementation in Federal and Unitary Systems, ed. K. Hanf and T. A. J. Toonen, pp. 335–54. Boston: Martinus Nijhoff.

Touraine, A. 1971. *The Post-Industrial Society*. New York: Random House.

UNESCO. Annual. *Statistical Yearbook*. Paris: UNESCO.

Valen, H. 1973. "No" to EEC. *Scandinavian Political Studies* 8:214–26.

Van der Eijk, C., and C. Niemoller. 1983. *Political Change in the Netherlands*. Amsterdam: Erasmus Univ. Press.

Van Putten, J. 1982. Policy Styles in the Netherlands: Negotiation or Conflict. In *Policy Styles in Western Europe*, ed. J. J. Richardson, pp. 168–96. London: George Allen and Unwin.

Veljanovski, C. 1987. *Selling the State: Privatisation in Britain*. London: Weidenfeld and Nicolson.

Verba, S., N. H. Nie, and J. Kim. 1978. *Participation and Political Equality: A Seven-nation Comparison*. Cambridge: Cambridge Univ. Press.

Verney, D. 1957. *Parliamentary Reform in Sweden, 1866–1921*. Oxford: Clarendon Press.

Vernon, R. 1984. Linking Managers with Ministers: Dilemmas of the State-Owned Enterprise. *Journal of Policy Analysis and Management* 4:39–55.

Vogel, J. 1974. Taxation and Public Opinion in Sweden: An Interpretation of Recent Survey Data. *National Tax Journal* 27:499–513.

Waara, L. 1980. *Den Statliga Företagssektorns Expansion*. Stockholm: Liber.

Wainwright, H. 1988. *Labour: A Tale of Two Parties*. London: Hogarth Press.

Wald, K. 1983. *Crosses on the Ballot*. Princeton, NJ: Princeton Univ. Press.

Waller, M., and M. Fennema. 1988. *Communist Parties in Western Europe*. Oxford: Basil Blackwell.

Wassenberg, A. F. P. 1982. Neo-Corporatism and the Quest for Control. In *Patterns of Corporatist Policy-Making*, ed. G. Lehmbruch and P. Schmitter, pp. 83–108. Beverly Hills, CA: Sage.

Weale, A. 1985. Why Are We Waiting? The Problem of Unresponsiveness in the Public Social Services. In *The Future of Welfare*, ed. R. Klein and M. O'Higgins, pp. 150–65. Oxford: Basil Blackwell.

Weaver, R. K. 1986. The Politics of Blame Avoidance. *Journal of Public Policy* 6:371–98.

Weaver, R. K. 1988. *Automatic Government: The Politics of Indexation*. Washington, DC: Brookings Institution.

Webb, S. 1988. Blow to Image of Refugee Haven. *Financial Times*, September 20.

Weber, Y. 1968. *L'Administration Consultative*. Paris: PUF.

Weigel, R. H., D. J. Hessing, and H. Elffers. 1987. Tax Evasion Research: A Critical Appraisal and Theoretical Model. *Journal of Economic Psychology* 8:215–35.

West, P. A. 1984. Private Health Insurance. In *Privatisation and the Welfare State*, ed. J. LeGrand and R. Robinson, pp. 111–15. London: George Allen and Unwin.

Westerståhl, J. 1971. *Ett Förskningsprogram: Den Kommunlae Självstyrelsen*. Stockholm: Almqvist and Wiksell.

Whiteley, P. 1981. Public Opinion and the Demand for Welfare in Britain. *Journal of Social Policy* 10:453–476.

Whiteley, P. F. 1983. *The Labour Party in Crisis*. London: Methuen.

Wilenski, P. 1986. Administrative Reform—General Principles and the Australian Experience. *Public Administration* 64:257–76.

Wilensky, H. L. 1975. *The Welfare State and Equality*. Berkeley, CA: Univ. of California Press.

Wilensky, H. L. 1976. *The "New Corporatism," Centralization and the Welfare State*. Beverly Hills, CA: Sage.

Wilensky, H. L., and L. Turner. 1987. *Democratic Corporatism and Policy Linkages*. Berkeley, CA: Institute of International Studies, Univ. of California

Wilson, F. 1983. French Interest Group Politics: Pluralist or Neocorporatist. *American Political Science Review* 77:895–910.

Wilson, V. S. 1988. What Legacy? The Nielsen Task Force Program Review. In *How Ottawa Spends, 1988/89: The Conservative Heading into the Stretch*, ed. K. A. Graham, pp. 23–48. Ottawa: Carleton Univ. Press.

Wolfe, J. H. 1974. Corporatism in German Political Life: Functional Representation in the GDR and Bavaria. In *Politics in Europe*, ed. M. O. Heisler, pp. 323–40. New York: David McKay.

Woolley, J. T. 1977. Monetary Policy Instrumentation and the Relationship of Central Banks and Governments. *The Annals* 434:151–73.

Worre, T. 1980. Class Parties and Class Voting in the Scandinavian Countries. *Scandinavian Political Studies* 3:299–320.

Yeatman, A. 1987. The Concept of Public Management and the Australian State in the 1980s. *Australian Journal of Public Administration* 46:340–53.

Zysman, J. 1983. *Governments, Markets and Growth*. Ithaca, NY: Cornell Univ. Press.

INDEX

ABOUT THE AUTHOR

B. Guy Peters was educated at the University of Richmond and Michigan State University. He has held faculty positions at Emory University, the University of Delaware, and Tulane University and is currently Maurice Falk Professor of American Politics and Chair of the Department of Political Science at the University of Pittsburgh. He was Fulbright Professor at the University of Strathclyde (Scotland) and Hochschule St. Gallen (Switzerland) and Hallsworth Fellow of Political Economy at the University of Manchester. He has also held visiting positions at the University of Stockholm, the LOS Center (Norway), the University of Zürich, and the London School of Economics and Political Science.

Professor Peters has a variety of teaching and research interests, which include comparative public policy and public administration, European politics, and American public bureaucracy. He was founding co-editor of *Governance*, an international journal of policy and administration, and co-founder of the International Political Science Association Research Committee on the Structure and Organization of Government. Professor Peters has also served on several state and local government commissions.

DATE DUE

MAY 3 1 92			